Re-platforming the Airline Business

Airline business models continue to be shaped by powerful forces relating to customers, complexities, and regulators. However, at the same time, there are emerging technologies that can help airlines cater to the needs of their changing customer bases and manage the complexities of the business.

In his previous books, Nawal K. Taneja has deliberated on these forces and how the airline industry is poised for disruptive change that could come from within or outside of the industry. He also discussed the point that the airline planning systems and processes in use are neither contemporary nor sufficiently integrated to meet the changing needs of customers who now are looking for outcomes, not products. In *Re-platforming the Airline Business: To Meet Travelers' Total Mobility Needs*, Taneja not only reiterates the need for transformation of the airline business but provides a map of the transformational process.

This book proposes that different sectors of the aviation industry, particularly airlines and airports, should consider using not just a wide array of technologies (artificial intelligence, biometrics, blockchain, and the Internet of things) but also specifically designed customer-centric platforms to make informed decisions and to develop and implement transformative strategies to meet travelers' total mobility needs. These technologies and platforms can enable airlines and airports to achieve scale and scope as well as agility and flexibility (through strategic partnerships) to offer intelligently aggregated travel-related services right now. Subsequently, they will enable various members in the travel chain to provide solutions to travelers' global mobility requirements, effectively and with better experiences.

Nawal K. Taneja, whose experience in the aviation industry spans five decades, has worked for and advised major airlines and related businesses worldwide. His experience also includes the presidency of a small airline that provided schedule and charter service with jet aircraft and the presidency of a research organization that provided consulting services to the air transportation community throughout the world. On the government side, he has advised departments of civil aviation, finance, economics, and tourism worldwide in matters relating to the role of government-owned airlines and their management. Within the academic community, he has served on the faculties of the Massachusetts Institute of Technology (as an associate professor) and at the Ohio State University (professor and later as chairman of both the Department of Aviation and the Department of Aerospace Engineering).

Re-platforming the Airline Business

To Meet Travelers' Total Mobility Needs

Nawal K. Taneja

Routledge
Taylor & Francis Group

LONDON AND NEW YORK

First published 2019
by Routledge
2 Park Square, Milton Park, Abingdon, Oxon OX14 4RN

and by Routledge
52 Vanderbilt Avenue, New York, NY 10017

Routledge is an imprint of the Taylor & Francis Group, an informa business

© 2019 Nawal K. Taneja

British Library Cataloguing-in-Publication Data
A catalogue record for this book is available from the British Library

Library of Congress Cataloging-in-Publication Data
A catalog record for this book has been requested

ISBN: 978-1-138-36867-5 (hbk)
ISBN: 978-0-429-42910-1 (ebk)

Typeset in Times New Roman
by Apex CoVantage, LLC

Dedicated to Angela, Matthew, Sophia, and Ravi

Contents

Figures

Acknowledgments

I would like to express my appreciation for all those who contributed in different ways, especially Angela Taneja (my business research analyst), Peeter Kivestu (transportation and logistics industry consultant at Teradata), Dr. Dietmar Kirchner (formerly a SVP at Lufthansa and now a senior aviation advisor and a cochairman of the International Airline Symposium Planning Committee), and Zhihang Chi (vice president and general manager of North America for Air China) for discussions on challenges and opportunities facing the global airline industry and related businesses.

The second group of individuals that I would like to recognize include, at:

- Air Canada – Mark Nasr;
- Airlines Association of Southern Africa – Chris Zweigenthal;
- Amadeus – Monika Wiederhold;
- Amsterdam Schiphol Airport – Guillaume Burghouwt, Richard Emmerink, Joyce Gardner, and Marieke Smit;
- Boom Supersonic – Phoenix Normand and Blake Scholl;
- CAPA-Centre for Aviation – Peter Harbison, Derek Sadubin, and Binit Somaia;
- Deloitte – Bryan Terry;
- Delta Air Lines – Steve Williams;
- Denver International Airport – John Leavitt and Stacey Stegman;
- Diio, FlightGlobal – David Hoppin;
- Google – Rob Torres;
- Huawei – Xi Lin and Xilin Yuan;
- IATA – Pierre Charbonneau, Stephan Copart, Eric Leopold, and Brian Pearce;
- InterVISTAS – Michael Tretheway;
- KLM – Liesbeth Oudkerk;
- Lufthansa – Jorga Ahlborn, Marion Blanz, Mario Kalsch, Max Kownatzki, and Christian Langer;
- Nationwide Insurance – Ian Czaja;
- OpenJaw Technologies – Paul Byrne and Colin Lewis;
- Québec City Jean Lesage International Airport – Thomas Brassard, Richard Bureau, Raymond Hout, and Bernard Thiboutot;
- Salesforce – Antonio Figueiredo and Taimur Khan;

- SITA – James Peters;
- Southwest Airlines – Adam DeCaire;
- Terrafugia – Chuck Evans;
- TravelSky – Xi Li, Thomas Ma, and Junwei Mao;
- United Airlines – Dave Hilfman, Soumit Nandi, and John Slater;
- Wencor Group – Ben Boehm and Raisa Ferdinand;
- WestJet Airlines – Louis Saint-Cyr, Ed Sims, and Alfredo Sims;
- Winding Tree – Pedro Anderson.

Third, there are a number of authors of books whose work and ideas have been referenced throughout this book. They include (with the second authors' names in parentheses):

- Allen Adamson (and Joel Steckel);
- Evert De Boer;
- Michael Dart (and Robin Lewis);
- Thomas Davenport (and Jeanne Harris);
- Richard Koch (and Greg Lockwood);
- Andrew McAfee (and Erik Brynjolfsson);
- Tracy Maylett (and Matthew Wride);
- Jacob Morgan; and
- Andrei Perumal (and Stephen Wilson).

Fourth, there are a number of other people who provided significant help: at the Ohio State University – Cynthia Overly and her staff, Robert Mendez and Ishwar Shreram; at Routledge of the Taylor & Francis Group (Guy Loft – *senior editor*, Aviation/Health & Safety; and Matthew Ranscombe, editorial assistant, Business); and at Apex CoVantage, Kerry Boettcher and Marie Roberts, project managers, Amy Freitag, editorial coordinator, and Sheri Levisay, copy editor.

Finally, I would also like to thank my family for its support and patience.

Foreword

Dick Benschop
CEO
Royal Schiphol Group

Connectivity by air is key to competitiveness in today's globalized society. A good quality of network minimizes travel costs for consumers, boosts trade and foreign direct investment, enhances productivity, and stimulates tourism.

The relevance of aviation in the global economy is reflected in the mission of the Royal Schiphol Group: *connecting the Netherlands*. And we have been doing well in terms of connectivity: in 2018 Amsterdam Schiphol ranked as Europe's second airport in terms of direct connectivity and hub connectivity.[1] The connectivity by air – powered by all our airlines – gives consumers and businesses in the Netherlands an almost unrivalled access to the rest of the world, allowing the Netherland to play its role as an open trade economy. According to our latest estimates, in 2017 we provided direct links to almost 50 percent of global and 80 percent of European metropolitan GDP.

This is a remarkable achievement: although Schiphol's catchment area is sizeable, it is certainly not the largest one in Europe. Of all European airports' catchment areas, Schiphol's catchment area ranked 29th, with 12 million inhabitants and 500 billion euro of GDP within a 100 km radius. Schiphol ranks behind London, behind the Ruhr area, behind Brussels and behind Paris.

In fact, the connectivity offered is much larger than what one would expect based on the local origin-destination (OD) market alone, thanks to the hub operation of Air France-KLM and its SkyTeam partners. By operating Schiphol as a hub, the carrier complements local OD traffic with transfer traffic and allows the Netherlands to benefit from a network that is much larger than the catchment area of Amsterdam is able to support. This is what I call the 'connectivity premium' of a hub airport.

To continue to connect the Netherlands in the future will require us to deal with numerous challenges. Let me briefly mention four of them.

The first challenge relates to expected industry growth in relation to airport capacity. Aviation demand is expected to double again in the next 20 years. However, airport capacity is not keeping up with demand growth. According to the latest estimates by Eurocontrol,[2] the number of 'Heathrow-like' airports operating near capacity will climb to 16 in 2040. However, in the densely populated metropolitan areas in Europe, expanding airport capacity – let alone building new airports – is a cumbersome task. Airports have to work hard to generate the needed public and political support.

The second challenge relates to the changing airline landscape and the type of traffic to cater to. Low-cost carriers are entering the (self-)transfer, premium and long-haul markets, facilitated by liberalization, new aircraft technology, and IT solutions. The market share of low-cost carriers in Europe is still on the rise, being close to 50 percent for intra-European traffic in 2017.

The growing share of these carriers and their predominant focus on point-to-point travel as well as general market growth have been main reasons for the decreasing transfer rates at major airports worldwide in the past 15 years.[3] We seem to move to a more point-to-point world, although hub operations and transfer traffic remain very important to connect all the dots on the map. We are also moving to a world in which the classic distinction between low-cost and full-service carriers is gradually fading.

The growth of low-cost carriers as well as hub carriers in the Gulf and Turkey provide airports, regions, and consumers with new connectivity opportunities. At the same time, the growing competition puts additional competitive pressure on the European hub carriers, which are so important for the connectivity premium at airports like Schiphol.

In this changing airline and capacity landscape, the question for airports is how to strategically position themselves for the future in terms of investments but also in terms of business model and value proposition.

Another challenge for the aviation industry at large is sustainability. The current share of aviation in global CO_2 emissions is expected to rise further above its current 3 percent level due to demand growth and the difficulty of making the transition to more sustainable aviation fuels.

Schiphol Group is putting a lot of effort into making our airports more sustainable. For example, at Schiphol we have electrified our airside bus transportation system, and we are doing the same on landside. Together with our energy supplier, we have invested in wind turbines for the supply of 100 percent renewable electricity. But in the end, the direct influence of airport operators regarding emissions is limited, as the majority of emissions are generated in the air. Technical solutions, operational measures, and market-based incentives will be needed for the industry to become more sustainable.

A final challenge relates to the consumer of tomorrow. As Professor Taneja has stated rightly in his books, passengers are increasingly expecting personalized and contextualized services and products – not only at the airport itself, but for their entire door-to-door trip. This will require our airports to digitalize and innovate to create a seamless airport experience that can exceed customer expectations.

To give one example, using biometrics, we shorten the waiting time for passengers at immigration and increase capacity. The use of big data and IT allows us to forecast passenger flows in the airport much better, better utilize our assets, and improve the passenger experience. However, meeting future customer demands also means working together and exchanging data with airlines, other airports, and landside transport providers. Ultimately, the whole passenger trip chain, of which airports are just one part, will be integrated. How do airports need to prepare for that? And what role do we want to play as airports in the world of 'mobility as a service'? Which companies are going to be the 'integrators' of the trip chain?

The challenges and questions for airports are numerous. It is here where Professor Nawal K. Taneja plays an important role as one of the industry's most important thought leaders. In this book, he discusses the important changes the aviation industry is going to face. As such, he provides useful guidelines for the strategies of both airports and airlines to navigate the future.

Amsterdam, Netherlands

Notes

1 ACI EUROPE, Airport Industry Connectivity Report, 2018.
2 Eurocontrol, European Aviation in 2040: Challenges of Growth, 2018.
3 DLR, "Development of Transfer Passengers at Key International Airports," Paper prepared for the ATRS Conference, 2018.

Foreword

Marco Benvenuti

Co-Founder, Chief Marketing & Strategy Officer
Duetto Research

Most senior executives spend the majority of their time focused on the business as it exists today, as they should. The very best also look ahead to the next fiscal year and maybe even a more strategic five-year plan. But how much time are you spending thinking about what comes after that?

That's what I love about this book and Nawal's challenge to airline executives. If you're only seeing evolutionary changes and not thinking about the revolutionary changes, you are going to be left behind.

It's the same challenge the hotel industry I know so well is facing. Disruption is all around us. Hotels, like the airlines, are in the midst of a digital transformation that continues to accelerate. We are watching an e-commerce revolution happen before our eyes.

Look at the growth of online travel agents like Expedia and Booking.com and how they've become the first choice for consumers. They've taken money from the pockets of hotel owners as acquisition costs have risen, and now Google and Airbnb are innovating to better meet consumer needs.

Why? According to several recent studies, the hotel industry as a whole has approximately a 2 percent conversion rate of consumers booking a room after visiting a hotel website. That means 98 percent of people aren't booking a room after visiting a hotel website. I'm not sure what the conversion rate is for airline websites, but I spent more than an hour shopping and booking a flight and hotel room for an upcoming trip this past weekend. It was painful.

Meanwhile, I spent a few minutes on Amazon buying stuff I don't need. Front and center, I saw a compelling deal of the day and recommendations on the next video I should stream or book I should buy. And it's just a few clicks and seconds to order.

When I go to the website of my favorite hotel in San Francisco and search for a room, I have to scroll down to the fifth choice to find the room type I've booked hundreds of times before. When I visit your airline website, it takes more than several minutes and clicks to find and purchase the ticket I want.

Amazon has 100 million members of Prime, and my bet is they also like to travel. Those are your customers too, and they want that same experience on your website. Do you have a plan to get there? Like the hotel industry, you have the power. You own the assets, have the service and provide the hospitality, and most importantly, you should have the most data and insights into the consumer.

But you need to connect the data and bring together all the systems providing it. This is what Nawal astutely sees as the future of the airline industry. It's the same on the hotel side. It is the re-platforming of the business, and the ability to bring together all that data in real time and connect technologies on both the marketing and operations sides of the business.

Although yield management may have started in the airlines, the hotel industry has moved further ahead and is on the verge of true dynamic pricing. Hotels with the right technology integrations are able to independently yield all customer segments, booking channels, room types and rate codes in real time. The industry calls this approach open pricing, and it goes beyond the more traditional method of hotel pricing that is centered around several "Best Available Rates" established based on different forecasted occupancy levels. With that approach, a tiered structure of sub rates is discounted by a percentage from whatever the BAR is for that date. For example, an 80 percent occupancy forecast might trigger a BAR of $200 and if the standard AAA discount is 10 percent less, that rate would become $180. If occupancy was forecasted to be 50 percent, BAR might be $100 and then the AAA would become $90. With the growth of digital distribution, there are many more channels and segments hotels price for, all with rates cascading down from that primary BAR.

This rigid approach limits the amount of price points a hotel can offer and the revenue it can capture because revenue managers are forced to either keep discounted channels open and accept lower rated business or close them during higher demand periods. With open pricing, those discounted rates can be flexed up and even made the same as the highest available rate being marketed, meaning offers never have to be closed and all channels can be kept open and available for customers shopping them.

Much of the hotel industry continues to use the fixed tier BAR approach because of closed and legacy systems that don't work well together, but the future of revenue and yield management is open pricing. By unifying data, hotels can move closer to the holy grail of 1:1 pricing and real personalization. This is the promise of the platform.

Imagine if you could connect all core technologies and bring together that data in real time. You could have one 360-degree view of your guest across the entire customer journey and could personalize offers, the on-property experience, and even marketing promotions after.

This is beginning to happen in the hotel industry. Companies with loyalty programs are driving more direct and profitable business by offering personalized prices to known guests. When the customer is logged in, the offer becomes private and rate parity agreements aren't violated. If commission costs are higher with online travel agencies, hotels should offer better rates on their own channels to win direct business and even larger discounts to known guests who historically spend even more on property with F&B, spa and other ancillary offerings. Pricing can and should be dynamic based on not only demand, but the guests' value to the business.

And the utility goes far beyond just pricing. Merchandising, like what room type or offer is displayed first, can be personalized based on what you know about the consumer.

Platforms open the door to connecting more than just what is in your own tech stack. For example, by connecting to Facebook, hotels can use its advertising platform to share real-time offers with consumers who may only be thinking about and lightly researching upcoming travel. By integrating with a CRM and Salesforce.com's Service Cloud, hotel operators could see and respond in real time to customer feedback on social channels.

The possibilities are endless. Imagine integrating all of travel into one platform, hotels to airlines to car rental agencies and more.

This is the future. Are you ready?

San Francisco, USA

Foreword

Zhihang Chi

Vice President and General Manager
North America, Air China

I get excited upon hearing about opportunities to leverage technology to make my company and our industry better. Who doesn't? For me, however, it is especially so because years ago, when I was studying for my PhD at MIT, we were at the cutting edge. We were one of the very people in the world who were using the Internet, or Arpanet, as it was called back then. We were sending email and playing Tetris on DEC Unix workstations. It was chill! Totally!!

So when Nawal said to me that his new book would be about using the newest technologies and leveraging the newest platforms in our business and asked me to write a foreword, it was a no-brainer. After all, the DEC was the coolest platform and the Arpanet was the newest technology.

The platforming, or re-platforming, as Nawal calls it, is a fascinating idea. Uber, Airbnb, WeChat, Facebook, Amazon, Alibaba, eBay are all very powerful platforms that have brought about profound changes to how we live and how we conduct ourselves. The fundamental problem that the airline industry has been struggling with since its reception is how to sell our product. Along the way, we've made tremendous progress and created very powerful and effective tools. Think of global distribution systems (GDS), airline websites, and departure control systems. Along the way, however, our customers' needs have progressed even more – so diverse that our capabilities have been overwhelmed. The New Distribution Capability (NDC) is IATA's response, which will come to our rescue. Progress in that area has been gradual, very gradual. Meanwhile, still more needs are being created, by our customers and ourselves alike.

So why reinvent the wheel? Why do we simply adopt solutions from other industries, especially the high-tech sector? Better yet, why don't we partner with them and consign some of our functions to them?

Sounds like a great idea. But . . .

It is worth noting that the high-tech industry and the airline industry are probably the diametrical opposites of each other. We are very capital intensive. One airplane can easily run us hundreds of millions of dollars. There are all the regulations that there can be that bind us rather snugly. Most airlines operate in a union environment that adds still more to our constraints and restrictions, while the high-tech industry is filled with whiz kids who are highly motivated, willing to work as many hours as need be on a salary. Incidentally, no computer will crash because an operator is too tired. While people love Steve Jobs and his cool gadgets, the airline industry, for reasons no one has been able to figure out, is a convenient target of gripe, denunciation, animosity, and hate, even though it's each passenger's decision and choice to step on the most miraculous engineering feat to be elevated to dizzying heights and hurtled at crazy speeds. There is no cleaner and more elegant solution than using one's fingers, or in this day and age, simply telling Siri, Alexa, or Cortana, to change a few parameters or a few lines of code at worst, and voila! In our industry, there is no such thing as a clean solution. Everything is a patchwork of Band-Aids, a product of compromise.

Bottom line, we try to survive in a rigid and rule-bound environment, while anything goes in the high-tech industry. With the investigation of Russian interference and the grilling Mark Zuckerberg had to endure, things may begin to change.

To digress from re-platforming, the crux of our industry's challenge is this intrinsic conflict between a rigid frame in which we are bound and the ever-changing needs of our customers, which require flexibility and efficiency in meeting them.

Democratization of air travel has been gathering steam. We see an explosion in air travel. Along with that explosive growth in traffic, we see needs that are so diverse that we struggle to meet them in our rigid system. Don't forget, not long ago, there was no first class or coach, let alone all the subclasses and fare rules. There was only one class on an airplane, which simply means air platform. Today's traveling public is equipped with such cool gadgets that the airline industry's monopoly over information is a memory of the past. Balance of power has been decidedly shifting in favor of our customers.

Nawal believes that a revolution is at our doorsteps. It'd better not be a revolution, because any revolution in human history would result in violence, in fallen heads and bloodshed. Ideally, we collectively should constantly evolve at as fast a clip as possible. It is up to each member of our community to work together to deliver the flexibility that our customers demand. Our culture needs to change from the traditional command-and-control model to a team approach. Our regulations need to migrate from a crude rule-based or rather a rule-of-thumb-based system to a more precise science-based approach. Our labor force needs to put our customers' needs first and at the same time be able to share in the fruit of labor. Lack of action on the part of any constituent will scuttle the effort. Fortunately, the reverse is also true. Any small step forward taken by any party may deliver a monumental impact. The truly explosive growth in U.S.-China traffic is made possible by one small policy change, the streamlining of visa processing. At a December 1, 2005 industry conference, when I fired my opening salvo in what turned out to be an epic campaign that involved stakeholders and allies from airlines, to city and state governments, to trade associations, even labor groups, I never thought we would achieve striking results beyond our wildest dreams. In 2005, the U.S. and Chinese carriers operated fewer than 80 flights a week, about 52 of which were operated by U.S. carriers and 25 or so by Chinese carriers. Today, that total has jumped to about 350, with a split of 190 operated by Chinese carriers and 160 operated by U.S. carriers. The sharp rise in the number of frequencies has primarily been driven by a massive growth in outbound traffic from China, from a quarter-million in 2005 to more than 3 million in 2017. In 2005, Air China was operating three times a week between LA and Beijing. On Chinese New Year's Day in 2015, we held a press conference attended by dignitaries such as Mayor Garcetti of LA to announce a third frequency between LA and Beijing, *daily*. In my remarks, I mocked myself for lack of vision, evidenced in my WeChat hashtag "doubledaily," a manifestation of my pride in having brought our frequency from three times weekly to double daily, which I thought was the utmost we would go. Incidentally, those 3 million visitors from China pumped $30 billion into the U.S. economy in 2017, according to data published by Commerce.

We should also learn from other industries. The banking industry is also heavily regulated and saddled with legacy systems. The retail industry has been directly affected, if not entirely made over, by platforming.

Los Angeles, USA

Foreword

James Davidson

President and CEO
Farelogix

"This book discusses how airlines can re-platform their business models to achieve operational excellence and marketing innovation through the achievement of scale and scope, as well as agility and flexibility. Intelligent engagement platforms can enable airlines and airports to overcome the constraints and complexities of their businesses and change their value propositions to meet the mobility needs of a growing number of passengers and the increasing diversity of their expectations. The critical success factors are not only the vision to deploy enabling technologies to achieve scale but also the laser focus on execution."

I fell in love with the airline industry at the ripe old age of twenty-two when I took my first flight on Mohawk Airlines. I was traveling from my hometown of Elmira, New York, to the Lake of the Ozarks, Missouri, to interview for a job I did not end up getting. While I can't recall what the job was about, I will certainly never forget that trip. That's where I became hooked on this business. Somehow, some way, the airline industry was going to become a serious and exciting part of my world.

Here we are several decades later reflecting on the airline business of the twenty first century. So, what's changed? At a cursory glance, once might say, "not much." 40 years later we still have tickets (so they're now electronic, big deal); fares are still filed in 26 miserable buckets; legacy technologies still reside at the heart of most airline systems. "Plus ca change"! Actually, such a view is misleading and overly skeptical. Because very quietly, under the surface and at long last, disruptive change has arrived in our beloved industry.

Today's discussions of airline distribution, technological innovations, and disruption refer to the *very real* concepts of new distribution capability (NDC), airline-controlled offer engines, retailing, new generation revenue management, customer experience, artificial intelligence, and machine learning. The airline industry meets digital transformation and data science!

Finally, the age-old airline staples of schedules, fares, and availability – to this day predetermined, static, and filed – will be dynamically generated through sophisticated scientific algorithms designed to deliver only the most relevant offer based on request input criteria that incorporates who's asking, propensity and customer scoring, available flight attributes, and more. The ability to optimize the offer, I predict, will have the most significant positive impact on the sustainability and growth of the airline industry since I took that first flight to the Ozarks!

The big challenge staring us in the face is the requirement for airlines to retool, or as the author states, re-platform both their technology and business model footprint. Brute force computational methods served us well in an environment of static information and established volume-predictable distribution channels. But they are no longer fit for purpose and no amount of cache, computing power, or IT muscle can change this fact. Already today, request and search volumes from new channels and new geographies put too much strain on our traditional technology applications and infrastructures. The addition of dynamic real-time calculation to the mix is the straw that breaks the legacy camel's back, compromising the airline's ability to effectively compete. This is, of course, unacceptable.

The good news is there is widespread acceptance across the industry – both from the folks who run the airlines and from those of us that supply new enabling technologies – that re-platforming is essential.

This re-platforming effort will require a steady and deliberate move from present day commodity and community-focused airline distribution technology to a much more disruptive airline-controlled set of offer management engines (e.g., shopping, pricing, merchandising, availability, and schedule building). These engines will interoperate dynamically in milliseconds to influence and optimize a relevant offer for every single trip request. The shear scale required to meet this transactional demand – unimaginable even just a few short years ago – is now on every credible airline technology provider's near-term roadmap.

No longer can airline marketing innovation be siloed from, or limited by, operational delivery. Existing airline systems, once the enabler and governor of the airline's distribution capabilities, have now, in many cases become the airline's "nemeses" in enabling their ability to compete. The notion of any airline simply delivering a price and a schedule "because that's all you can do" is at best archaic and at worst a formula for disaster. Investment in transformation is a competitive must.

The path to digital transformation challenges airline executives to redefine what drives success. Historically, the relationship between customer experience and revenue has been viewed as a trade-off. In the new world, consumer experience and incremental revenue generation are both forward-looking distribution drivers, coexisting in a win-win retailing and operational ecosystem. Delivering the right offer at the right time and place leads to a more favorable customer experience (one they are willing to invest in using a "second wallet" according to Atmosphere Research Group). The ability for the airline to generate incremental revenue will soon be the highest goal of revenue management professionals, as they optimize the offer for every single trip request, regardless of distribution entryway. For the first time, airlines have a wonderful opportunity to strike a new balance in their relationship with customers and would-be customers, while exceeding revenue and retention goals. Now, that's a value proposition!

This book outlines a roadmap for ever airline manager and executive to attain that balance between meeting the customer expectations and delivering sustainable new revenue to the airline. May you innovate fast and well.

Miami, USA

Foreword

Kim Day

CEO
Denver International Airport

Over the past two decades, seismic shifts have occurred in the aviation industry that have fundamentally changed the way we and our passengers travel and transact business. The result is less expensive airline tickets and fewer on-aircraft amenities for non-premium passengers, and in response, airports' offerings are rivaling the most exclusive shopping and dining destinations. Clearly, the advent of the smartphone and the empowered, app-fueled traveler are among the chief forces that continue to change our industry's landscape.

But at Denver International Airport (DEN), we believe it's a mistake to overly simplify these shifts as being driven solely by quickly advancing technology. While its true consumers are doing more than ever with their smartphones, it's also true customers are craving more personal attention than ever, and they're seeking to customize their "experiences" and "pleasures." This point is discussed throughout Professor Taneja's book.

But sometimes it's just a matter of the basics. I recently overheard a visitor to the Metropolitan Museum of Art in New York City acclaim the virtues of warm water and paper towels in the restroom. Even as she took full advantage of the Met's prodigious technologies, she found comfort in some very simple pleasures.

What's a business to do? Should leaders stake their companies' futures on advanced technology alone? Or should they eschew technology and instead cling to old-fashioned customer service? The tension between such divergent forces is enough to shred business plans and keep aviation industry executives awake at night.

It isn't and won't ever be enough again to lean fully to one side or the other. We must learn to find our balance on constantly shifting sands, and the secret to defining that balance is to listen – listen to our passengers and listen to our carriers and other stakeholders. We clearly need to stay flexible and nimble and to be open to new ways of thinking and conducting business, but we don't have to guess what our travelers and airlines want; we just need to ask them.

And as we are asking people and partners what they want, we also have an opportunity to learn from others and other industries about what they're doing and what's working for them.

For example, as we continue to reimagine the way security functions at our airport, we've partnered with the Transportation Security Administration (TSA) and consulted with organizations that think differently about security than airports: casinos, amusement parks, service delivery companies, and more. If we were to simply brainstorm with organizations like us, we would return with solutions with limited creativity and application. As it is, our resulting solutions are providing unique queueing concepts that support risk-based assignments to lanes, paired with emerging screening equipment that allows for enhanced security in conjunction with an improved passenger experience.

Consulting with existing partners has already enhanced DEN security by inviting off-duty TSA explosive sniffing dogs to "live-train" in our facilities. This no-cost activity places uniformed canines and their handlers around the airport in plain view of the traveling public, incrementally hardening our security and helping to train and hone the skills of amazing animals.

As DEN renovates its tented terminal and adds gates in response to airline demand, we're developing solutions to enhance passenger experience through a unique strategic partnership that allows us to incubate, rapidly develop, and deploy innovative solutions in a low-risk setting. The best part about this development method is its reliance on immediate customer feedback to quickly focus on those innovations that are most meaningful to people.

Incidentally, even though DEN is undertaking significant expansion projects today, we are committed to keeping the costs to air carriers competitive. DEN can expand at incrementally lower costs due to our vast expanse of land available, thanks to the visionary decisions of past leaders. They relocated the airport to 53 square miles on the eastern edge of the city, allowing us to better plan for future growth, eventually increase from six to 12 runways, accommodate more than 100 million passengers, and contain noise on our property.

Among the first efforts of our innovation trials will be to reimagine an airport bathroom and offer the latest innovations in restroom comforts – from new sink, stall and lighting design, to other yet unimagined improvements, and of course . . . warm water and paper towels. Customers will give immediate feedback, letting us identify the changes most desired before large-scale rollout.

And we continue to work with our airline partners. One area of interest involves the use of "push messages" that proactively reach out to known customers with helpful and interesting information. It's easy to imagine a near-future application that can alert a passenger that a connecting flight is delayed, an expected gate location is changed, and even suggest that a favorite coffee shop is located nearby . . . would they want to order a latte and pick it up on the way?

I get more than 150 cold-call emails and calls each day that offer new solutions to airport problems. Honestly, I delete them all. We don't just go to aviation meetings looking for ideas; instead, we head to other industries' meetings and try to see what ways we can use their technology, processes, and innovations. One recent payoff is a "See/Say" smart-phone app that effectively deputizes our employees to share photos of possible concerns with a click of a button and maybe a quick photo. Using the app, employees quickly report safety concerns and customer and maintenance issues such as malfunctioning conveyances, untidy restrooms or spills. And each time an issue is reported, a reassuring response is quick to come.

My vision of the airport of the future is a facility that balances intuitive and reliable technology along with low-tech indirect response to users' requests. It's also an airport that stays flexible and nimble to reinvent itself as preferences and this dynamic industry evolve. But ultimately, we want to ensure a friendly face with a helpful attitude is with you all along your way.

Denver, USA

Foreword

Gaëtan Gagné

President and CEO
Québec City Jean Lesage International Airport (YQB)

Who is an airport's real end customer? This question has haunted me ever since I became involved in the airport industry, in 1997. In 2006, it became clear to me, however, that *Passenger First®* should be our primary value, and, in retrospect, I am more than ever convinced that we made the right choice back then.

Airports are an amalgamation of stakeholders, including airlines, tenants, concessionaires, government entities, boards of trade, the general population, politicians, etc. and, at some point in time, we might ask who, in fact, is the real end customer? If trade-offs are needed when making decisions, who should come first in our ranking of people to be served?

I asked myself a similar question when I was the CEO of a life insurance company prior to joining YQB. Whose interest should be served first when dealing with the client? The client, or the distribution network serving the client; in that case, the insurance agents and the brokers? Even in those days, decades ago, I came to the conclusion that our entire team focus should first and foremost be directed, not on the "number of policies," as I was once told by a so-called expert, but rather on the satisfaction of the clients, and certainly not on the distribution network serving them. At the outset, this mindset led me to put in place one of the first direct-sale life insurance companies in Canada. Actually, time has proven me to be right. Years later, I am pleased to see that financial regulators now encourage direct sales to customers, the intermediaries being replaced, when possible, by smarter technologies.

I strongly believe that, both in the financial and airport industries, the person on whom the emphasis should be placed is the person who brings the most value to our business. Remember the old saying "Follow the money"? Instead, I would now suggest, "Follow what brings added value." The key word here is indeed "value." Value for us, as airport authorities, but also, and above all, value for the people we serve, the passengers. If our primary customers recognize the value of what we do for them, it will necessarily reverberate onto our own organization's value, be it measured through a better reputation or through better financial results.

Concretely, let me give you three illustrations of what we mean by *Passenger First®*. Québec City is the second city in Canada in terms of volume of snowfall. Around five years ago, we asked ourselves, "Is it possible for our airport to alleviate our passengers' hassle of cleaning off the snow from their cars when they come back from a sunny vacation in the south?" The answer was yes . . . once we decided to build a 1,150-stall parkade to alleviate that annoyance to our primary customers.

Another illustration is that, almost a decade ago, we observed that airline ticket prices in our area were very high. After analysis, we discovered that the root cause of the problem was a critical lack of capacity. Again with the passengers in mind, we invested some $500 million to build a domestic and an international terminal, leading to more gates being offered and allowing more airlines to land at YQB. The results were almost immediate. Increased airline competition has contributed in reducing ticket prices by as much as 71 percent in some cases.

Consider also this last example. Boarding an aircraft off-bridge in sub-zero temperatures was another major irritant for our passengers. To avoid that, we decided to heavily invest in covered and heated bridges, thus allowing our passengers to circulate freely between the terminal and their aircraft.

It makes sense to put the *Passenger First*® at the heart of any business strategy. As Nawal K. Taneja also points out in this book, this is the only way to adapt to a new reality where consumers are taking control of their own plans, thanks to new technologies, to the detriment of traditional intermediaries, who are losing their predominance. We are also convinced that it is vital to become a world-class company, because passengers will have all the tools they need to demand nothing less in the services we provide to them. By directing all our decisions toward satisfying the needs of passengers and treating them as a world-class company would, we will not only develop our full potential but also that of our entire region, as put forward in our mission.

This recent quote from one of our passengers tells it all:

Being at YQB: it is like spending time at a huge VIP lounge.

To be successful with a *Passenger First*® strategy like ours, the strategy must be embraced by all those having to deliver this unique experience on a daily basis, i.e., our own employees. More than that, it must also be shared by our partners' employees. This way, passengers are at the very center of all the airport activities, be they face-to-face encounters with passengers, or behind-the-scene operations, like snow removal or baggage handling. In fact, we so firmly believe in this core value that we have begun training all YQB employees, be they ours or those of our partners, in order to make sure all staff adhere to this fundamental value on which our common success depends.

This strong belief that *Passenger First*® should be our primary concern was also reinforced by an Oxford University course I recently took on the emerging blockchain technologies. Although my staff had some ideas about how this digital phenomenon would affect us, I wanted to learn more about it myself. What I discovered during the course convinced me even more that blockchain and related technologies will change the way we do business, another topic discussed in this book. Not only that, it also clearly demonstrated to me that this idea of *Passenger*

First® will only be strengthened, due to the fact that the new technologies will allow for airports, airlines, and government bodies at airport sites to better deliver what passengers are really looking for at airports.

There is clear evidence that the *Passenger First*® primary value has worked. YQB has achieved an almost 7 percent compound annual passenger growth rate over the past 15 years, going from 608,000 passengers per year in 2002 to close to 1.7 million in 2017.

Interestingly enough, Nawal K. Taneja and I recently had a one-on-one discussion on the future of our industry. We both shared the opinion that we are at a turning point. This book, along with the previous ones in this series, is an excellent tool to understand what challenges, threats, and opportunities lay ahead.

In short, what does the future hold? The airport's primary clients will likely be the passengers. Technologies and a world-class service are key elements to strengthening the close relationship with passengers, and I suggest that any strategy placing the emphasis on other airport stakeholders is simply destined to miss the mark.

Québec City, Canada

Foreword

Jeffrey Goh
CEO
Star Alliance

The record of the airline industry in innovation and creativity has been remarkable. Since the birth of commercial aviation, we have seen the deregulation of the industry, which also paved the way for new entrants (and exits, of course), which gave birth to new and innovative products and development of new markets. The concept of codeshares enabled airlines not only to build partnerships but to access markets that otherwise may be less accessible for reasons of scale and economics. Indeed, the concept of partnerships has continued to evolve. Joint ventures that permit airlines to coordinate commercially, with antitrust authorization, have become an attraction that is capable of extracting, arguably, up to 80 percent of the value that may be expected from a merger or acquisition. Cross-border equity investments are gradually emerging, although still rare and limited in scale, as the industry, almost uniquely, continues to be regulated by ownership and control restrictions.

All of the foregoing is but snippets of an industry resilient at its core and driven by the need to be ever-evolving. Critical challenges have often led to creative and ground-breaking solutions, from loyalty programs to reward and retain valued travelers, to global airline alliances with worldwide reach and expansive frequent-flyer program (FFP) propositions, to modern aircraft technology for efficiency of operations and market reach.

But for the industry, there is a new imperative taking shape – that is, customer experience. Customer expectations are changing. They are mobile first. They expect information on demand and services at fingertips. They are always connected in an increasing world of connected travel. Studies estimate that by 2020 there will be over 50 billion Internet of things devices, and by the same year there will be over 5 billion smartphones in use. Increasingly, smartphones will play a central role in the Internet of things, particularly as they connect to multiple devices on the ground, in the airport, and in the air, on board the aircraft. Mobile technology has not only become integral to personal experiences but has become a key enabler to the digitalization of customer experience, including the use of biometrics.

None of this is new, of course, but it is a current reality that customers have come to expect and demand instant gratification, and this has been aided by digital and mobile technology. To meet these evolving customer and service expectations, the airline industry needs to evolve, to leverage data for customization, and, equally important, to be agile. In comparative terms, the airline industry is behind the curve in digital development.

Take the case of GO-JEK, a ride-hailing (motorcycle taxi) app in Indonesia that has seen a meteoric rise to become a logistics platform since it was founded in 2010. Soon after it began operations, GO-JEK recognized that its cadre of drivers could not be kept occupied all throughout the day because of low demand during off-peak hours. The ride-sharing business on its own would not be sufficient to achieve scale and network effects. So, to keep its drivers busy all day, it developed other lines of business that leveraged the ride-hailing platform. Hence, the birth of Go-Send, Go-Food, Go-Mart, Go-Clean, and even Go-Massage! The key point is that GO-JEK would not have been able to develop and integrate the new lines of business onto its existing platform without an agile strategy and a technology architecture that is flexible.

The airline industry needs to catch on to such agility, to reinvent itself. Segments of the industry are well-advanced but there is certainly much room to be better. It has to evolve with the new norm, in product and service development, no less in thinking and processes.

All of this is to say that technology has and will continue to play an instrumental role in shaping the future of the industry, both as enabler and disruptor. It has changed the way in which airline operations can be managed – aircraft parts management through blockchain technology, revenue management through artificial intelligence, or network planning through automated algorithms. It has had a profound effect on customer experience and its management, and will continue to do so. The joint venture between Amazon Echo/Alexa and Kayak has introduced an experience through voice technology in travel planning that was unimaginable only a few years ago. Digital technology has ushered in a new era of experience. The opportunities to learn more about customer behavior and personalize offerings according to customer preferences by leveraging data – the new oil – has never been more real. Digitalization and customization are set to be the next battleground for distribution.

An important foundation for such progress has been the platform economy, where consumers and providers are connected, often with minimal capital expenditure and mostly with operating expenditure. Uber, Airbnb and, of course, Go-Jek come to mind. In this connection, the global airline alliances stand at a unique intersection in delivering a seamless digital customer experience through platforms that act as middlewares connecting digital services of its members with one another and with customers. The Digital Services Platform of Star Alliance has enabled, among other things, its members to offer seat selection capability for a customer traveling on a multi-airline itinerary, an experience which until recently proved a challenge. Also significantly, the interactions with customers continue to take place through the interfaces of the members.

To that end too, as digitalization of customer experience progresses, airlines and enterprises will need to see themselves as a partner in the travel experience ecosystem. How can they create an end-to-end experience in the customer journey through an ecosystem made up of accommodation providers (hotels, Airbnb), baggage recovery management providers (Unicoaero), or "last mile- transportation providers (Ubertaxi, Hyperloop)? Transforming from enterprises to ecosystems, however, requires a strategic shift in mindset and business model. It is not a task to be underestimated.

Let's take a step back for a moment, and ask: Are we at risk of a race to the bottom in our chase for more digitalization opportunities and experience? The volume of digital initiatives, in breadth and in depth, direct and indirect to the industry, risks creating a disjointed customer experience. Digital "silofication" risks customer confusion and, eventually perhaps, apathy.

Airlines are digitalizing. Airports are digitalizing. Concessionaires are digitalizing. Customs and border protection agencies are also digitalizing. But there are few signs that they are moving in an orderly fashion. Yet each of these stakeholders plays a key role in delivering a more seamless customer experience. Take the airports, where printed boarding passes continue to be required so that a security officer has the ability to stamp on it once the passenger exits the security screening. This is hardly congruous with the age of mobile technology and electronic boarding passes in a smartphone – where does the stamp go? Still, at other airports, there are no less than five touch points at which a passenger is required to present the boarding pass, paper or electronic, and passport or a form of identification, because at one or more of these touch points it is a different stakeholder in that customer journey through the airport.

Institutions such as IATA, ICAO, ACI and alliances have a critical role to ensure that the progress toward a better digital customer experience is rational and orderly and, above all, have added value propositions. Digitalizing for the sake of it will risk a disservice to customer experience. If we are serious about delivering a seamless digital experience, we need to be serious about a more coordinated approach at key touch points of the customer journey that are less about commercial advantage and more about better customer experience.

For now, let's make no mistake. The digitalization train has left the station. The platform economy will enable digitalization opportunities to an even greater extent in better meeting customer preferences and expectations. That journey of digital transformation necessarily calls on airlines to question, beyond the dichotomy posed in this book on re-platforming the airline business – of between managing aircraft and marketing – and to adapt its existential landscape from an enterprise to an ecosystem. Quintessentially, it is about adapting and fitting business to emerging technologies, not simply about changing technology to fit business.

Frankfurt, Germany

Foreword

Greg Hyslop
Chief Technology Officer
The Boeing Company

On any given day, a population about the size of Paris or Los Angeles flies on a commercial airliner somewhere in the world. Twelve million people leapfrog across the globe to conduct business, visit family and friends, study abroad, and discover new places and cultures.

Since the dawn of the jet age, air travel has grown steadily from the province of the relative few to a viable choice for the broader population. It's become our physical World Wide Web and an integral part of modern life. And yet, while 4 billion passengers will step aboard an airliner this year, flying remains out of reach for most of the world's population. Less than one in five people have ever flown and just 1 percent of all world trade ships by air, according to Boeing's research.

Simply put, our primary modes of travel and transport are still very much on the ground, particularly for shorter distances. And the infrastructure required to maintain the status quo on the ground – roads, parking lots, and garages – are economically inefficient.

Technological advances, changes in the commercial aviation business, and key socioeconomic factors will radically alter that picture in the coming decades. As Nawal K. Taneja explains in this book, the rate of transformation will shift from evolutionary to revolutionary. We're already seeing a variety of disruptive changes that will shape the future of travel and transport.

Boeing is a leader in changing how the world moves people and goods. Our efforts are founded on a century of innovation, extensive research, a commitment to safety, and our mission to connect, protect, explore, and inspire the world. We see trends between now and 2050 that support activity quickening the pace of change.

By mid-century, two-thirds of us will live in urban areas. This change leads to one undeniable truth: The value placed on time will increase. Same-day delivery for goods ordered online is already a reality in many places. We pay extra in a variety of contexts for the privilege of not waiting in line.

People and goods will continue to move through the air. Boeing estimates that the global commercial airplane fleet will double to about 48,500 aircraft over the next 20 years. This growth will intensify current pain points on the ground for travelers – transport to and from airports, among them – as well as aviation's effect on the environment – issues the industry is striving to address.

We believe that aviation will fundamentally change the economics and eco-system of flight to meet the increasing demand for safe, efficient, affordable, and sustainable transport for all distances. We've identified five major areas that are ripe for change:

1 **Solutions for developing countries:** The substantial expense to build aerial and surface transport infrastructure challenges us to reconsider the relationship between traditional airplanes, airports, and automobiles – and how we might bypass this paradigm. First-time fliers whose alternative is a long bus ride may have different expectations regarding the speed and amenities of their journey. Vertical takeoff and landing aircraft that are slower than jets but operate without runways could make air transport more prevalent in developing nations, especially those without expressway systems.

2 **Low-stress travel:** A two-hour flight (between Seattle and San Francisco, for example) represents just one-third of a passenger's journey. It takes another four hours to get to and from the airports, wait in line to drop off bags and pass through security, and board and deplane. The inefficient flow of people and goods costs time and money – encouraging travelers and businesses to explore other transportation modes.

   Technological solutions, some of which are already being tested, could create a faster, less fragmented journey using a new generation of air vehicles as part of a connected transport future.

   Imagine this: You board an autonomous flying taxi at a corner down the street to avoid highway traffic to the airport. Biometrics detect your arrival in the terminal and automate your flight check-in. You simply leave your bags at a designated station, thanks to tracking technology. Manual security checks are largely alleviated by artificial intelligence that assesses threats. Augmented reality then tells you where to find your gate – and coffee.

3 **Bringing flight closer to home:** With the world's population expected to reach nearly 10 billion by 2050, on-demand, low-stress mobility will be necessary to efficiently connect people and goods. This will require a safe and reliable next-generation air traffic management system that allows piloted and autonomous air vehicles to coexist in the same ecosystem.

4 **Connectivity and big data:** Analytics are already helping airlines and their passengers, and that trend will continue. Health management services will enable operators to replace parts before they wear out and forecast the weather and flight conditions with greater real-time precision to minimize delays and cancellations. The flying experience will reflect passengers' preferences. Imagine a cabin that digitally morphs into a custom product tailored to their individual needs – whether they want to work, relax, or sleep.

5 **Sustainability:** Cleaner, quieter, and more affordable airplanes will accommodate aviation's growth while protecting the environment. Two significant efforts involve developing the supply of sustainable aviation fuels on a commercial scale and leveraging higher energy-density, lighter-weight electrical propulsion solutions.

Over the past century, aerospace has transformed the world. Humans progressed from riding on horses to flying on airplanes and spacecraft. As Nawal K. Taneja recommends, all stakeholders need to contribute to the acceleration of our industry's transformation to meet air transport's future needs. We at Boeing are proud of the role we've played in this momentous journey, and we're committed to providing mobility solutions that will improve the lives of people around the world.

Chicago, USA

Foreword

George J. Khairallah
CEO
JR Technologies

The business case for re-platforming is not self-evident. Massive capital investments have been made by airlines in their existing passenger services system (PSS). We might think that these investments were made simply to acquire and maintain a PSS but that is not the only cost. In the mid-1990s, when airlines wanted to leverage the Internet to go direct to consumers they quickly realized that they did not have the infrastructure for it. They did not own the systems to return basic information like the price of an available seat, they did not have a clear view of who their passengers were. Although they had a good understanding of their market segments from an indirect distribution perspective, they did not have enough data to lead a successful direct distribution strategy. Today, the average airline operates between 200 and 600 software applications to compensate for the gaps and inadequacies of their PSS. The costs associated with building, acquiring, customizing, and maintaining these applications are not negligible.

The dependencies of the various airline divisions on the PSS and these peripheral applications make it extremely difficult to simplify core processes and eliminate functionality that the passenger no longer requires. The revenue management, marketing, and revenue accounting departments, to name but a few, rely on the same data, but require separate data feeds, separate data storage, separate interactions with third parties, and complex labyrinth-like flows for each division to access the information it needs to meet its objectives. As a result, for example, the airline knows the actual revenues of a given month six to eight weeks after the end of the month. It knows the effectiveness of its marketing strategy three to four months after the fact.

Besides the costs related to the complexity inherent to the current setup, we have to consider other important issues. One of these is velocity, measured in terms of speed to market. Today, any change in airline product design takes 12 to 18 months to be available to consumers through the indirect channels. Changes in baggage policy, for instance, took years to be reflected in the distribution channels, and it required the involvement of government regulators to get the change implemented by the GDS. We have also to consider the cost of agility, measured in terms of the speed required to align distribution process flows to new business models. The lack of agility inhibits innovation and enforces commoditization.

The business case for re-platforming needs to account not only for the technology and human aspects but also for the opportunity costs that are directly related to this lack of velocity and agility in the current airline distribution model. From this perspective, a write-off of investments made in PSS and peripheral applications is dwarfed when compared to the limitations that the current distribution technology models impose on an airline's growth and its ability to adapt to new market conditions.

The core principle behind platforming, as discussed in this book, is to make available a real-time, customer focused, central source of truths to data consumers. Data consumers can be internal to the airline such as operations, revenue management, marketing, and accounting. They can also be external such as content aggregators, airports, operations teams, third party services providers, and the like. Most importantly, from a customer service perspective, information is made available in real time to passengers and service providers involved in the delivery of services to the passenger throughout the journey.

The minimum components of such a platform need to include the ability of the airline to control its offers, record and manage orders and changes to orders, process payments, and track deliveries of services and products.

Offer management in this case is in direct relationship with product design, which is traditionally a marketing function. Offer management orchestrates a number of items: the definition and description of services, including rich media; the pricing of the offer; and the definition and description of third party add-on services that some consumers may require to facilitate or enhance their journey. A good offer management system reduces time to market to hours and days rather than months and years as is currently the case.

Order management records the orders with a focus on the service delivery. This requires record keeping not only of purchased items but also their delivery status, their price, the taxes, and the details of the service delivery partners such as lounge providers, ground handlers, and the like. All parties involved in delivering services throughout the journey must have access to the information needed for them to deliver the service, and they also need to update the order management system with the status of each delivery. The passenger, in turn, has real time access to same information.

Offer and order management systems need to be closely integrated and their data need to persist beyond the transaction to provide real-time business intelligence such as offer-to-order conversion rates. Real-time business intelligence can facilitate rapid intervention by the revenue management and marketing teams as they get advance notice of buying patterns. The availability of such data will enhance the value of data lakes that machine learning engines rely on to predict and correct certain revenue trends.

Payment hubs, such as the IATA Financial gateway, facilitate interactions between the order management systems and the payers and the vendors involved in the journey. Like any payment hub this service needs to support a vast array of payment solutions beyond cards and cash. It needs to support dynamic currency conversion, fraud detection, and real-time settlement upon service delivery.

This in no way means that every airline needs to build all the systems and all the connections to all the vendors and service delivery partners, whether internal or external to the airline. This does mean, however, that each airline needs the capability to store, control, and communicate. What we call an "NDC Platform" is akin to what Microsoft or Apple calls an operating system. Microsoft and Apple do not need to develop all the connections and all the software. Thousands of third party applications exist today on the Apple and Microsoft Stores. What they need to do, however, is expose a standard that allows third parties to communicate with these operating systems, while retaining control of access rights and data storage.

By now the reader will surely ask: if the business case for re-platforming is valid and the technology and know-how are available, why is adoption of these new concepts so slow, practically even non-existent. The answer lies in the human factor. From within, airline management looks at current processes, PSS, hundreds of peripheral applications, retraining of employees, and is overwhelmed by the scope of such a change. From outside the airline, IT solution providers who are currently making billions of dollars stand to lose significant revenues because eliminating complexity results in leaner less expensive systems. As a result, the marketplace is ripe with mis-information, blurring the vision for a real digital transformation in the industry. Existing major players do not hesitate to abuse their dominant position in certain markets to stifle innovation and prevent change. Some promising new players are underfunded. Others may have the funding but are lacking in industry know how. They both hesitate to enter a highly competitive arena, where current PSS/GDS providers have a decade-old hold on the industry.

Yet the light at the end of the tunnel is clearly visible. A number of airline groups have taken the travelers' total mobility needs to heart and are investing heavily in new platforms. Our hope is that Nawal K. Taneja's book, on re-platforming the airline business, will encourage more airlines to look beyond perceived limitations, and heed the voices of their customers.

Chania, Greece

Foreword

Taimur Khan

General Manager, Vice President –
Travel, Transportation, and Hospitality, Salesforce

The ubiquity of computing on mobile, sensors, and PCs has been subject to the concept of Moore's laws: processing power doubling every 18 months and unit costs dropping. The travel industry is subject to a similar Moore's law, but with improvement in an additional axis: air traffic has increased, costs to the traveler have dropped, and at the same time safety has improved. The accident rate/million flights in 2017 was 1.08, down from 2.01 over the five-year period from 2012 to 2016, and cost to travel has dropped by 50 percent in the last 30 years, while fuel costs have rocketed up. We as travelers take safety and reliability under normal (non-weather-influenced) factors take this for granted: as business travelers, we will fly on the day of the meeting, conduct business, and return, while remaining productive through Wi-Fi at 30,000 feet while in transit.

To bring the travel to this level of efficiency and safety took a concerted effort from the industry. The concept of crew resource management (CRM) was first introduced in the 1980s and has been a decades-long journey to improve crew collaboration and avoid accidents. Today, crew resource management is a common practice on a global scale. This is one of numerous examples that illustrates the same point: discipline and effort has gotten the industry to where air travel has become a predictable experience.

Over the last decade, a revolution has been taking place in consumers' preferences, as discussed also by Nawal in his series of books on the airline industry. Research shows that 65 percent of today's consumers are likely to switch if a company doesn't anticipate their needs; 75 percent of consumers want their provider to anticipate needs and make relevant suggestions. This is the age of New CRM, 'customer relationship management': it's about knowing your traveling customers and serving them in a way never done before. This is most obvious in media and retail but has touched every major industry in the economy. The consumer expects an on-demand, frictionless experience where they are in control. In order to grow and build loyalty, media, retail, and manufacturing industries have made this transition and developed new business models and customer experiences:

- Netflix groups its audience into one of several thousand taste clusters so it can make appropriate recommendations.

- Adidas delivers exceptional value and branding by harmonizing the e-commerce and in-store experience to drive brand differentiation, understand customer tastes, and improve loyalty.
- Kone transports more people in one day than the entire airline industry combined: 1 billion people utilize Kone elevators/escalators daily. Building intelligence into its elevators has enabled Kone to be proactive with its customers. Sensors monitor various aspects of the elevators and send real-time data that are used to detect usage patterns and surface any issues with the product. The company can engage with customers proactively in event of outages or potential maintenance issues and also understand future needs based on actual use.

Consumer expectations for hyper-personalization are now extending to travel and will be key to brand differentiation. The quality of the customer experience can have lasting effects. An exceptional customer experience can create a lifetime revenue opportunity with loyal customers. But a bad travel experience can turn into lost revenue and a social media nightmare for a brand. Media and retail by comparison are much more perishable: you can always hit pause on a bad movie recommendation, or return a retail item that didn't work out.

The intersection of sensors, mobile, artificial intelligence (AI), and immense computer power through the cloud makes it possible to collect data from external sources that consumers choose to share, analyze it, and act on it at the point of the engagement with a brand to deliver a hyper-personalized customer experience.

The hospitality segment in travel has recognized this trend and is going through a re-platforming to hyper-personalize their engagement with guests. Hotel brands are embracing digital to meet rising customer expectations, making every guest-facing associate more informed at the point of engagement, saving costs, and most importantly having a more complete understanding of each traveler's needs. This understanding of needs and preferences allows them to anticipate the traveler's need and provide a superior customer experience that leads to a positive revenue impact. This digital re-platforming is occurring in parallel to their business model shift to an asset-light model where greater than 90 percent of the properties branded by the largest companies are owned by operators and not the brands themselves.

Airlines are in early phases of this journey. From a business model aspect, the airline industry has taken the first step of unbundling the core airline seat product into discrete components: seat, bags, meals, premium. From a technology standard, adoption of NDC will for the first time allow the offer package delivered through any channel and remove blind spots when a traveler is coming in through third-party channels. However, these are just foundational steps toward the merchandising vision the airlines aspire to for owning the traveler experience. To do it well and effectively, airlines will have to re-platform:

- Use digital to get the basics right to an end state where, regardless of touch point with the traveler, the experience is the same and regardless of which airline employee or where, the same information is available at the point of engagement. This does not happen today. Unless you are a premier flier, these seamless touch points do not exist across the gate agent, the reservation staff, and cabin crew. In an age of information asymmetry, in which the traveler has more information and has it earlier than the airline employees, fliers are forced to repeat information and resort to traditional phone interactions.

- In the rare cases these touch points exist, they only exist after travelers are past the inspiration and research phase and are purchasing the ticket or already on their journey. At this point travelers have already gone through the 'friction' and time investment of researching what they want to do. According to some estimates, there are as many as 50+ touch points across devices and various travel providers. This is the least likely place for an airline to differentiate or 'merchandise,' because at this stage the traveler has already invested the time choosing the cheapest option. Re-platforming helps get the airline to understand and influence the early inspiration phase, as discussed in this book, where the traveler is open to options and airlines can differentiate on value.

- Airlines need to understand travelers beyond what's in their existing transactional systems, which only represent a partial picture of the traveler. There is a broader traveler profile in their off-airline behavior, such as through social channels and physical location, that can give a deeper understanding of a traveler's preferences. Travelers who exercise the option to share their personal data can remove a lot of friction from the research phase and get more of a concierge-like digital experience. As an example, 40 percent of travelers under 35 prioritizing travel destinations based on how "Instagram-able" it will be (source: Schoefields Survey). More than half the consumers are willing to share personal data for easier purchasing and personalized offers (source: Salesforce Research).

- Air travel is about getting to a destination safely and without hassle, but ultimately getting on an aircraft is a path to their end goal. By re-platforming, the airlines can be in a better position understand their travelers' tastes and preferences on why they are taking the trip and be better able to monetize the @destination spend. This goes beyond a transactional relationship around marketing the fixed and limited ancillary items that can be sold before/during a flight but almost nothing after. The @destination spend for a traveler can be 2–3 times of what they spend on airfare.

- Re-platforming helps with the readiness to embrace new technologies such as voice interfaces and future travel assistants as part of an integrated traveler journey. It's easy to plug in a new gadget as a one-off, but unless they have the traveler history, preferences, and context, they add little value in terms of user experience. Imagine a hotel brand providing the guest's favorite music streaming platform and a voice assistant in the room. The voice assistant has to have context on the individual using it for it to be valuable. The music streaming platform is not very relevant if it doesn't identify the traveler and preferences on what the traveler likes to listen to on a business trip vs. leisure.

- Finally, re-platforming gets the organization existing channels of engagement ready for the future. Voice calls on mobile networks are on a downward annual decline of 10 percent to 20 percent over the next five years. Travelers will always need channels of engagement, but they will choose those channels and often switch between them. The large number of contact centers used as the primary method of engagement were set up when toll-free numbers came about. These contact centers have to be converted to traveler engagement centers where the engagement teams are given the capabilities needed to be successful. Re-platforming will help airlines adjust to the change so they are not left with a voice-based channel of engagement that's going to go the direction of telex and fax in terms of its usefulness and relevance.

We are also seeing the first indication of asset-light models in transportation. Flixbus is a digital-only company and a bus and rail provider in Europe and recently expanded to the US. It's an early example of how a digital platform can power a fast-growth transportation business by understanding traveler needs and is an indicator of what's to come in other modes of travel. The company is experiencing exponential growth in its short five-year history: 120,000 daily connections across 1,700 destinations in 28 countries. Local partners are responsible for the day-to-day running of routes. Flixbus handles network planning, marketing, pricing, quality management, and customer service.

The concept of crew resource management ('safety' CRM) did not exist a generation ago: the airline industry embraced safety as a platform. This has been key to continued appeal of travel that has contributed to the industry's growth trajectory. The industry's next growth will be defined by a different type of CRM ('customer' CRM). This customer CRM is anchored on the principle of understanding needs of the traveler and being able to deliver to that need. Re-platforming is not about a single technology or a specific product. It is a mindset of having the right digital framework and the accompanying mindset in place that provides a foundation for agility, while also providing a mechanism to connect with and make use of newer technologies like AI, voice assistants, and virtual reality as their use cases become relevant.

San Francisco, USA

Foreword

Ed Sims

President and CEO
WestJet Airlines

There is an old adage in the airline business, that he or she with the lowest cost wins. This adage remains as true today as it has since the inception of commercial air travel. It is not often that another axiom comes along to live alongside this one, but this is exactly where the aviation industry finds itself, and it is this: He or she with the data wins, or at least has a better chance of winning in conjunction with a lower cost!

Having the data is only part of the solution, however. Consumers are not buying your product, nor are they signing up simply because you have data. People purchase an experience based on how you make them feel, not simply the product itself. So data must be relevant, timely, and leveraged with a view to building a better experience. The examples may be overused, but Uber and Airbnb aren't doing anything revolutionary – it's a ride from point A to point B or a place to lay your head while you're traveling. It's the experience that is the revolution. As an airline, we fly people from one city to the other in an aluminum cylinder with wings that looks much the same as our competitors', and at the same speed and altitude. Harnessing the power of data and driving a superior cost advantage to make the experience better and cheaper than the competition will be the game changer for us all.

Nawal K. Taneja's new book tackles this dichotomy in great detail. Is it data or cost that wins? The answer is yes! *Re-Platforming the Airline Business* underscores the need to leverage the power of data and platform-based business models in order to discern which product offerings have become commoditized and which can provide true differentiation in the market.

As a relative newcomer to Canada, I am quickly learning that this is the very crossroads at which WestJet finds itself as we transition from a low-cost, point-to-point airline into a high-value, global network carrier. Platform-based business models are the future; it is only a matter of time before consumer expectations grow exponentially (again), and they will seek out those airlines that get their needs – needs they may not even realize they have today. For those who assume that disruptors won't impact or penetrate the "too complex" airline world, you are buying yourself years at best, months at worst.

Calgary, Canada

Foreword

Xiao Yinhong
CEO
TravelSky Technology Limited

In recent decades, cross-regional and cross-cultural cooperation have become common sense. The understanding and exchange among countries and cultures are gradually increasing. The world is in some senses getting highly integrated. According to the "Belt and Road Initiative" of President Xi, the aviation industry plays an even more important role in building a human community of a shared future.

In the past few years, the global economy has been in a steady growth, with the oil prices and interest rate at a low level. The global aviation industry has seen passenger flow, passenger load factor, and profits hit historic high levels. However, this year, with the growth of oil prices and labor costs, IATA lowered the annual profit expectation from 38.4 billion US dollars, set last December, to 33.8 billion. Therefore, doubts about sustainability of growth arise. This gives alarm to players in the aviation technology ecosystem, including the airlines and airports, and the IT solution providers and agencies. We are in a changing industry, though slow with regard to our expectations; however, there is always a burden in recognizing the right direction and properly following the trend. Furthermore, we have always been willing to make our direction the right one and lead the trend rather than follow it.

In the aviation industry, the linchpin has been the airlines, but it is unclear whether airlines will still play this role in the future. Furthermore, the concept of the aviation industry is being challenged as provider-centric. Indeed, from the traveler's perspective, more and more other providers from other industries are also getting into the picture, for example, hotels, ground transportation service providers, etc. To some extent, "customers do not care about the product," or the provider of the product, "they care about the result, and the experience." We have to reshape our business with yet-to-be-decided new boundaries, if they still exist, and make collaborations with all existing and potential service providers, with a customer-centric perspective, in a most efficient manner to meet the expectations on customer experience and to create additional value. Only then can we, as old folks in the aviation industry, stay relevant.

More specifically, in the aviation technology ecosystem, in which I have been serving for more than 30 years, there are always doubts and challenges, and we have been puzzling about making the right decisions. Where are we going according to our current road map of resource allocation and investment? Are we satisfied? What is the desirable future scenario? How can we be closer or faster to that future? What additional efforts or inputs are required to achieve this?

This new book by Professor Taneja managed to provide some interesting thinking, and I couldn't agree more, especially on the concept of "re-platforming" according to "traveler's needs." Also, it is very true that the airline business is divided into two aspects, operations and marketing. I would like to talk more on marketing, which has been more challenged both from business model and technology innovation perspectives, and from both the traveler's demand as well as new players in the picture.

As a CEO of an IT service provider in the aviation industry, let me try to describe where we are and how we feel at the moment. We have been a platform, sitting in the middle of the traveler and the airlines, with transactions in the millions, conducted 24/7. We used to share the glories of both aviation and IT, while now, we are like a "second-rate punk" comparing with fast-growing Internet technology companies, say Google, Amazon, and BAT. New technologies are profoundly changing the world and our lives. Artificial intelligence, machine learning, biometrics, blockchain, big data, etc., are used in all walks of life. However, the aviation industry has a limited or less-than-expectation application of new technologies. There has been a feeling of the need for change, but the gaps between expectation and implementation are significant.

To be able to resolve the challenges of aviation, we have to think beyond the aviation industry. As an aviation information technology provider, we have to reshape the legacy platform specifically designed for the airlines to new platforms that are able to provide a broader spectrum of customer-centric services.

Let's ask and answer the following specific questions so that we get closer to the expected platform.

1   Is there a significant difference between the business model of the airlines from the hotels? I do not think so, especially from a marketing perspective. We check the availability of a flight seat very much the same way as the availability of a hotel room, both of them categorized by various levels of service with respective fares. The same goes for the booking, the payment, and the process of check-in. The global distribution system consolidates the air and hotel booking into one "super" passenger name record, and so did the subsequent airline websites and mobile apps. In the scenario of national distribution capability, this combined service record is called "One Order." And we can see both airlines and hotels are managing to somehow provide the "platform" service for other service providers; for example, you can make an airline booking on Marriott.com or have a bundled package including a hotel from CathayPacific.com. Both of them have very obvious intentions of providing better services to the traveler with one-stop shopping, and thus, the "narrow" business is expanded, at least from the marketing perspective.

But who has more privilege in this "order"? The airlines? The hotels? Which one will become more important? Of course, it is possible for an airline or a hotel to successfully transform into a platform provider, like the GDSs have been doing, largely thanks to the application of new technology and connecting directly to the traveler. However, it is worth emphasizing that this is no longer a business boundary expansion but rather a complete shift of business model. Logically, the old fashioned GDSs and other IT service providers in a related industry will have more of a chance to fulfill the role of such a platform. However, the old-fashioned businesses have to prove that they are competent in making good use of new technology and to change to an infrastructure of traveler-centricity, where no provider will have more privilege to the "Order" than the traveler himself.

2 Is there a significant difference between the airline booking process and the addition of new items into the shopping cart on Amazon? I think not. I had been struggling to avoid this answer, but failed. I have to acknowledge that all the shopping behaviors – air travel, hotel booking, and the common commodity retailing – have no significant difference. Neither does the support to customers after sales. If you buy a product on Amazon, Amazon will be responsible for its delivery and after-sales services. The same is true with air retailing. Its range goes far beyond ticket sales. The airlines need to meet passengers' demands after they bought the tickets. The demand surrounds both after-purchase problems passengers meet, like flight delay, lost luggage, etc., and new demands, like prepaid seat selection, finding a parking space in the airport, in-flight entertainment, etc. To pay close attention to passengers' after-purchase behaviors, and to solve the problems and respond to new demands in time will boost passengers' satisfaction level and create additional revenues for airlines. The question is how to efficiently meet passengers' various after-purchase demands, because companies in other industries, like Netflix, have set a high bar for customer service by providing comprehensive and flexible personalized service, and thus the threshold for customers' degree of satisfaction has been rising. In comparison, airlines seem to lag behind in terms of customer service and are not able to meet passengers' expectations. To turn the tide, airlines should have keen awareness of all the touch points in passengers' itineraries and find out the pain points on each touch point, so that the airlines can offer targeted products and services. While providing customer-centric standard services, airlines should also expand personalized services, as after-sales personalization has been an area with many passenger demands and large revenue potentials.

To realize personalized services on all after-sales touch points, airlines have to depend on a mature platform. The platform should not only be able to offer standard and common services but have a future-oriented design, meaning it should be an open platform with scalable capacity and be able to support mutual transformation between the platform and personalized solutions. But is the current platform mature enough?

Like in the foregoing, since airlines and hotels can share the same platform to be able to provide seamless traveler experience, why not make use of the common retailing platform for travel? Technology-wise, I don't see any threshold. How soon will this happen? It is already happening, but still far from enough in terms of the current maturity of the retailing business model and the readiness of new technology. It seems that these new giant technology companies express insufficient interests: they show up at the gate but do not board. There are a number of new entrants into the travel industry, relatively small, with new technology approaches and less burden on the legacy environment; however, they also lack the business background. These new entrants act more to play a role of partial solutions and tend not to be the ones to completely replace the legacy systems.

Why do the new entrants show insufficient interests in taking the overall role to be the dominant players? Because there are big ugly problems in the current legacy environment that they are not easily able to overcome, and this is not just a matter of technology. Professor Taneja pointed out many times throughout this book, the "complexity" of the business, operation as well as marketing, and also overall management. So it is not a question of capability, but rather it is a question on expectation of profitable margin, and the current airline industry has far less profitable margin compared to other new emerging industries. Being involved for nearly my entire career in the airline industry, it is awkward for me to admit this.

When will the airline industry become more attractive to new entrants? I think at least one of the many prerequisites will be the accomplishment of re-platforming the business. This new platform will not only be able to satisfy the traveler's demands but also will be able to collaborate in the most efficient manner, with all providers on the supply side. The new platform will explore the potential needs of the traveler by shifting into new business areas, using innovative new technologies, and only by adding additional value would travelers be willing to spend more money, from convenience and efficiency to enjoy products and services and even get the feeling of freedom, and more.

Such a new kind of platform, both from the concept of business and technology, will, at least, contain two layers and would require the combined force of both the new entrants and the current players. First, the condition of the old-fashioned legacy environment will be taken care of either by incremental enhancements or full replacement; the bottom line is that it will not be a constraint on new services while providing stability under a reasonable cost. Second will be a new environment for the traveler's demands. This new environment will adapt to the trends of the consumer, possibly following the approaches of the new Internet companies, and it has to create a high profit margin by making good use of the most up-to-date innovative technologies.

However, there are lots of uncertainties preventing management in the industry from making satisfactory decisions. We have to struggle to balance risks and opportunities. Although "the rate of transformation, has been mostly evolutionary, rather than revolutionary," there is a more tightened schedule for decision every day, and staying where we are might be tactful, but also carry significant risks.

I think that by reading this book, the audience may get a different perspective that could help the development of our industry.

Recently, along with the aviation and tourism market fluctuation, the risks and uncertainties in the economic development of China have also constantly emerged. But we still believe that the global economy is in gradual recovery and China's economy shows sustained growth. In 2017, China's civil aviation registered steady and rapid growth for the sixth consecutive year. TravelSky played a very important role as the leading IT service supplier in China's aviation and tourism industry.

Alongside the growth, the size of the Chinese market also poses challenges for TravelSky, regarding management, security, regulation, customer service, etc. In particular, both from operational and marketing perspectives, solutions of Travel-Sky have to reach the industry's leadership level. These solutions have to be made under industry supervision (especially regulations on security) and with continuous low costs and in a timely manner. Although this makes the mission nearly impossible, TravelSky has been managing well for more than 30 years, and with the thinking of "re-platforming" according to "traveler's needs," we will be able to render better decisions in the upcoming 30 years.

Chinese airlines are on a fast pace of developing international markets, and the system service providers from the rest of the world are also taking steps to enter China. We are confident in the foreseeable future that TravelSky may well play the dominant role, with a unique position to cope with demands that are large in number as well as diversified in variety. Nevertheless, how to make good use of the exponential and innovative new technologies to satisfy the new business model, to deliver even better and more valuable services, and to continuously create high profit margins and sustained growth, remains a challenge.

Beijing, China

1   Introduction

Book theme

The airline business has seen continuous rapid, although evolutionary, change over its last hundred years – through strong but stable growth enabled by a combination of new technologies on both marketing and operations sides of the business. Going forward, airline business models will continue to be shaped by these forces, but in ways that will no longer be evolutionary, but revolutionary. This book lays out the case for this step change. Revolutionary change will emerge from forces discussed in this book, forces that are moving ever faster to create change in two diametrically opposed directions at the same time. When persistent, dramatic change occurs in opposing directions, "earthquakes" happen.

The case for revolutionary change

The airline industry has two primary functional areas that are rapidly diverging toward opposite ends of the business management spectrum. On one side is the management of operations – crewing, fueling, flying, and maintaining an aircraft fleet. The pressure in this domain is driving toward relentless efficiency and low-cost production. After decades of rapid technological changes, many parts of operations have now become a commodity business. Ground operations, flight operations, and maintenance are just three examples. In these areas of the airline business, success is defined by the efficiency of the operator. This is not to imply that the challenges are minimal, as all three are far from routine operations. Rather, it is that managing exceptions in their operations requires great skill. Nevertheless, there is now sufficient scale in these operational areas of the business so as to allow for the emergence of specialized players who are truly low-cost producers.

On the other hand, there are volatile and in some cases opposing changes that continue to occur on the marketing side of the business as increasingly diverse customers focus on experience and personalization. The marketing of travel is in a great turmoil. The demands of customers and emerging markets are leading to a dizzying array of outcomes. Whether it is the dismantling of the complex schemes of revenue management strategies, new social media channels, the myriad of new routes, carriers, and pricing options, or decisions relating to strategic alliances and joint ventures, nothing about airline marketing is clear. If anything, the emergence of underdeveloped markets as a prominent source of revenues will add to the continued disruption of the airline marketing focus. However, the capability to provide and manage customer experience is in an early stage, given the changing customer base.

Five forces management must face

Going forward, the picture of how airline management will navigate these two major management domains – operational excellence and marketing innovation – remains quite unclear. These two domains are moving in opposite directions in some ways, directions that will demand very different management skillsets. Operations demand relentless efficiency; marketing demands relentless innovation. The book will provide a framework for better understanding the management challenges in each domain and the likely outcome of this struggle. The book starts by laying out two sets of forces that are acting in the aviation business. It turns out that these two sets of forces also are in opposition to each other. Consequently, there are five forces in total.

There is a set of three positive growth-related forces that are operating at a pace faster than ever before. First, there are *disruptive market dynamics* resulting from ever-new forms of low-cost products. Even while this is playing out, new, better, and more customer-oriented distribution channels are emerging, making accessibility to these new forms of low-cost products a substantial market growth force. Second, there will be *explosive demand growth*, with demand emerging in markets that have never had service before and new travel demand segments emerging in existing markets. New forms of demand will also be generated from the fulfillment of new customer expectations, based on the growth of concepts such as mobility-as-a-service (MaaS). Third, there will be *transformational technology changes* centered around three distinct technology dimensions: (1) marketing concepts enabled by mobile technologies, for example, MaaS, based on the smartphone platform; (2) new aircraft technologies that will redefine air travel from the very shortest range (flying taxis and flying cars), to the longest range (nonstop service in such markets as Sydney-London and Singapore-New York), to the fastest mode in commercial operations (next-generation supersonics); and (3) new software capabilities, such as artificial intelligence, blockchain, biometrics, and video, that will deliver everything from personalization to customer experience to comprehensive search.

There will also be a set of two constraints that will conspire to limit growth. The impact of these constraints may largely be felt by the existing players; new players will also feel these constraints, but the impact will be asymmetric, as new players will design solutions that fundamentally work around such constraints. The first of the opposing forces is the complexity and *"tyranny of the installed base"* of technologies. Simply said, the technologies created yesterday and utilized by legacy players do not have the capability offered by newer technologies. Newer players coming along, created by the market dynamics mentioned earlier, will have an edge in capturing the lion's share of the new growth by utilizing exponential technologies, emerging almost daily, but which are oftentimes too disruptive for legacy players to rapidly embrace at their scale. The second of the opposing forces will be ***regulatory and operational constraints***. History shows that regulators are falling further behind in their ability to deal with new players. Think about how Uber managed to launch service in 100 countries, even while taxi regulations largely stayed in place. And, as far as capacity constraints are concerned (for example, capacity limits at airports), new players will develop solutions to work around these constraints, for example, through the use of secondary airports and long-range aircraft to by-pass constrained hubs. Yet these effects will be asymmetric on the players in the industry.

Emergence of platform solutions

One likely resolution of this seismic change, which forms the heart of the book, will be the re-platforming of the business. Why platform models? Because they have the ability to absorb the changes created by these two sets of opposing forces. Platforms are simply the most efficient ways of connecting buyers and sellers in any market, and a way of providing a clearinghouse for mixing players that are experiencing the asymmetric effects mentioned earlier. Platform-based business models are different. They enable the interface between a broad spectrum of sellers and buyers and thus represent the point where value is added and where profits are generated. Airline managements will likely need to separate those functions that for them represent commodities from those functions that can lead to differentiation. Some managements may choose to differentiate through a step-change gain in efficiency and become the lowest-cost operators. Other managements may choose to differentiate by becoming the most skillful marketers.

A management choosing the market direction may focus on a marketing platform for four reasons. First, a platform can enable an airline to gather and integrate relevant data from internal and external sources. Second, a platform can help develop business intelligence and customer intelligence through a synthesis of data, using new technologies, such as artificial intelligence. Third, a platform can facilitate the sharing of relevant and timely information within the travel chain. Fourth, a platform can connect buyers with the different suppliers of travel – that is, airlines offering seats and services companies offering everything from upgrades, to ancillary services, to destination services, to complementary travel products, such as limos, and so forth. A marketing platform largely enables the connection of the broadest range of new services to the greatest ease of access by the largest number of buyers. One can see the same kind of thing emerging on the operations side. An operations platform could exist primarily to (1) collect, integrate, and synthesize data, and, (2) connect suppliers of capacity – that is, aircraft operators, pilots, maintenance and ground services, lessors, and manufacturers of new types of aircraft – with buyers, where the buyers may largely be marketing entities with access to end customers. These marketing entities could be conventional airlines, "new virtual airlines" that own no aircraft, information entities such as Google, or retailers such as Amazon.

Opportunities for airline management

How long will it be before serious players emerge in one of these domains, for example, marketing, to drastically change the status quo? Will a Google or another player finally conquer the complexity of navigating the price-shopping pain of trip planning? Will an Uber or Airbnb or a similar business find a way of connecting customers with airlines that have seats to offer across a wide range of markets? We do not know. What is clear, however, is that the current situation is so complex and disorienting that the marketplace is ripe for disruption. Simultaneously, innovative technologies (both on the vehicle and the marketing sides), coupled with the emergence of new-generation platforms, threaten to consume management bandwidth at an accelerating rate. Management may well need to choose between using new technologies to focus on creating marketing price-service options, channels, and the go-to-market approaches on the one hand and on driving to be the low-cost operators of flying capacity on the other hand. Ultimately, developing or joining a platform may well be an increasingly popular option.

Previous books in this series presented some forces and their potential impact to disrupt from within or outside of the industry. Also discussed was the point that the airline planning systems and processes in use are neither contemporary nor sufficiently integrated to meet the changing needs of the now always-connected customers or the serious potential threat of new competition from outside of the airline industry. Customers are looking for outcomes, not products – for example, customized solutions to their mobility requirements that really matter – and current airline products are not moving in that direction. At the same time, new travel-marketing companies are getting ready to develop fast new business models to position themselves between airlines and their customers, enabling more customer-friendly travel guidance. Although *Re-platforming the Airline Business: To Meet Travelers' Total Mobility Needs* reiterates the need for transformation of the airline business and to some extent the airport business, this book will showcase the landscape of data- and technology-driven transformational processes that will need to emerge from a combination of human and intelligent technology to make more informed and faster decisions. However, there is also a need for a step-change in corporate culture on the part of both management and the workforce, as well as the development of enlightened regulatory policies.

This book proposes that different sectors of the aviation industry, particularly airlines, reconsider their business models from production to customer centricity by using not just a wide array of technologies (biometrics, blockchain, conversational interfaces, the Internet of things, and new forms of transportation, for example), but also by specifically designed, customer solution-centric, and experience-centric platforms established between airlines and the customer community. Any one of the technologies discussed is sufficient to dramatically change the airline business. The combination of these technologies, in both the marketing side and the operational side, is likely to be groundbreaking and likely to stretch the bandwidth of management to accommodate and transform simultaneously. That is why a risk of new entrants that sharpen their skills and are purely focused on one or the other of these aspects is particularly threatening to incumbents.

There is also the likelihood of changes created by the platform economy. Platform-based business models are different. First, they represent the interface between a broad spectrum of sellers and buyers, and they represent the point where value is added and where profits are generated. Second, they facilitate the making of informed decisions to develop and implement transformative strategies to meet travelers' total mobility needs and the needs of service providers to make a profit. Third, internal data-powered platforms, a building block of the larger travel-services platforms, will enable pioneering airlines to achieve scale and scope in their businesses and create agility and flexibility. It is these internal data-powered platforms that will help bring about processes that (1) dynamically bring in line the higher investments in an airline's fixed assets with demand that is variable and (2) provide some control over how the data is shared with respect to the value delivered and the value received.

Sectors of the global aviation industry are fully aware of the need to transform their business models to adapt to the changing nature of economies that are becoming increasingly digital, sharing, on-demand, and convenience based. The transformation is not just to remain competitive but to remain relevant. However, progress relating to a significant level of transformation, at least in the case of almost the entire airline sector, has been relatively slow, due to:

1 Different stages of development of businesses within different sectors of the aviation industry, calling for widely different strategies and their timings.

  • A range of airlines, from those fighting for their survival to those that are not only making huge amounts of profits, but are strategizing to position themselves to achieve sustainable and profitable growth.

2 The difficulty of shifting from supply-driven and product-driven business models to demand-driven and solution-driven business models.

  • The sequential setup of airline organizations continues to be to first acquire capacity, then schedule it, and finally fill it on a seat-by-seat, flight-by-flight basis, precluding the ability to implement new holistic approaches to harmonize supply and demand.

3 A significant gap between the capabilities of the legacy technology systems and processes and the contemporary, not just customer-centric, but experience-centric, technology systems and processes that are needed to engage with customers and employees to provide personalized services.

  • This challenge is a lot more difficult to overcome. Although most management do have a reasonable understanding of what experience is for different segments of customers at different times and at different touch points, systems and processes are not available to identify, measure, and track customer experience, let alone employee experience.

4   A gap between the inspirations of marketing executives and the capabilities of the business to execute the inspirational concepts.

- Executives suspect that big data can provide customer and business intelligence. However, there is a big gap between knowing that big data can generate actionable customer insights and actually developing and implementing strategies based on customer insights.

5   The inability of the traditional functional silos within airline organizations to develop, let alone execute, substantially different business models.

- Managers within different functions have their own objectives and their own strategies without system-design perspectives.

6   Management's view of the unusual levels of complexity within some aviation sectors of the industry to bring about step-changing transformation quickly.

- Although technologies exist to handle complexity, the challenge is not only to define complexity but also to define its costs.

7   Resistance to the implementation of fail-fast initiatives even in areas that do not relate to safety considerations.

- Is management willing to evaluate projects within the fail-fast framework based on an analysis of big data? Even for projects not related to safety, some airline managers spend years evaluating projects, compared to their counterparts in the technology sector, who take months.

8   Lack of unity within different sectors in the travel chain, with each sector planning to "own the customer."

- Would airlines be willing to share data with airports, car-rental companies, hotels, etc., when there is even a challenge to share data within different divisions of airlines?

9   Infrastructure constraints, particularly at congested airports around the world.

- How would a major global airline, such as Cathay Pacific, develop a low-cost division and operate it out of its own hub, in this case, Hong Kong International Airport?

10   A perception that the "total" costs of a full set of emerging technologies will be high, if one includes the replacement costs of the legacy systems that are considered to be "reliable."

- While airline managers recognize that a number of legacy systems are obsolete, they consider these systems critical for an airline's operations.

Based on the aforementioned observations, while some airline executives have been hesitant to change their prevailing business models and business processes, a few pioneering airlines are developing a clear vision of business transformation. They are beginning to push the frontiers of innovation to develop and implement distinct and bold business strategies to drive value by enabling emerging technologies to change the structure, performance, and conduct of the airline industry. They are planning to accomplish the transformation in both areas at the same time, operational excellence and marketing innovation. They are already starting to go beyond incremental changes by undertaking faster planning network cycles instead of the traditional once or twice a year, considering developing pricing systems that are dynamic, and reworking loyalty systems that add more value for customers and airlines. Some of these pioneering airlines could even decide to separate those functions that represent commodities from those functions that can lead to differentiation. Some managements may choose to differentiate through a step-change gain in efficiency and become the lowest-cost operators. Other managements may choose to differentiate by becoming the most skillful marketers. Platforms will likely be important to both management choices. Platforms can be used to dramatically minimize costs in areas representing commodity products and offer meaningfully differentiated services in other areas to build brands and loyalty.

This book is about re-platforming the airline industry. The re-platforming aspect is because the aviation industry, in general, is not new to the use of platforms, even though the systems were not called "platforms" at the time of their development. Within the airline sector, early forms of platforms were developed by IATA and SITA, for example, to coordinate inter-line operations and bank settlement systems and communications, respectively. Other examples of early forms of platforms developed and used by airlines include the filing and access of fares, computer reservation systems, loyalty programs, regional carriers to provide feeder services at major hub-and-spoke airports, global distribution systems, and strategic alliances among airlines. Technological standards like Airinc and Spec 2000 were jointly developed to ease air-to-ground communication or share spare parts. These early types of platforms enabled airlines to deal with, to some extent, the complexity and constraints of the industry while providing safe, efficient, and increasingly affordable forms of air travel.

Within the airline sector, however, older-generations of platforms, while still operational, are not capable of transforming either different sub-functions within marketing or different sub-functions within operations to reduce costs dramatically and/or to increase revenues while improving both customer experience and employee experience. This limitation is understandable, since older generations of platforms were not designed to provide scale, scope, and flexibility for airlines and to focus deeply on customer service, let alone customer and employee experience, relative to the contemporary perspectives. From the beginning, the complexity of logistics caused airlines to focus more on operations than on marketing, even though the IATA pricing and inter-line regime did enable passengers to travel around the world on one ticket. Similarly, the business model of most airports focused more on operations than marketing. However, as with some airlines, some airports have also been increasing their focus on marketing to adapt to the needs of their customers – full-service airlines, low-cost carriers, and, in turn, their customers. Moreover, these customers' needs are changing. Once airlines and airports start to operate within a newly designed platform framework, different airlines and different airports can strategize their actual and potential business models at different points on their respective platform continuums.

The need for re-platforming the airline business is also clear because some technology businesses, working with customer-centric and experience-centric platforms, can easily help travelers create personalized and total trips with flexibility and with the ease of changing the trip components in real time and on a contextual basis. Think about what has already happened in the hospitality sector. Take, for instance, the concept of time-sharing properties. New-technology businesses, such as Airbnb, already re-platformed the business, not only by capitalizing on the deployment of a web-based system but also by taking the concept of experience, authenticity, unique properties and locations, and detailed information (including relevant images) to facilitate comparison to new heights. Airbnb could step forward, for example, and extend its platform to offer a comprehensive set of travel-related services. Airbnb is reportedly extending its core business into new areas, such as relocations and off-site locations. The relocations relate to longer-term rentals of properties. The off-site locations relate to meetings and a wide array of activities at off-site properties. In addition to these features is the value of Airbnb developing a powerful loyalty program that places a much greater focus on experience? The existing platform has already disrupted the distribution space in the hospitality sector by becoming a powerful competitor to the likes of Expedia and Booking.com. Such operators of platforms could include a much more comprehensive search (based on voice, for example) and rankings (based on input from social media). They could also include such services as prediction of fares and on-time performance and recommendations on the use of alternate airports to provide different price-service options, as well as the deployment of emerging payment systems.

Chapter outline

Chapter 2 provides a brief description of the three major forces and the two constraints and their impact on airlines, airports, and, to some extent, on aircraft manufacturers. Also presented are the results of a forecast by IATA in a report called the *Future of the Airline Industry 2035*[1] and the results of a forecast by Eurocontrol in a report called *European Aviation in 2040*.[2] Each of both reports contains four scenarios of the future between now and 2035 by IATA and between now and 2040 by Eurocontrol. In this book, an assumption is made that passenger traffic will continue to grow in line with the middle two scenarios discussed in the IATA report and the middle two scenarios discussed in the Eurocontrol report. Within this context, this book discusses three forces – market dynamics, customers, and technologies – and two constraints – complexities and regulators.

Relating to the first force, market dynamics, we can expect a much larger expansion of low-cost carriers and the emergence of new travel marketers. Relating to the second force, customers' demand for air travel has not only been growing, but it has also been shifting with respect to geographic locations as well as changes in consumers' expectations, attitudes, and preferences. The third force, the proliferation of enabling technologies, promises to help different sectors of the aviation industry to cater to their business needs – relating to market dynamics and customers – and manage the complexities of their businesses as well as the fulfillment of the regulatory requirements of governments. As for the complexity of the business, there has been, and continues to be, (1) an increase in the fragmentation of service providers and (2) a wide gap between the capabilities enabled by the operational systems and the dramatically changing needs of customers, for example, not just for service, or even experience, but seamless experience. As for the potential changes in policies of regulators, there are impacts in five areas of the aviation industry – bilaterals (relating to airline networks), airline ownership and control (relating to organizational structure), aircraft emissions (CO_2, noise, and so forth), security (digital and physical, relating to customer experience and the privacy of data), and infrastructure, airports, and air traffic control systems (relating to capacity). Among the dozens of enabling technologies available to adapt to the three forces and to handle the two constraints, only six are discussed in this book: mobile, biometrics, blockchain, artificial intelligence, Internet of things, and new forms of air and ground transportations.

Chapter 3 is about transforming and bonding two major functions within airlines and airports, marketing and operations. From the strategies being followed in the industry, it is evident that the commercial side of the airline business has received a lot of attention for transformation relative to the operational side. For example, personalization is beginning to appear, facilitated by technology, along with an attempt to break down the silo system. Some airlines have started to create 360-degree views of their customers to make the right offer to the right customer at the right time with the right price and through the right channel, a consistent theme stressed throughout the series. However, the objective now is to generate additional revenue and improve customer experience at the same time. Furthermore, consider now a possible parallel situation on the operational side. How about using technology and a breakdown of the silo system to get 360-degree views of maintenance situations, to get the right part (and the right mechanic and with the right tools) for the right plane at the right time and at the right location?

The first section of Chapter 3 discusses different aspects for making airline marketing more mainstream. Airlines have clearly achieved much success in marketing their services in the past three decades. However, if one looks at the development in the last ten years that led to evolutionary changes in airline marketing, the forecast of developments in the next ten years is for changes that are revolutionary. Such forecasts call for making airline marketing mainstream. The second section presents some ideas on how to lead the operational side of an airline into the digital era – flight operations; maintenance, repair, and overhaul; and ground operations. Digitalizing these operational areas will reduce operating and investment costs and enable the generation of additional revenue through an increase in the time available for the aircraft to be in the air. The third part discusses the need for and some ways of bonding the commercial and operational functions to enable management to implement transformational strategies more efficiently and more effectively. The fourth part highlights the need to prioritize employee experience in the digital age to access and use relevant information to improve customer experience as well as their own experience.

Chapter 4 discusses how airlines and airports can implement a number of transformative strategies discussed on both their marketing and the operations side by leveraging (1) the ecosystem of technologies discussed and (2) solution-centric platforms that provide scale and flexibility to grow in the digital era with sustainable profits. The first part of Chapter 4 points out the evolution of platforms. The second part provides an outline of a framework for developing a new generation of intelligent engagement platforms to enable airlines to work around their conventional and new complexities while helping travelers meet their total mobility needs. This part provides information on some important building blocks that encompass three central levers – vision for the business, enabling technologies, and design thinking. And design thinking, in turn, calls for a clear definition of and a focus on customer and employee experience and the expectations of both in the digital era. The third part discusses the idea of rethinking design thinking related to platforms as well as internal airline products and services. With respect to the latter, two examples are discussed – customer-contact centers as well as cabin configurations and services. The final part discusses some operational considerations relating to the use of platforms.

Chapter 5 discusses the need and some ways to transform the value propositions of airports just as airlines are changing their value propositions to adapt to the three major forces and the two constraints discussed in this book. Only the value propositions of airports relate not only to their customers (airlines and retailers, for instance) but also to their ultimate customers (passengers). In addition, just as competition is increasing for airlines, it is also increasing for airports to capture larger shares of the growth in passenger traffic and to divert existing flows of traffic. Moreover, just as airlines work with a large number of complexities, although to different degrees and in different areas, airports face a similar challenge. The first part of the chapter discusses four major challenges facing airports: lack of sufficient capacity to meet the expected growth in demand, structural changes within the airline industry, the growing need of customers for experience throughout the travel journey, and the growing concern for the environment. The second part presents some ideas on how platforms and technologies can enable airport management to transform their business models to address the four challenges discussed in the first part. The last part suggests that airports need to develop their own scenarios relating to the future – for example, the development of "virtual airports" as well as the role of new forms of transformation.

Chapter 6 presents a thought-provoking scenario of an intelligent engagement platform developed with the support of a far-thinking airline. The first part presents some challenges and opportunities for the airline to develop a platform based on an open system and operated by an independent group of the airline to offer dynamically curated and integrated travel. Based on the deployment of the mobility-as-a-service (MaaS) concept, explored by "smart cities" around the world, a travel-based platform makes available a high level of totally integrated end-to-end journeys provided by multiple service providers through strong collaboration within the travel value chain. The shopping phase of the platform even includes digital assistants, taking, for instance, voice search to new levels. The platform even coordinates the services of no-frill and full-service airlines from around the world to meet the needs of budget travelers to travel from anywhere to anywhere, with convenience related to shopping, traveling, and changing travel plans with significant flexibility. In this scenario, the platform integrates numerous internal platforms and external data platforms to develop and manage itineraries with the use of a suite of technologies and apps. One example of an embedded app in the platform would be the services of fare-prediction companies. Such apps provide not only good information for travelers, information relating to the optimal time to make a booking, but they also integrate with other embedded apps that have access to data on consumers' preferences. The platform offers solutions to the mobility requirements of travelers at all levels of the pyramid. For all travelers, the platform framework provides 24/7/365 support to monitor the progress of travelers and provides different levels of support depending on the relationship with the traveler.

Chapter 7 provides a perspective, based on the three forces and the two constraints discussed in this book, on what is on the horizon for the aviation industry and how to stay ahead of the transformation curve through innovation. Mobility-as-a-service (MaaS) provides an example of a challenge that is also an opportunity. However, it has two important requirements: (1) faster response time to match demand with supply, and (2) de-complexing the airline business. Faster response time, in turn, requires understanding the digital environment and focusing much more on business transformation than on the development of digital strategies. De-complexing the airline business calls for the need to navigate strategically between two domains, operational excellence and marketing innovation. The key to balancing the impact of the opposing forces while preempting the entry of new travel marketers is to develop and operate intelligent engagement platforms that handle travelers' total mobility needs.

Finally, Chapter 8 provides a broad set of thought leadership pieces, contributed by practitioners with experience in a broad spectrum of sectors within the aviation industry worldwide. These pieces cover both the commercial side and the operations side of the business.

Book audience

The main audience of this book series continues to be senior level practitioners of differing generations of airlines and related businesses worldwide as well as government policy makers. Why government policy makers? Government policy makers create an environment in which various sectors of the aviation industry can transform their business models, leading to the creation of mutual value – value for businesses and value for their customers and employees. The content continues to be at a pragmatic level, intended to spark some dialogue within the functional divisions and to explore alternatives to enable managers to think critically about the viability and stability of their prevailing business models as well as the need for new business models.

Based on the author's personal work experience in the global airline industry, as well as through a synthesis of leading business practices appearing in a wide body of literature (referenced throughout the book), this book builds upon concepts contained in previous books in this series. For example, forces relating to shifts in customer behavior and expectations, as well as customer-based and business-based technologies, have been discussed in previous books and in various levels of details. However, first, this book updates the material, as in the case of forces relating to customers, and provides additional details, as in the case of technologies. Second, while the previous books have emphasized the "why" part for transformation, this book provides some details on the "how" part.

Once again, as in previous books, based on input provided by readers, this book contains numerous forewords and thought leadership pieces (in Chapter 8) for readers. The forewords provide value for readers from the perspectives of a diverse group of senior executives from traditional and new businesses on the overall theme of the book. The thought leadership pieces provide value from the detailed viewpoints and perspectives of different practitioners in different areas of responsibilities and from their bases in different parts of the world.

Notes

1 "Future of the Airline Industry 2035," IATA, Geneva, Switzerland, 2017.
2 "European Aviation in 2040: Challenges of Growth," Eurocontrol, 2018, Edition 2.

2 Managing the intersection and convergence of disruptive forces

This chapter provides a brief discussion of how three mega forces and their convergence and intersection, as well as two constraints, are affecting different sectors of the aviation industry and in different ways. This set of three forces (market dynamics, customers, and technologies) and two constraints (complexities and regulations) has a narrower context than the much broader context discussed by IATA or Eurocontrol in its report.[1] In 2017, IATA issued a detailed report (produced by the School of International Futures) called the *Future of the Airline Industry 2035* in which it aggregated numerous forces into four different scenarios for the global airline industry in 2035 to help airlines plan their strategies with respect to both opportunities and challenges.[2] Figure 2.1 shows these four scenarios, developed around two axes: geopolitics (calm vs. turbulent) and data (open vs. closed). One interpretation could be that the traffic growth would be positive and at the highest level within the scenario of *Sustainable Future*, negative growth within the scenario of *Resource Wars*, and the traffic growth would be positive under the other two scenarios (*New Frontiers* and *Platforms*) but at a lower level than within the *Sustainable Futures* scenario.

As previously mentioned, the potential forces discussed within the IATA and the Eurocontrol reports are at a much broader level than the forces discussed in this chapter. Geopolitics, in the IATA report, for example, presumably include terrorist incidences that have had temporary but serious impact on some destinations, like France, Spain, Tunisia, and Turkey. Assuming that waiting for a clear view of where the geopolitical situations are going is not a reasonable strategy, as they are likely to change anyway, this book touches on only the three forces, their convergence and intersection. However, the discussion of these two sets of forces tries to relate to their impact from the perspective of the short, medium, and long terms. Take the case of new forms of transportation, air and ground. The short-term horizon will be impacted, for example, by the increased adoption of cost-efficient, ultra-long-range, narrow-body aircraft. The medium-term horizon will be impacted by the entry of driver-less cars and urban air mobility (UAM) vehicles. The long-term horizon will be impacted by the entry of small hybrid-electric aircraft in regional markets, the Hyperloop, the small supersonic jets, and the flying cars.

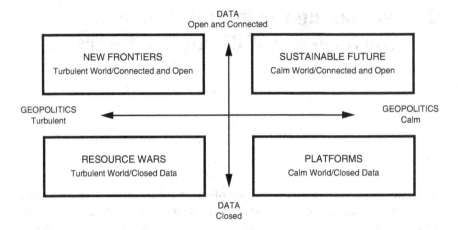

Figure 2.1 Four Scenarios of Future Growth in Air Travel

Source: IATA and the School of International Futures Report: Future of the Airline Industry 2035, p. 15.

The first major force is the changing dynamics of the market, producing more competition from inside and outside of the airline business. The second force is the expected growth and changes in traffic as well as changing consumer behavior, expectations, and attitudes. The third force, the emergence of exponential technologies, however, will not only be powering the first force (changing market dynamics) but will also facilitate managements of different aviation businesses to adapt to the two constraints. The first constraint is the increasing levels of complexity and the continuations of the constraints of legacy systems. The second constraint is the changing role of regulators in different sectors of the aviation industry.

With its focus mostly on the global airline and airport business sectors, this book suggests that dramatic transformation within these two sectors can be achieved by not only leveraging the emergence of exponential technologies but also by developing intelligent engagement platforms to provide mutual value in businesses that have operated in a linear basis. The value will be mutual in that it will benefit both businesses and their customers and employees. The value provided to customers relates to price, or various aspects of experience, or both.

As for businesses, mutual value can be created on continuums for both airlines and airports – different values for different businesses (and their segmented customers and employees) depending on their unique situations: stages of development, degrees of risk-aversion, visions of the future, length of planning horizons, understanding and acceptances of the roles of technologies, and so forth. Within the industry, the potential value of emerging technologies and platforms is clear. One only needs to look at the success of some world-renowned technology businesses. As Tom Goodwin pointed out in an article in the March 2015 issue of *TechCrunch*, Uber owns no taxis, Facebook creates no content, Alibaba has no inventory, and Airbnb owns no real estate.[3] Yet, their market capitalization is enormous relative to the market capitalization of conventional businesses.

All three forces and the two constraints are discussed only briefly, as they have already been discussed at some length in the author's previous books in this series. However, the discussion on these forces is updated in this book and, in the case of the ecosystem of technologies, it is presented in more detail, including some examples on how these technologies can cater to the needs of businesses to deal with complexities to fulfill the needs of businesses and the needs of their customers.

Market dynamics

The first major force is the ongoing increase in competition within the industry. Business models of existing airlines are changing and, in some cases, converging. Low-cost carriers have been increasing their services in long-haul markets for some time. More recently, they have begun to implement strategies to penetrate the business segment of the market. Full-service airlines are trying to hold on to the price-sensitive market by such initiatives as either the development or the expansion of their low-cost divisions and the introduction of highly restrictive basic fares. Singapore Airlines' Scoot now flies to Europe (Athens and Berlin) and the US (Honolulu). The International Airlines Group established a low-cost division, Level, in 2017 to fly long-haul routes. In June 2018, IAG announced that Level would expand into short-haul markets to compete with European low-cost carriers such as Ryanair, easyJet, and Lufthansa's Eurowings. Full-service carriers are also competing with carefully designed unbundled basic fares and are leveraging their frequent flyer programs, alliance partnerships, and more comprehensive in-flight entertainment systems.

In North America, to cater to the needs of the truly price-sensitive market, ultra-low-cost carriers are expanding their services, such as Spirit Airlines in the US and the start of Swoop, a new division of WestJet Airlines, based in Canada. Airline competition is increasing among the full-service carriers. First, it was from the entry of the Persian Gulf-based carriers. Now it is from the carriers based in China, who are not only growing their international destinations but will also transform their operations at major airports in China into much larger hub-and-spoke systems. Further expansion would take place from China's Belt and Road Initiative (BRI) with the goal of strategic global expansion. In Africa, Ethiopian Airlines has been expanding at a phenomenal rate to compete with the Persian Gulf-based airlines in markets linking China with Africa. Just one example: passengers can now connect via Addis Ababa between Beijing and Accra in Ghana, Angola in Luanda, Lagos in Nigeria, and Lusaka in Zambia.

In the US, according to some analysts, despite the fact that more than 80 percent of the market share in domestic markets is handled by just four carriers, competition has increased and consumers are benefiting. For example, in a report published by Compass Lexecon, the average number of city-pairs in domestic markets has increased from 3.3 in 2000 to 3.5 in 2016. Moreover, airline ticket prices are close to their historical low level even though fuel prices have increased and there have been a number of mergers.[4] Regarding the change in airline services and airline fares on a worldwide basis, Figure 2.2 shows the increase in the number of unique city-pair connections worldwide between 1995 and 2017 and the decline in the real cost of air transport. This data shows the ongoing increase in airline competition on a worldwide basis, competition that is offering choice to consumers.

In addition to competition from within the industry, linear-business-based airlines will most likely also face competition from outside of the industry from new travel marketers, such as Airbnb, Amazon, and Facebook, as well as new transportation service providers, such as Uber. The new travel marketers will use technology to create new, customer-friendly platforms as layers between the traditional airline service providers and their customers. This development will pose the biggest challenge for the traditional airlines, if, instead of collaborating with airlines, these technology businesses decide to compete in the distribution space. Airbnb could capitalize on its competency to market "local experience" and "authenticity" to expand in the air travel sector. Amazon is already reported to be exploring verticals where consumer expenditures are high and in which Amazon has no significant presence. Facebook, having focused on advertising and messaging, could develop a new strategy that capitalizes on its capability to facilitate billions of messages between consumers and businesses, not to mention its travel-related bots. As for Uber, its concept of an all-electric flying vehicle will seat four passengers and a pilot, fly at speeds of 150–200 miles per hour at an altitude of about 2,000 feet, and have a range of 60 miles, with a single charge.

The key ingredient is the mobile platform to research, compare, rate, book, and stay with the customer during the entire trip to find solutions to situational

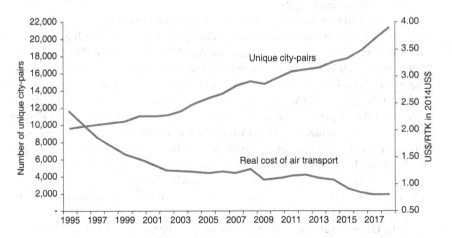

Figure 2.2 Connectivity and the Cost of Air Transport

Source: IATA Economics Department, Using Data from ICAO, IATA Statistics, SRS Analyzer and IATA's Own Forecasts, as presented by Brian Pearce at IATA's Aviation Data Symposium, Berlin, Germany, June 19, 2018.

challenges in the end-to-end journey. There could be an integration of a number of such platforms with different service offerings, starting with the aggregation of content from existing services and fares from airlines and other mobility services (similar to the services offered by major online travel agencies (OTAs) – Expedia, Ctrip, and Priceline), but with en route "concierge" services. One critical competency of a platform operator would be to search all airlines, not just those with membership in such organizations as IATA, and work, on a personalized basis, with the flexibility of the traveler – time of the year, day of the week, time of the day, connecting airport, stop-over desires, and so forth. Some of these travel marketers may even try to book space on existing airplanes (similar to what some forwarders do on cargo aircraft) and then market their allotments with their own products. Others could try to offer a much more comprehensive service, mobility-as-a-service (MaaS).

There is lot to learn about airline customers, not just when they are planning a trip and actually traveling but information about their everyday lives outside of travel. What are they buying? Where are they shopping? How are they shopping? How overwhelmed are they? In a person's life, a very short amount of time is spent traveling, except for the small percentage traveling on business. Where is their loyalty when shopping for other products and services? How do non-airline vendors measure loyalty? The new travel marketers will gather data from many sources other than from the shopping and booking process associated with travel and during the actual travel itself. The starting point for this data is the data from the partners in the travel chain (airlines, hotels, car-rental companies, credit card companies, and so forth), followed by the information in social media – Facebook, WeChat, etc. It is the knowledge from this data that will help the new travel marketers generate relevant offers to meet travelers' total mobility needs.

The movement to change business models applies not just to airlines but also to airports and aircraft manufacturers. Smaller airports are going after the long-haul, low-cost carriers that have been investing in advanced narrow-body aircraft with excellent payload-range features. One only needs to look at the strategies developed and implemented by Norwegian Airlines in recent years. JetBlue could easily start to serve the transatlantic market with the use of Airbus 321LR, leveraging its strength at Boston, JFK, and Fort Lauderdale Airports, not to mention its brand and its business-class cabins. Low-cost carriers can offer not only lower fares but also some options preferred by some travelers. Think about the progress that has already been made in transporting passengers from the US to Europe via Iceland. Fares can be lower and connections made in Iceland with less of a hassle. Then there is the opportunity for a stopover to visit the local areas in Iceland.

Aircraft manufacturers have also been developing new generations of wide-body aircraft capable of flying ultra-long-haul routes, such as Sydney to London, Heathrow, on the one side and to New York, JFK, on the other side. Qantas has already flown nonstop between Perth and London, a nonstop flight with a Boeing 787–9 that took just over 17 hours covering a distance of 9,240 miles. Take the case of the market between Singapore and the US. In 2016, there were no nonstop flights. At the beginning of 2018, there were 21 nonstop flights, and by the end of 2018, it is reported that there will be 41 nonstop flights. Such flights will increase competition among existing hubs to attract passengers who are willing to make connections. Moreover, aircraft manufacturers are also trying to grow their revenue in the aftermarket. Boeing, for example, is reported to be aiming to grow its aftermarket business revenue from US$20 billion to US$50 billion in the next ten years.

Customers

Relating to customers and the expected growth and changes in the demand patterns for air travel, the global travel and tourism landscape has been changing for numerous reasons, affecting all sectors of the aviation industry:

- shifts in the power of economies and demographics;
- shifts in the nature of economies (such as the focus on sharing and on-demand services);
- growth of the middle classes in emerging markets;
- rapidly evolving consumer trends relating to attitudes and expectations of consumers using smart devices;
- lowering of overall travel barriers, for example, relating to travel visa requirements;
- reductions in travel costs, both ground (for example, through the use of Uber) and air;
- proliferation of technologies relating to consumers and businesses; and
- increases in connectivity.

As a result, the demand for air travel has not only been growing, but it has also been shifting with respect to geographic locations as well as changes in consumers' expectations and attitudes. Take the case of growth first. According to charts published by IATA, the global passenger demand (based on an origin-destination basis) will double between 2016 and 2036. One reason is that passenger traffic appears to grow faster when economies are growing, and economies are forecast to grow at high rates in many populous Asian emerging markets. As for a shift in the demand relating to geography, again, according to the data developed by IATA, the year 2018 could be a pivotal year when the percentage of passenger origin-destination traffic within developing markets becomes higher than within advanced markets. See Figure 2.3. Adding more to the evidence in the shift in passenger traffic, consider also an analysis by Airbus that concludes that between 2016 and 2036, passenger traffic between emerging countries is forecast to grow at 6.2 percent per year, increasing its world share from 29 percent in 2016 to 40 percent in 2036.[5] As further evidence of the shift in demand, consider the rankings in the top ten air passenger markets, 2036 vs. 2016. The US shifts down from number 1 to number 2 and the UK shifts down from number 3 to number 5, while India moves up from number 7 to number 3 and Indonesia moves up from number 10 to number 4.[6] See Figure 2.4.

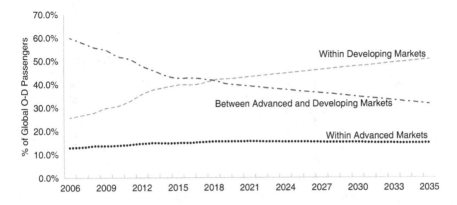

Figure 2.3 Global Passenger Demand: Developed and Developing Markets

Source: Reconstructed from a chart presented by IATA from its 20-year passenger forecast in the seventh World Passenger Symposium, Barcelona, Spain, October 2017.

These shifts in traffic can be explained by such developments as the relaxation of aviation regulatory policies and the expansion of low-cost carriers. This is an area where government policy makers can adapt contemporary regulatory polices to facilitate the growth in traffic and the generation of mutual value for service providers and customers. Consider, for example, Japan, a country with its inbound tourism increasing at phenomenal rates in recent years. The United Nations World Tourism Agency reported the number of inbound foreign visitors in 2012 to be 8.6 million and in 2017 to be 28.7 million. According to the Japanese National Tourism Organization, this number is expected to reach 40 million by 2020! Reasons include, among others, (1) growth in the segments of the middle class in emerging economies, (2) relaxation by the Japanese government of travel visa requirements as well as some customs and immigration rules, (3) a weaker Japanese yen, which has made Japan a less expensive country to visit, and (4) the expansion of services provided by low-cost carriers. This trend in inbound foreign visitors to Japan will strengthen even further with the increase in the number of seats offered by low-cost carriers in Northeast Asia. In this region, currently about 25 percent of the total seats are offered by the low-cost sector, compared to over 50 percent in Southeast Asia.[7] While a desirable trend for the Japanese economy, such an increase in traffic is an example of a significant pressure being placed on the aviation infrastructure.

Other recent examples of favorable government policies include the decision by the government in China to ease the restriction in its policy of only one airline per long-haul international route, which has been in effect since 2009. This change in policy will produce products that are more competitive for consumers and a more efficient utilization of resources for airlines. A second example is the signing of an open-skies agreement between the US and Brazil, which will open

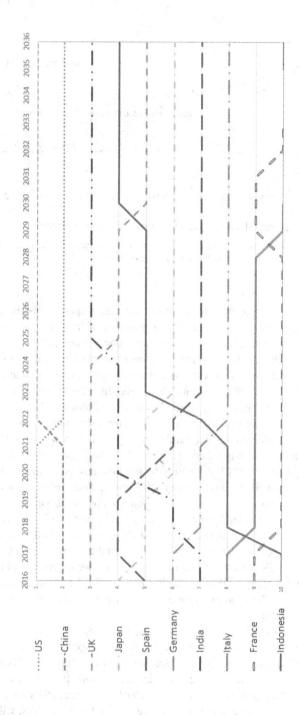

Figure 2.4 Top Ten Air Passenger Markets 2036 vs. 2016

Source: Reconstructed from a chart presented by IATA from its 20-year passenger forecast in the seventh World Passenger Symposium, Barcelona, Spain, October 2017.

up more service opportunities for airlines, with a potential for more competitive pricing policies to benefit consumers.

As for shifts relating to consumers' purchasing decisions, a Euromonitor International highlights ten emerging forces shaping consumer behavior, shaped in some ways by the accessibility of mobile technologies and the Internet.[8] Following are three examples extracted from this insightful study, which is based on actual surveys. First, consumers are now focusing less on ownership of products and services and more on flexibility and sharing. This trend is evident from consumers' willingness to give up car ownership and rely more on consumer-centered on-demand ground transportation. Consider the impact of this trend on the reduction of capacity of parking facilities at airports, not to mention the impact on revenues generated by the parking facilities at airports. Consumers' attitude toward flexibility will change even more with the entry of driver-less cars, which will clearly affect short-haul air transportation. Second, the increase in the use of augmented reality, enabling consumers to "see" before they buy, enables consumers to "try" on clothes and accessories before they buy. How about "seeing" a 360-degree and 3-D view of a particular seat on a long-haul flight prior to making a booking? Third, people are leaning away from the conventional 9-to-5 jobs in the corporate sector to self-employment. These people are clearly looking for flexibility. According to the surveys cited by Euromonitor International, "nearly 50% of respondents across all generations aspire to being self-employed."[9] What impact would this trend have on airlines' views of the traditional business segment or corporate travel? Another trend is not just the increasing concern of the public for the protection of the environment but the increasing engagement relating to, for example, pollution – carbon dioxide (CO_2) and noise.

Technologies

Proliferation of enabling technologies, the third force, in fact, promises to help different sectors of the aviation industry cater to their business needs – facilitating the management of complexities of their businesses, the fulfillment of their needs and the needs of their customers, and compliances with the regulatory requirements of governments. As an example, some airlines want to become sophisticated retailers, while customers may want not just convenient travel services but solutions to their mobility problems, not to mention a seamless experience throughout the entire journey. These technologies and technology-enabled platforms can bring about significant reductions in operating and investment costs, enhancements in revenues, and step-up changes in customer service and customer experience by reducing complexity and managing the growth and shifts in traffic as well as customers' expectations.

Among the dozens of enabling technologies available, only six are discussed in this chapter. The choice is difficult given the existence of many other value-adding technologies such as 3-D printing, digital twins, technologies embedded in wearables, and drones. On the other hand, some technologies not discussed directly overlap with those that are discussed. For example, AI can include machine learning and robots, context awareness, natural language processing, and computer vision, as well as the areas of virtual reality and augmented reality, although the last two are related, but they are not the same. Similarly, the Internet of things can also include machine learning and digital twins. The six technologies discussed are:

1   Mobile Internet connectivity for customers to facilitate their travel and manage their own expectations.
2   Biometrics to facilitate security clearance and aircraft boarding processes.
3   Blockchain to transform within the commercial and operational spaces.
4   Artificial intelligence – coupled with machine learning as well as augmented and virtual realities – to make customer engagements more meaningful, and augmented reality to enhance customer experience in a different way and to increase sales.
5   The Internet of things, facilitated by the wireless connection of physical objects to the Internet, to enable objects to be connected to each other and with people.
6   New forms of air and ground transportation to improve travel experience.

Mobile

Mobile has already enabled more and more consumers to research and arrange travel more effectively and to engage with service providers before, during, and after journeys. However, there is much more value that mobile can add for consumers; for example,

- integrate apps and provide access to full content more easily;
- facilitate frictionless end-to-end mobile experience; and
- continue to add more functionality to mobile devices, such as the ability to re-book flights and open room doors in hotels or access rented cars.

Moreover, 5G communications promise to provide greater reliability and much faster speeds for downloading contents. In addition, 5G communications (coupled with the Internet of things – IoT) will result in "a smarter and more connected world." The big change expected, however, will be in how consumers plan their travel. For example, whereas in the past most consumers planned their entire trip before starting the trip, in the future they may wish to remain flexible in some areas of the trip and may choose locations and activities in real time and on an on-demand basis, given that they can communicate and interact with suppliers of services on a 24/7/365 basis worldwide. Moreover, travel-related service providers, leveraging mobile capabilities as well as other technologies such as AI and consumer analytics, can interact with consumers to fulfill their "on the spot" needs.

Smart mobile devices, coupled with location-based mobile apps, are already providing travelers with more options and greater flexibility to plan their travel. At the same time, more and more travel service providers, like airlines, as well as activity providers, like sightseeing businesses, are building their mobile channels of communications that are more user friendly and provide better customer experience. For example, service and activity providers are enabling travelers to use their mobile devices not only to obtain information on the services available but also with the capability for travelers to obtain reviews. Moreover, it is not just commercial service providers but also communities (locations at destination) that are able to use the IoT technology to engage with travelers to provide information on local events, as well as to manage the identities of people for travel on local transportation systems.

Some experts claim that mobile devices and embedded technologies (artificial intelligence and machine learning) will soon be able to "predict" their users' needs in real time. In other words, technology will anticipate the challenges the user will face and look for solutions, like a delay in a flight, send a message to the people expected to be affected, and provide options for new itineraries, using different airlines, hotel accommodations, car rentals, etc. Then the passenger will not need to wait until a delay message has been received from an airline and then use the mobile device to look for options. Imagine mobile devices used like Amazon's Alexa, working as a concierge for people on the move with queries, matching location and the preloaded itinerary.

Biometrics

A number of airlines and airports worldwide have already started to implement biometric-based processes in which facial-recognition and finger-printing technologies are linked with the information obtained through scanned documents (passports and boarding passes, for example) to facilitate security clearance, aircraft boarding, and movement through immigration and customs facilities. This technology is also about to facilitate the implementation of self-service options, like checking in, dropping off baggage, entering an airport lounge, boarding an aircraft, and passing through immigration and customs areas. Under discussion is also the use of "single-token travel" facilitated by biometrics. With this system, a passenger can show a selected form of identity, like a passport, at the first biometric location, like a kiosk, to enable the creation of a biometric marker that would then facilitate travel through all points. However, while biometric technology will clearly improve the airport experience, concerns are being raised about data privacy and data security issues.

Blockchain

Blockchain, a distributed ledger and a form of a data structure and a data-flow framework, is reliable, transparent, more accessible, and secure. Information is stored in blocks – hence the name blockchain. Security is there, as the information stored in blocks is verified, it is visible, and it can only be altered with the full knowledge and approval of the community using the blockchain. Moreover, since every authorized user can access the information, there is no reason to keep multiple copies of the data.

Currently, data sits in different subsegments of major segments, like crew management in flight operations or sales in commercial operations. As such, there are multiple sets of data in multiple warehouses, with very limited capability to exchange data even if the data were in a consistent format. The blockchain framework can improve not only the flow and exchange of data but also regain some trust and integrity by reducing, if not eliminating, complexity. Within this framework, there is no single group or even subgroup that owns the data. The ownership, processing, and storage is at the enterprise level.

Blockchain technology promises to provide different ways to transact services, make payments, and share information with less friction and with greater transparency, trust, and security. This technology can help to reduce costs, increase revenues, and improve customer service and experience. The thought leadership piece by Maksim Izmaylov in Chapter 8 provides an excellent background about the value blockchain is adding to transform the aviation business. Consider some examples of the blockchain technology on the commercial side of the airline business. It could change fundamentally the role of and charges related to intermediaries. Airlines having direct access to customers can reduce distribution costs and provide better ways to engage with customers by providing, for example, more personalized content. Consider the use of blockchain in the areas of loyalty, like tokenizing miles that can then be used anywhere, e-ticketing, payment systems, and distribution. The role of blockchain in e-ticketing involves the use of smart contracts – relating to terms and conditions – and tokens, leading to "tokenized tickets," facilitating the transfer of tickets among partners in the travel chain. There are, of course, some questions. For example, if an e-ticket is issued through the blockchain mechanism, can that reservation be transferred to another person, either because the plans of a traveler changed or because the buyer bought the ticket in the first place, on a speculation basis, to make a profit? The purchaser could be an individual person or a tour operator. Similarly, if an airline ticket is purchased on a platform as part of the total product, can it be sold to a different person? Would airlines set up conditions for resale? Consequently, while the blockchain framework could change the role of conventional intermediaries, it would also create new intermediaries.

In the near future, online bookings are expected to exceed off-line bookings. Consumers already have power in that they have more capability to search for more choices. As such, service providers will need to make their products and services much more accessible to consumers within the consumers' framework of search and booking, for example, on their smart mobile devices. They will need to enable consumers to find not just the lowest price but also the best price-service option, not to mention see the full content. Customers want a seamless end-to-end experience. How will these requirements get resolved during the online shopping phase? Distributers, OTAs – traditional, such as Expedia, and digital, such as WeChat (owned by Tencent) and Alibaba – are becoming technology businesses, and they are changing their business models to reflect these trends as well as differentiating their brands.

On the operational side, blockchain can enable step changes in tracking assets, physical and human. Physical assets can be aircraft, individual parts, maintenance equipment, baggage, and catering trucks. Human assets can relate to the location of flight attendants, gate agents, ramp agents, and mechanics. The bottom line is a substantial reduction in costs (operating and investment) and an increase in the revenue-generating capability of assets, as well as the higher value relating to customer experience through higher levels of operational excellence. As for its use within the travel chain or within different partners working on a platform, it can help with the transparent and secure flow of data with the capability of authenticity and traceability. The last two attributes are important in the maintenance area, for example, relating to registration of parts and maintenance records with a complete history. As mentioned in the second part of Chapter 3, Lufthansa is already reported to have started its *Blockchain for Airlines* initiative (BC4A) to bring together various parties in the area of maintenance, repair, and overhaul.

In the near term, blockchain can facilitate the development of a "single source of truth" relating to data used within different aviation sectors, like airlines and airports. This technology was used in the project called FlightChain to develop a "single version of the truth" for information relating to flight status.

Artificial intelligence, augmented and virtual reality

Artificial intelligence (AI), according to Microsoft, will "shape the next phase of innovation" and will undoubtedly influence all phases of travel, from online searches to pricing and experience, before, during, and after travel. AI – along with machine learning and digital assistants – promises to enable service providers to offer relevant, targeted, and coordinated travel options and customer-facing solutions to travelers' mobility requirements. Machine-learning technologies can add much value to the development and presentation of meaningful content. With respect to AI and predictive analytics, a recent survey conducted by OAG Aviation Worldwide shows that consumers have strong interests in predictive pricing technologies and services to predict flight delays and cancelations on the day of travel as well as during the booking process.[10] In addition, from the point of an airline, the use of AI can provide better prediction tools to manage delays, for example, to assure that one delay has the least impact on the next delay. Prediction tools will encompass delays relating not only to aircraft but also to crews. Within this context, the desire for reliable information about on-time performance will influence both the quality of search engines and the brand of airlines and airports used.

The use of AI depends on the availability of a large quantity of data, and the aviation industry has a large quantity of data. However, will passengers want to share their personal data, other than the straightforward type of data, such as email addresses, possibly even home or office addresses, or even telephone numbers, and preferences, such as seat location? What about deeper personal data?

AI systems can only learn from data, and they need to have continuous data to improve. If customers are not willing to share data, then how far can AI move forward? While people are willing to share data through social media networks, will they do so when asked by airlines and airports, unless they can be assured of not only the privacy and protection of data but also the governance of data, for example, relating to where else the data will be transmitted and shared? Passengers are obviously interested in pieces of information such as what to do when flights are delayed or canceled, and possibly recommendations on activities at destinations.

Artificial intelligence can help in the areas of customer service and customer experience and improve operational effectiveness. Of course, airlines are continuing to make improvements using technology in areas such as the look and feel of their websites to make them more engaging, in order to improve customer experience and to improve conversion and sale. In addition, airlines are developing self-service kiosks, airport information display systems, and systems such as Alexa to answer questions and help customers plan trips. Airlines are also beginning to explore the use of machine-learning algorithms to identify patterns in activities relating to customers and operations and predict prices in real time. AI can also be used to test different web designs compared to the conventional A/B testing methods.

Artificial intelligence can also help airlines in the area of pricing and revenue management, not just looking at how demand is changing but also external factors such as actual and expected changes in the price of fuel. While AI can help management in revenue management decisions, the challenge appears to be if revenue management controllers have sufficient confidence in the AI technology (with machine-learning analytics) for the systems to make decisions instead of overriding the recommendations made by the AI-powered systems. Airlines have always had good techniques to forecast the no-show rate for controlling inventory in managing revenues. Now the no-show forecasting techniques can be improved by using AI to determine not just how many passengers may not show up for a flight but which specific customers and, possibly, why. For example, it may be possible to forecast which frequent flyer passengers could most likely switch flights, based on their past behavior, weather forecasts, and many other types of data – such as route characteristics and flight schedules.

Within the broader framework of AI are technologies related to augmented reality (AR), virtual reality (VR), and mixed reality (MR) – technologies that are about to go mainstream in smartphones. To see AR from the consumer point of view, one only needs to look at the impact made by the introduction of *Pokémon Go* – a game released in 2016 in which virtual creatures – called *Pokémon* – appear in a player's real-world location. Now, an increasing number of smart devices are becoming available with the capability to support AR applications. AR is technology that enables virtual objects to be placed in a physical environment and the user to interact with the virtual objects in the physical environment. Think of some current applications such as "seeing" yourself in different clothes or accessories, "seeing" a piece of furniture in your home or office, or "seeing" how a car would fit in your driveway or garage. Augmented reality blends the boundary between physical and digital worlds. To use this technology, consumers can use traditional digital devices such as smartphones without the need to wear special goggles. Within the context of travel, a person could "see" how she would fit into the economy-class seat on a long-haul flight. Augmented reality will also play an important role on the operational side of the business. Consider how a mechanic working on a complex component of an aircraft on the ramp could "see" the manual immediately without having to go back to the maintenance shop to bring back a huge binder.

Apple offers a software development kit for developers, called ARKit, to build AR apps for iOS to be used in Apple's products, such as the iPhone and the iPad. Google has a similar kit, called ARCore, that adds AR functionality to Google's Android phones. Microsoft has developed HoloLens, a head-mounted device that enables AR applications – enabling a user to engage with digital content and to be able to interact with holograms in the local environment, blending the physical and the digital worlds.

In addition to augmented reality, virtual reality (VR) technology that can provide an interactive computer-generated experience, shows numerous applications in the aviation industry. First, the entertainment area uses goggles or headsets to view 3-D films. AR and VR techniques can facilitate the demonstration of projects in customers' own environments. On the operational side, VR can help reduce the time required for training cabin crews. AR shows tremendous opportunities in the area of maintenance through communications with remote locations, for example, access to expertise located elsewhere. The use of wearables by experts at remote locations enables them to see what the mechanic on location is seeing, and then a "virtual reality" hand can be used to assist the mechanic on site.

Next, there is mixed reality (MR), which becomes possible from the inputs of humans and the environment with the processing capability of computers to create mixed reality experiences. Within the aviation industry, SITA Lab and the Helsinki Airport have been experimenting with the use of HoloLens, for example, to analyze and manage airport operations in a mixed reality environment. Information can come from multiple sources, such as the movement of aircraft and passengers and the use of gates and security facilities, as well as the use of mixed reality (a combination of AR and VR) to create unique views of the operations at an airport at different times. Applications exist in the areas of operations, for example, maintenance and training.

Finally, there are chatbots that will soon have advanced capability for understanding spoken language and understand different languages. These chatbots will enable travelers to have access to all kinds of travel-related information 24/7/365 and across all of their mobile devices. However, more work needs to be done in this area yet. For example, the questions asked to chatbots must be in specific ways. On the other hand, AI can make chatbots smarter not only to meet customer needs better but also to help sell more. For example, consumers could show images of destinations to chatbots and chatbots could come up with recommendations. This capability relates to computer vision, where the system looks at a digital image and relates to the physical world. Still, while travelers are perfectly content in getting the information from chatbots, they also want access to human beings if needed to get more comprehensive answers or resolve issues and, perhaps most important, reduce stress.

Internet of things

The Internet of things (IoT), wireless connections of physical objects (using sensors and beacons) to the Internet, is enabling objects to connect with each other as well as with people, facilitating the collection of data and analyses, and continues tracking – exchange of data. Connecting devices with data will improve operations and customer experience. IoT sensors, coupled with machine learning (an application of AI), and digital twins will enable dramatic improvements in the efficiency of operations and improvement in customer service and experience through listening, engagement, empowering, and providing timely and personalized information and services. Sensors embedded in objects produce data about what is happening in real time. Data is transmitted in real time to other sensors over a network where information can be synthesized using analytics – again, in real time. Technology embedded in networks can identify patterns and anomalies, adding value on the commercial side (communicating with chatbots, information on parking spaces, location of bags, etc.) as well as on the operational side (management of assets, such as aircraft and parts, for example).

The idea behind this technology is not just to push information out in a broadbrush manner but communicate information in a two-way framework and on a personalized basis, curb-to-gate-to-gate-to-curb. IoT can add value in helping target the right customers for the right product offers at the right time, subject to the issue of privacy, of course. If the lounge is not fully occupied, then making a time- and location-sensitive offer with digital payment methods would save crowding at the gate. Passengers lost at airports can get not only directions (wayfinding) on their mobile devices but also the estimated walking time to get to particular points, such as gates. Travelers with a physical disability can get information on the location of a wheel chair. Those concerned with the status of their bags can keep track of the luggage at it moves through an airport.

On the operational side, sensors have been deployed in aircraft engines for some time, providing vital information on engine performance and fuel consumption. This information provided much value in the area of maintenance planning. However, the deployment of IoT will improve connectivity to the point that actions can be taken in a much timelier manner, whether the actions relate to maintenance or fuel consumption. An engine can have more than 5,000 sensors generating many gigabytes of data per second. It is IoT that enables data to be sent and received in real time from the aircraft, while in flight, to the maintenance staff on the ground, enabling maintenance to analyze the situation even before the aircraft lands with the right solutions and, if possible, the aircraft to be repaired at the gate instead of being taken out of service. For engine manufacturers this intensification of connectivity, facilitated by IoT systems, will not only help in the area of predictive and prescriptive maintenance and logistics but also in changes to the business models of engine manufacturers in terms of taking the power-by-the-hour to the next level. Moreover, digital twins, virtual models of real-world products, processes, or services, can help to examine future scenarios, with the digital twin situated at a different location than the physical twin. This technology is already producing incredible benefits for industrial companies – aircraft engine manufacturers, for example – to interpret, forecast, and optimize the performance of their products, processes, and services. As such, technology is making the engines smart. On the airspace side, the IoT will facilitate the development of advanced airspace systems – SESAR in Europe and NextGen in the US – through significant increases in connectivity and the flow of information through the airspace. Specifically, the new systems enabled by the IoT will help create much more efficient flight plans and improve the timings of takeoffs and landings.

While sensors are already reporting vast quantities of data, there are some challenges. The first challenge relates to the volume of data generated. The volume is increasing at such a fast rate that the current bandwidths of available links are becoming inadequate, relating not just to the volume and speed but also to the quality of the service. The second challenge is in the collection, processing, and analyses of the data generated, for example, to analyze pieces of unrelated data to lead to outcomes that are more effective. Machine-learning technology is beginning to overcome this challenge by enabling systems to learn and improve progressively from the new data. The third challenge relates not to the collection of the data or its transmission but to the ownership, the control, and the sharing of the data. The fourth challenge relates to the data privacy and data security issues.

New forms of transportation

As for new forms of transportation, driver-less cars are getting very close to becoming mainstream. They will be followed, most likely, by the flying cars, one version of which is under development by the Terrafugia Company and is depicted in Figure 2.5, a, b, and c. Such a version of the flying car will totally transform travel. See the thought leadership piece by Chuck Evans in Chapter 8. The primary benefits will be in the planned areas of reductions in energy costs and reductions in emissions and noise. The propulsion systems could be all electric or hybrid electric. Consequently, a vehicle such as Bell's electric vertical-takeoff-and-landing (eVTOL) aircraft may have not just lower operating costs, but it could have new applications such as urban mobility. Uber is already flight testing some full-scale vehicles, with plans to offer commercial service in 2023, and achieving scale by 2025. Electric propulsion is reaching maturity and will play an important role for civil aircraft in short-haul markets, regional and urban.

Next, consider the entry of the 55-seater supersonic aircraft being developed by Boom Technology. This will also transform travel in transoceanic markets, transatlantic and transpacific, as well as in numerous high-profile markets, such as Tokyo-Singapore, given the potential to fly most of the time over water. The aircraft could even offer shuttle service in markets such as Tokyo and Hong Kong. See Figure 2.6. Such an airplane is now viable, given advancements in

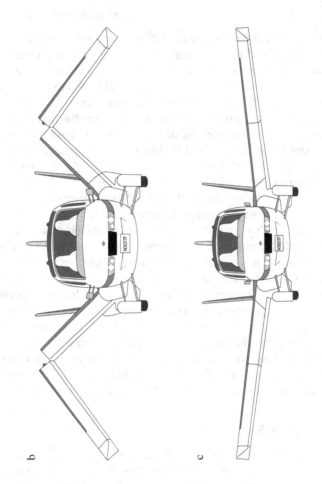

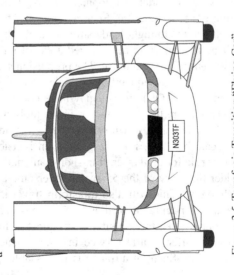

Figure 2.5 Terrafugia Transition "Flying Car"

Source: Terrafugia, Inc.

Figure 2.6 Boom Supersonic Aircraft
Source: Boom Technology

technology, such as next-generation propulsion, computational fluid dynamics (CFD), and carbon fiber composite material. Think about the impact of such an aircraft, offering fares comparable to the current business-class fares, especially once the aircraft fleet achieves scale.

Other potential game-changing vehicles include the small hybrid-electric aircraft operating in regional markets, flying taxis, and, eventually, the Hyperloop, that could transport passengers at speeds approaching 700 miles per hour. It has even been suggested that a version of the Hyperloop can enable much faster connections between city centers and airports, particularly the new mega airports under development. Business models of both airlines and airports will change significantly with the introduction of these new forms of air and ground transportation. The future of mobility relates to the delivery of platform-enabled, door-to-door, multi-modal trips with seamless experience throughout the journey and at all touch points.

Complexities

Complexity of the business and the constraints of legacy systems have always been considered major transformational challenges for airlines. With respect to complexity, while other business sectors also deal with complexity – automobile, pharmaceutical, and petrochemicals, for instance – airlines consider their sector exceptionally complex for numerous reasons that many analysts and managements have already discussed for years. The main point is that while other businesses are also subjected to similar constraints such as tight government regulations, perishable inventory, high degree of seasonality, dependency on weather and constrained infrastructure, and intensity relating to labor, fuel, and capital, the aviation industry is constrained by all these and other factors simultaneously.

As for the legacy systems, there has been, and continues to be, a wide gap between the services enabled by the operational systems and the dramatically changing needs of customers, for example, not just for service, or even experience, but seamless experience. To deal with these complexities and constraints, airlines have continuously been developing sophisticated subsystems and processes within their two major functions – commercial and operational. However, the introduction and implementation of multiple airline sub-functional systems within each of these functional systems has made the airline business more, not less, complex, for the following reasons.

1   Integration among systems within the siloed operational space and within the siloed commercial space has been handled through human interfaces that further added to the ongoing complexity.
2   The need to work with legacy systems and contemporary systems at the same time has resulted in enormous complexity.
3   The growth in the membership in strategic alliances increased, not decreased, complexity, not only in terms of different carriers working with different systems, but in some cases there is cooperation among members, and in other cases, there is competition. Moreover, the cooperation-competition situation can change and has changed among the same members at different times and in different markets.
4   Complexity increased with the increase in merger activity. Merging airlines had different systems and subsystems developed by different vendors at different times and with different technologies.
5   Instead of decreasing, complexity began to increase with the development of airline groups, for example, the IAG and the Lufthansa Groups. Integration efforts undertaken by managements of airline groups, while well intentioned, have been challenged due to a lack of effective data environments and, in some cases, corporate culture.
6   Complexity increased when airlines began to establish low-cost subsidiaries. In 2017, 10 of the 30 largest airlines had low-cost carriers in their groups.[11] Full-service airlines have not been able to cross-pollinate the low-cost culture.

7   Complexity increased when low-cost carriers began to penetrate the business segment. In 2017, 9 of the 10 largest low-cost carriers were targeting business travelers.[12]

8   Complexity increased even further due to airlines' need to deal with not just social media but multiple mobile devices that are having an enormous impact on traveler experience.

9   Security-related compliance requirements have been increasing resulting in an increase in complexity.

10 Increases in the amount and flow of data have increased complexity in the aviation industry. Consider the transmission of additional data to meet governments' security-related requirements. Moreover, complexity could also increase significantly from the application of government regulations relating to, for example, oversales and voluntary and involuntary denied boarding. In addition, there are potential regulations relating to the privacy and security of customer data.

11 There is a high level of complexity relating to the introduction of new types of fares with a wide array of rules and conditions. This complexity increased with the sale of a broad spectrum of ancillary products and services and increased even more with the movement toward the implementation of dynamic and personalized fares.

12 The desire for customer experience is increasing more than ever, and it is calling for airlines to shift their focus from conducting transactions to engaging with customers and building relationships, a change in processes that are increasing complexity.

13 Complexity relating to distribution has increased with new players entering the marketplace, some to actually offer a different channel of distribution, some to help airlines become better retailers (dynamic pricing to maximize revenues per customer), and some to help customers to identify the best fare options relating to airlines as well as the optimal timing of bookings.

14 Congestion at major airports around the world and piecemeal solutions, especially those relating to the allocation of slots, continue to increase complexity.[13]

15 Finally, complexity relating to payments has been increasing with the growth of networks of global airlines, involving different currencies and government regulations.

Consider the first point: within typical airline commercial subgroups – marketing, sales, customer service, and loyalty, for example – there are different systems, different data sets, and different assumptions. These systems and data sets are not sufficiently integrated. Managers in the operational space also have different systems and different data sets relating to flight operations, ground operations, and maintenance, repair, and overhaul. They are not sufficiently integrated, either. Additionally, the sub-systems within the commercial space and the operational space are not integrated using technologies. To the degree integration exists, it is provided by people who make the systems work, but not in an optimal manner. The result is lower levels of financial and operational efficiencies. Similar situations exist within the airport sector, where different divisions, like hub planners, retail planners, operations planners, and space planners, work with different systems, different data sets, and different assumptions. Consequently, systems and processes used by different divisions lead to non-optimal results from the viewpoint of different stakeholders – airlines, concessionaires, garage operators, security staff, and so forth.

Consider the seventh point: EasyJet is changing its business model to feed longer-haul flights of lower-cost carriers, for example, Norwegian and WestJet. EasyJet has announced that the connecting services will begin at London Gatwick Airport and expand to Amsterdam, Barcelona, Geneva, Milan Malpensa, and Paris Charles de Gaulle. Connecting services represent one way of generating incremental revenue through connection fees, reported to be between 2 and 25 percent of the total fare. The partnership with Norwegian could also be expanded to include airports slots at London Gatwick Airport.

As a result, complexity continues to exist and, in many cases, has increased within the commercial function and the operational function. In addition, the gap between operations and commercial areas has increased, affecting operating and investment costs, revenues, and customer experience, as well as employee experience. One way to get a better handle on complexity is to understand it within a three-dimensional space, suggested by Peruman and Wilson in their "complexity cube."[14] They suggest that complexity be measured in three dimensions – product, process, and organization. The product dimension relates to not just the number of products and services but also their variety and subcomponents. In the case of a large full-service airline, think just about the number and variety of routes, aircraft, cabin configurations, and fares. The process dimension relates to, again, not just the number of processes but their complexity and interdependence. Think about just the number of processes involved in handling a major disruption due to the closing of a major airport for a day, in the case of a major weather-related situation. The third dimension relates to the organization with respect to the resources required to produce, price and sell the services. Again, think about the organizational structure and processes required to manage just the operations of a full-service airline, let alone their low-cost subsidiaries and their alliance partners. However, while the degree of complexity is clear, what is not clear is the cost of complexity.

The airport sector also continues to deal with enormous complexities, although to different extents and in different areas, compared to the airline sector. For example, airports are not only regulated at the federal government level but also constrained to incredible levels and by multiple sets of regional and local governments. Next, there are the complexities resulting from the often conflicting interests of the multiple customers – airlines, retailers, government agencies, service providers, and vendors. Then there are the complexities related to the exceptionally long-term planning horizons involving not only the sources of funds but also the uses of funds to build new facilities. Think about the implications of a decision by a major global airport to change its focus from being a hub to becoming a destination, or a combination of the two. The development of the Jewel Changi Airport in Singapore is a case in point.

Regulators

Regulators in the aviation industry continue to have a major impact in, at least, six areas:

1 bilaterals relating to airline networks;
2 airline ownership and control (relating to organizational structure);
3 security (digital and physical, relating to customer experience);
4 airline retailing;
5 aircraft emissions (noise, carbon dioxide, and so forth); and
6 infrastructure, airports, and air traffic control systems (relating to capacity).

Government policies in the first two areas, bilateral agreements and control and ownership rules, seem to be becoming more liberal, in most regions, impacting airline networks, alliances, and JVs worldwide. For example, given some relaxation of the government policies on both sides, China and the US, carriers of both countries have expanded their services, and traffic increased substantially, especially with the changes in the visa requirements by the government in China. Again, going forward, the aviation policies could become part of the much broader US-China trade agreement. Even in Africa, a protectionist region in general, 23 nations signed a single aviation market to increase connectivity and stimulate economic growth. There could also be further consolidation, for example, relating to the ultra-low-cost carriers in the US as well as the smaller full-service carriers in Europe. However, government policies could also become more restrictive, depending on geopolitics. Consider, for example, the US-UAE Open-Skies agreement. It enabled the Persian Gulf-based carriers to expand enormously. However, going forward, depending on the direction of the geopolitical situation, the agreement could place restrictions on, for example, fifth-freedom rights.

Intervention of regulators will change the business models of airlines and airports in numerous other areas. Consider, for example, the current discussion as to if the European Commission should get involved in the charges proposed by airlines for bookings made through the systems of third parties, such as GDSs. Consider also the impact of a potential decision by the European Commission to look into the flight and hotel search engines operated by technology businesses, such as Google. It was mentioned earlier that regulations now exist in the areas of oversales and voluntary and involuntary denied boarding. Next is the concern for an increase in governments' requirements and charges relating to emissions, changing the business models of airports and airlines. However, government regulators could allow better relationships between airports and airlines, as evidenced in some countries such as China, Ethiopia, Mexico, and Turkey. Governments could also enable more dynamic control within the airspace with enabling technologies producing an increase in airspace capacity, for example, reducing aircraft separation and allowing aircraft operations on converging runways without premature alerts. Then, there is the potential decision of a congested airport to determine if it wants to expand its capacity or manage its demand by limiting operations or implementing economic initiatives. All these changes will impact different sectors of the aviation industry.

Consider three other areas. First, 3-D printing (also known as additive manufacturing) will have enormous impact on the supply chain within the global aviation industry. It will provide flexibility relating to maintenance activities and it will lower inventory costs. Currently, parts produced through the 3-D printing process relate to the use of plastics and titanium. Eventually, there could be a mixture of materials – plastics, metals, ceramics, etc., – and their use in the manufacture of complex parts. High volumes of components and some components with a lower number of parts would reduce the weight of an aircraft, which would, in turn, reduce the amount of fuel required. Moreover, aircraft manufacturers would no longer be required to maintain numerous parts in warehouse after the production of aircraft has been stopped. However, there are at least three questions relating to government regulations. First, how fast can regulators (say the Federal Aviation Administration in the US and the European Aviation Safety Agency) keep up with innovations in 3-D printing technology? The approval process could be lengthy in that complex parts will be designed from the ground up instead of the use of conventional and accepted methods. Second, there is also the concern for security. Hackers could get access to digital blueprints and the control of printers. Third, how fast can the industry achieve scale, moving from low volume to high volume?

Second, all-electric or hybrid-electric aircraft have not only the potential to transform travel in urban and short-haul markets but also reduce the impact of noise and emissions. However, operations of such vehicles is subject to government approvals. The regulatory approvals would not only relate to the use of such technology, for example, electric propulsion but also the airspace for conducting flight tests, as well as actual flights. It is reported, for example, that Uber is visualizing air taxis operating between skyports, spaced a few seconds apart in dozens of skylanes.[15]

Third, there are questions regarding the number of pilots in the cockpits of commercial aircraft. Partly to deal with the current and potential shortage of pilots and partly to reduce operating costs, there are ongoing discussions on the use of one pilot in the cockpit of commercial aircraft. Currently, the minimum number is two, presumably, one pilot to fly the aircraft and the second one to assist as well as monitor. There are a number of other considerations such as workload, work intensity, and pilot incapacitation. Some technologists are suggesting that the second pilot could work from the ground during the work-intensive stages of the flight, takeoff and landing. Although, from a technological point of view, aircraft could fly with one pilot or even no pilot, the questions are if regulators would approve such operations and if passengers would fly on these airplanes. Would government regulators be willing to allow all-cargo flights to be operated with one pilot in the cockpit and one on the ground?

Technology-enabled transformational strategies

The technologies discussed earlier, as well as their convergence and intersections, are creating numerous potential opportunities for transforming the airline business. Below are just a few examples that are discussed in this book.

1   Simplify the shopping process, which continues to be quite complex relative to innovations introduced by other business sectors.
2   Adapt more effectively to customers' needs, which have been shifting from the need for just basic services to the aspiration for personalized services and experiences.
3   Transform conventional business processes to reduce costs and offer much lower fares in more fundamental ways than just through the introduction of lower-cost subsidiaries and the introduction of basic fares.
4   Provide a simpler access to air travel if an airline really believes that it is a commodity business. Examples could include exceptionally simple shuttle services.
5   Deploy platforms to exploit the benefits relating to the development and introduction of new forms of air and ground transportation systems.
6   Use technologies to develop intelligent engagement platforms to achieve scale to find solutions to mobility problems, during regular and irregular operations, of all customers, not just those in the top-tier status.

Finally, while most business sectors, including aviation, are amid a fundamental change led by digital technologies, the digitalization process relates not just to technology but also to people, as well as corporate culture. Technology is simply an enabler and, in some cases, possibly, even a driver. However, the successful achievement of outcomes, solutions created to travelers' mobility requirements, depends on people – employees, partners, and to some extent, even customers. Why customers? For one thing, millennials are not just consumers but also employees, and, in some cases, partners. Additionally, consumers can build their own personal apps, probably simple ones, by deploying voice. These apps can even be changed frequently, given the ease of undertaking "programming" aspects. Moreover, all three – employees, partners, and customers – are going digital to varying degrees.

Notes

1   "European Aviation in 2040: Challenges of Growth," Eurocontrol, 2018, Edition 2.
2   "Future of the Airline Industry 2035," IATA, Geneva, Switzerland, 2017.
3   Tom Goodwin, "The Battle Is for the Customer Interface," *TechCrunch*, March 3, 2015.
4   Daniel M. Kasper and Darin Lee, "An Assessment of Competition and Consumer Choice in Today's U.S. Airline Industry," A Compass Lexecon Report, June 26, 2017, pp. 6–7.
5   "Growing Horizons 2017–2036," *Global Market Forecast*, Airbus, 2017, p. 24.
6   Andrew Matters, "Industry Performance & Outlook," A Presentation at the IATA World Passenger Symposium, Barcelona, Spain, October 2017.
7   "Current Market Outlook: 2017–2036," Boeing Commercial Airplanes, March 2018, p. 38.
8   Alison Angus, "Top 10 Global Consumer Trends for 2018: Emerging Forces Shaping Consumer Behavior," *Euromonitor International*, 2018.

 9 Alison Angus, "Top 10 Global Consumer Trends for 2018: Emerging Forces Shaping Consumer Behavior," *Euromonitor International*, 2018, p. 16.
10 OAG Aviation Worldwide, Travel Tech Innovation: Market Report, "Evaluating Travelers' Appetite for Adoption," 2018.
11 "Growing Horizons 2017–2036," *Global Market Forecast*, Airbus, 2017, p. 36.
12 "Growing Horizons 2017–2036," *Global Market Forecast*, Airbus, 2017, p. 36.
13 "The Fight for Slots," *Flight Airline Business*, May 2018, pp. 30–3.
14 Andrei Perumal and Stephen A. Wilson, *Growth in the Age of Complexity: Steering Your Company to Innovation, Productivity, and Profits in the New Era of Competition* (New York: McGraw Hill, 2018), pp. 8–14.
15 Graham Warwick, "Urban Expansion," *AviationWeek & Space Technology*, August 20– September 2, 2018, p. 53.

3 Transforming and bonding airline marketing and operations

From the digital strategies being followed in the airline industry, it is evident that the commercial side of the business is being transformed with digital technologies in areas relating to retailing, customer experience, personalization, and distribution. Leading airlines have been attempting to create 360-degree views of the increasingly changing expectations of customers to make the right offer to the right customer at the right time with the right price and through the right channel. The object is to generate additional revenue and improve customer experience at the same time. While progress has been made in these areas, first, there is still a need to make marketing mainstream if airlines are to adapt to the step-changing dynamics of the marketplace in the next ten years to capitalize on opportunities. Second, the commercial side of the airline business has received much more attention for digital transformation relative to the operational side. Consider, for example, the value of using digital technology to get 360-degree views of maintenance situations to get the right part, the right mechanic with the right tools, for the right plane at the right time, and at the right location. While progress has been made in both areas, more on the commercial side than the operational side, as stated earlier, it has been relatively slow on both sides due to the continued lack of sufficient integration, not only within each of these two functional areas but also between the two functional areas. This chapter starts with discussion on making marketing mainstream, followed by a discussion on leading operations into the digital age. Next is a perspective on bonding these two major functional areas within airlines – marketing and operations – while improving both customer experience and employee experience. A similar need exists within the airport sector, a subject covered in Chapter 5.

Making marketing mainstream

Based on the forces discussed in the previous chapter, marketing needs to become mainstream, facilitated by technologies, to adapt to the dramatically changing market dynamics and customer expectations. To put this in perspective, let us step back ten years and examine briefly the marketing activities at the time. Ten years ago, for example, there was little focus on retailing in the context of today and relatively little focus on customer experience. Today, airlines aspire to take retailing to new heights in the marketplace in which customers are looking for consistent and relevant experience at all touch points. Looking further ahead, say the next ten years, what could be the needs of customers? Could customers be looking for solutions to their total mobility requirements? To put retailing in perspective, the following section provides a quick review of where the airline business was ten years ago, where it is today, and where it could be ten years from now.

Looking back ten years

Low-cost carriers worldwide had a capacity share of just under 20 percent ten years ago, although there was a wide variation in the degree of low-cost penetration across the world. In the US, the airline sector was going through a major restructuring process. Delta and Northwest had announced their plans to merge. The three Persian Gulf-based super connectors were continuing to grow rapidly. Just as one indicator, Dubai International Airport handled just under 40 million passengers in 2008, representative of the traffic handled by such airports as Amsterdam, Bangkok, Hong Kong, Houston, and Singapore. Ancillary revenue of the airline industry was in the range of US$10 billion, with the highest percentage of total revenue in the hands of low-cost airlines, such as Allegiant in the US and Ryanair in Europe. Ancillary revenue as a percentage of total revenue was only about 5 percent at the industry level, again with a wide variation among carriers worldwide.

Most airlines, with the exception of some low-cost carriers, sold their tickets through the traditional indirect channels, global distribution systems and travel agents. Although airlines had capped and later cut travel agent commissions, the distributors reinvented themselves and continued to grow. Although IATA had successfully completed its game-changing, electronic-ticketing program, digital marketing activities within the airline industry were minimal. Airlines were still promoting their services through the regular media channels – print and TV, for example. Content was important, of course, but it was delivered within the contexts of "push" marketing, with messages going out to all customers. The blockchain technology was just beginning to get discussed, with its potential role in the transformation of the financial sector.

Mobile search, along with booking activity, was minimal given that the Apple iPhone had only come out in 2007. Social media was just emerging. An estimated 10 percent of the population used social media. Consider, for example, Twitter, launched in 2006, one of the three major channels, the other two being Facebook and LinkedIn. Based on the information available in the media, there were less than 10 million active users of Twitter per month, and the messages transmitted text only. However, social messaging began to play an important role in people's lives.

Customer service in the airline industry had been discussed for decades. Jan Carlzon, president and CEO of SAS, had written the book *Moments of Truth* in 1987. Sir Colin Marshall, CEO of British Airways in 1995, made customer service a priority.[1] Yet the industry continued to face challenges in creating high levels of customer service, and customer satisfaction continued to be low relative to many other business sectors.

The Uber concept did not exist ten years ago. The business was founded in 2009 and the service and the mobile app were launched in 2011 in San Francisco. The concept of Airbnb, developed around 2008, did not begin operations until 2011, and the self-driving car was barely visible. WAYMO, a self-driving car business and a subsidiary of Google's parent company, was formed in 2009. There was no discussion of the development of a small hybrid-electric aircraft to operate in regional markets or the development of a small commercial supersonic aircraft. Both Zunum Aero and Boom Supersonic were formed in 2014.

Now

Low-cost carriers worldwide have a capacity share of about 30 percent, with a wide variation across the world. The airline industry in the US has gone through a major restructuring process with the completion of mergers between United and Continental (2010) and between American and USAir (2015). The three Persian Gulf-based super connectors have achieved enormous growth. One indicator, the Dubai International Airport, handled just under 40 million passengers in 2008 but increased to just under 90 million passengers in 2017, overtaking London's Heathrow Airport and the Los Angeles International Airport and becoming the world's busiest airport in terms of international passengers making connections. Ancillary revenue could approach US$100 billion in 2018, now with major carriers participating in the stream. It now represents about 10 percent of the total revenue at the industry level, with substantial variation at the carrier level.

IATA has already made enormous progress in moving forward its new distribution capability initiative that has been enabling airlines to start changing their distribution processes. A number of leading carriers have been pursuing strategies to distribute their products directly to customers. Major GDSs and travel agents (online and offline) continue to play an important role, and there are a number of new metasearch platforms. Leading airlines are now exploring the use of blockchain technology to transform airline distribution. Digital marketing is now the buzzword with airlines developing initiatives to adapt to changing consumer behaviors, as consumers are increasingly shopping online. Web search activity is more prevalent on mobile devices than on desktop computers. However, the higher level of activity on mobile devices relates still only to search. The majority of consumers are still booking through their desktops. Social media has become a major force. It is estimated that about 80 percent of the US population now uses social media. Again, according to information available online, there are more than 300 million active Twitter users per month. The size of the message has increased (from 140 to 280 characters). It is now possible to attach images and videos to messages. The number of social channels has increased, now to include the likes of Instagram, SnapChat, YouTube, and WhatsApp. The popularity of social messaging has been increasing at a phenomenal rate, exemplified by the usage of WeChat.

Airlines are now beginning to consider delivering content within the framework of "pull" marketing aimed at targeted customers. Content has started to move away from text and toward images and videos. Airlines are clearly focusing on customer experience, given the experience provided by the likes of Amazon and Uber, businesses that are now used as references. Even some of the ultra-low-cost carriers have begun to pay attention to customer experience aspects. Take, for example, Spirit Airlines, that is improving its check-in process and its in-flight experience by offering, with a fee, a high-end Wi-Fi system to stream, surf, and text. Additionally, airlines have begun to explore the use of technologies such as artificial intelligence and augmented reality to bring about step changes in customer experience. Consider, for example, the use of chatbots and self-service re-accommodation systems during irregular operations.

At the beginning of 2018, it was reported that the market capitalization of Uber was about US$70 billion, a business that did not exist ten years ago. The number of countries where Uber has service appears to be approaching 100. After transforming the taxi sector with its ride-sharing service, Uber is now experimenting with electric VTOLs, with service beginning in 2023. Airbnb has been totally transforming the hospitality sector, and now the airline sector is beginning to feel some pressure. Expedia has been reported to want to become a global platform, with a potential to launch its own hotel brand to capitalize on the changing market dynamics between "hotel brands, hotel owners, and the online agencies."[2]

On the air transportation side, Zunum Aero, backed by Boeing Horizon X and JetBlue Technology Ventures, is planning to fly its prototype aircraft by 2020, with the aircraft in commercial service in 2022. Boom Technology is planning to introduce between 2023 and 2025 its 55-seater supersonic aircraft, capable of flying at a speed of Mach 2.2 with a range of 4,500 nautical miles. There is also ongoing interest in other new forms of transportation. Two examples include the prescription-based services provided by airlines such as Surf Air and the viability of seats on private jets.[3] On the ground transportation side, the self-driving car is almost here. In the middle of 2018, there was discussion in the media of Google starting a paid ride-sharing system using the self-driving car. Interest in the Hyperloop is increasing, and Virgin Hyperloop One, a US-based technology company, has already begun the initial stages of the commercialization process.

Looking forward ten years

In order to justify the suggestion for airline marketing to go mainstream, it may be helpful to develop a scenario that looks ten years ahead in a context similar to the one relating to the last ten years. Based on the developments of the last ten years, low-cost carriers worldwide could have a capacity share approaching 50 percent, especially from their expansion in international markets. The long-haul low-cost carriers could increase the current cost gap of about 20 percent between full-service carriers through innovations in operational strategies, including the development of alliances. Consider IndiGo Airlines, based in India. Despite some current setbacks, its current fleet, about 170 aircraft, could expand to over 500 in the next ten years.

It could serve numerous international markets, including destinations in Europe and all over Asia. A couple of major low-cost carriers based in Europe and a couple based in the US could start offering transatlantic services. Low-cost divisions of major full-service airlines, such as Singapore, Qantas, IAG, and Lufthansa, could expand their services worldwide. The airline industry worldwide could go through another restructuring process with further consolidation, in Europe, the US, and the UAE. Not only could the super connectors continue to grow, but also new China-based super connectors would most likely emerge, facilitated, in part, by China's "One Belt One Road Initiative," to take advantage of the changing air traffic patterns around the world. Although ancillary revenues would continue to increase at a reasonable pace, the big change would relate to the types of air-ground price-service options provided. For example, for a fee, say X percent of the fare, a traveler might be provided a guaranteed arrival within Y hours of the scheduled time.

IATA would have succeeded in a number of areas to simplify the airline business. Two game-changing examples would be the success of its ONE Order and ONE ID initiatives. The ONE Order relates to the concept of a single customer order record that replaces the multiple and rigid booking, ticketing, and payment methods. The ONE ID makes the security process more efficient for passengers and more effective for governments. Third-party distributors would still handle a significant portion of the air travel business, but there would be new breeds of travel marketers who handle the total mobility needs of different categories of customers, leveraging a broad spectrum of content and digital assistants. They will most likely be using specifically designed platforms that are solution-centric and experience-centric. Web search activity would be almost completely conducted on personalized mobile devices, coupled with AI-enabled digital assistants, which work in the dynamic and interactive modes. Wi-Fi would be literally everywhere. It would be very fast and very reliable, and 5-G networks would become available around the world. Bookings will be made through mobile devices, as the process would have become much easier, relating, for example, to price comparisons, availability of relevant information, and fast check-out processes. Additionally, there would also be greater security relating to websites. Social media would have new channels, and each one, using new technologies, would have developed new ways of learning about its audience and ways of monetizing that audience. The new channels would have mastered the use of such technologies as AI, machine learning, augmented reality, and virtual reality to show specifically curated content in each social ad for each individual.

Digital marketing would have enabled travel service providers to really adapt to changing consumer behaviors. The new travel marketers would now make access to relevant content easy, fast, and in real time. Consumers would be interacting with the content and engaging with content providers on a one-to-one basis to customize the experience in the end-to-end journey. Subscription-based airline services and seats on private aircraft would finally have become available through platform operators, who would have worked out the challenges relating to networks, customers services, and logistics. In other words, digital marketing would be adapting to the digital lives of individuals.

Mobility-as-a-service (MaaS) would have gone from an idea to new forms of services. Urban transportation, for example, could be available via Uber flying taxis, and driver-less cars would have totally changed transportation in short-haul markets, reducing, for example, the number of short-haul flights connecting to other short-haul flights, with connections at major hubs, helping to reduce congestion at major hubs. Electric vertical-takeoff-and-landing vehicles could offer air mobility in urban areas. In short-haul markets, there could even be flying cars. Hybrid-electric airplanes could be offering nonstop services in thin markets with ranges up to 700 miles. Fifty-five-seater supersonic airplanes could be flying across the Atlantic and the Pacific. The network-fleet-schedule offers of major global airlines could be expanded. An airline such as BA could be offering cost-effective nonstop transatlantic service from London City Airport, with the next-generation of the A220 (the rebranded Bombardier's C-Series aircraft), from London Heathrow, service with the next-generation supersonic aircraft across the Atlantic, and nonstop service in ultra-long-haul markets such as London Heathrow-Sydney with advanced versions of the Boeing 787 and the Airbus 350, as well as subscription-based services in various markets. Moreover, advanced technology, coupled with redesigned processes, would finally be delivering consistent customer experience throughout the travel journey.

This medium-term perspective and the scenario demonstrate that while changes in the last ten years might have been considered to be evolutionary, changes in the next ten years will be revolutionary. These changes will be facilitated by the commercialization of exponential technologies, the introductions of new forms of ground and air transportation, the implementation of totally redesigned processes, and the entry of a new breed of travel service markets. The new technologies will enable travel service providers and travel service marketers, the new travel distributors, to create significantly new value propositions for existing and new customers. The structure of the industry would be very different. For example, while the capacity share of the low-cost carriers might approach 50 percent, some carriers in this category could have merged, and some could be part of the larger network carriers. Further consolidation could also reduce the number of full-service network carriers. However, the mega full-service carriers would be more innovative in creating and delivering value through platforms to rebuild their customer bases by keeping up with changing customer expectations by providing, for example, personalized solutions to meet travelers' total mobility needs.

New focus on retailing

Airlines are exploring new ways of retailing with respect to their traditional methods as well as new products and services to add more value for their customers while generating new streams of revenue and profitability. To participate proactively in the retailing revolution, do airlines need to go beyond their core competencies – flying and selling seats – by exploring the use of new technologies and platforms? For example, airlines basically sold seats at prices to clear inventory, a process resulting in price-driven competition and product commoditization.

More recently, they adopted the mindset of selling from a "store" that has more products and services than just seats. This process improved margins and profits. Next, the "store" can expand to sell mobility solutions. Figure 3.1 shows how a retailing platform can provide a flexible system for suppliers of different travel-related products and services to meet the needs of different segments of customers. The platform will also be an open system to support technology developers to incorporate innovative value-adding retail-related features.

First, an internally integrated retailing platform within an airline will need to be connected directly with other platforms such as those operated by hotels and third parties, such as Airbnb. This connection will provide seamlessness. An integrated platform will enable seamless coordination of two aspects, supply and support: supply of all the elements of the end-to-end journey and real-time support prior to the trip, during the trip, and after the trip. The supply-support platform will lead to differentiation in an otherwise commodity business. The platform would provide the capability to make tailored recommendations based on knowledge of customer preferences, past purchases, and behavior. For example, for a particular individual and in a particular situation, perhaps the short-haul part of the trip would be better on a ground mode of transportation than on a regional carrier. In another situation, how about offering the ground transfer on Uber rather than the hotel shuttle?

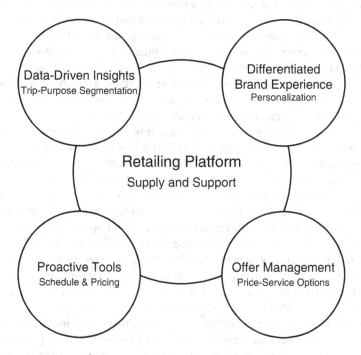

Figure 3.1 A Framework for Transforming Airline Retailing

Within the framework of Figure 3.1, merchandizing will now be conducted within the platform of the operator, which could be an airline or a third party. The product mix will relate not just to the product mix of services from the airline (seat, lounge access, etc.) but from a broad spectrum of related businesses (ground transportation, hotels, destination activities and events, etc.), and it will be created through the platform. Airlines currently face a challenge of how to show on an airline's website, in depth and breadth, the availability of all the products and services to meet a customer's end-to-end needs. The platform will overcome this challenge for an individual airline to display the full spectrum of products and services, as well as the services of other service providers. Retailers with physical stores have expertise in placing items on shelves in eye-catching ways. What would be the equivalent of that on a website? Where would higher-margin items be placed on a website? Platforms will overcome these challenges, with the success depending on the brand of the platform.

Consider some challenges facing airlines that are aspiring to become top-brand retailers. Sometimes airlines are mentioned as having legacy mindsets. However, the legacy nature has related more to data, analytics, and systems than to mindsets. Consider data. While airlines are beginning to have access to more and more data, the data that they currently have is not sufficient to generate a 360-degree view of even a small segment of customers. There is even a hidden challenge within this challenge: namely, the willingness to share data on the part of data holders, leaving aside the issues of protecting the data and respecting the privacy of data. The second challenge for an airline is to access the inventory in real time of closely related or distantly related products and services. It is hard enough to even work in a seamless manner with a limited number of related businesses such as hotels, car-rental companies, and railroads, given the wide-ranging (and widely changing) inventory buckets of each supplier. The task becomes much harder in working with a *full spectrum* of suppliers of distantly related products and services, such as ad hoc events and activities at destinations like sports, live shows, and sightseeing, and the availability of their products in real time. As for analytics, airlines have had a reasonable number of descriptive and diagnostic analytics to determine what happened and why. The limitations have been on the side of predictive and prescriptive analytics to determine what could happen and what should happen to, for example, some proposed retailing tactics.

As for systems, two limitations continue to exist. First, numerous planning systems in the commercial area (e.g., revenue management, pricing, reservations, and loyalty programs) and the operations area (e.g., flight operations, ground operations, and maintenance, repair, and overhaul) are of different vintages. In addition, they are not sufficiently integrated, either within the commercial or operations areas or between these two areas. What is needed is the willingness to change the organizational structures and to use enabling technologies to integrate various subsystems within the commercial and operations areas, as well as to bond the commercial and operational areas, topics discussed later in this chapter. The second systems constraint relates to the use of older-generation passenger services systems (relating to an airline's reservation system and the departure control system). This constraint has limited the implementation of contemporary retailing initiatives.

The retailing strategy now is to overcome these challenges to (1) make shopping easier and (2) deliver experience consistently. Unlike some other businesses, complexity in the airline industry relating to shopping relates to the complexity of itineraries, not to mention providing solutions at scale. Identification of the pain points of an individual customer is not the problem. Providing solutions that encompass both the physical and digital features of the product and meet the practical and emotional needs of the customer is the challenge. Moreover, delivering consistent service and experience for the entire end-to-end journey is a challenge, given that many products and services provided are not under the control of an airline. Even this challenge could be resolved. However, does an airline want to be perceived as the aggregator of the package of products and services to meet the end-to-end needs of a customer and be seen as the entity responsible for the seamless experience throughout the journey? These are important questions.

The solution for airlines to address these challenges while becoming leading retailers is to work on platforms. Some platforms would be internal to integrate the subsystems within the commercial and operational areas as well as to bond these two functional areas. Some would be external to achieve scale, scope, and flexibility to create and capture new levels of sources of value for customers and the airline. Below are a few examples of the ways intelligent engagement platforms can facilitate the development and delivery of end-to-end products and services within the much broader travel ecosystem.

- Platforms can provide scale to enable airlines to meet the needs of all passengers, not just those within the top-tier status or those traveling at much higher fares in premium cabins.
- Platforms can provide agility for airlines to keep up with technology that is moving at a fast rate and that is enabling consumers to expect much higher levels of customer service and experience with other business sectors.
- Platforms can provide user-friendly ways to identify and sell a wide array of travel-related products and services in personalized ways and make payments much more convenient while reducing transaction fees. Platforms can also track the fulfillment of customers' needs in real time, throughout the journey, and at all touch points.
- Platforms can provide customers greater control of their travel, whether it is relating to inspirational research, to shopping or in-flight services (like preferences relating to an environment to work, be entertained, or just rest) or to change plans easily during normal or irregular operations.

A behind-the-scenes platform will help find the right offer for the right customer at the right place. With respect to the last point, consider the timing of offers relating to ancillary products and services. Should ancillary products and services be marketed at the time of the booking or during the time between the booking phase and the day of travel, and for some products and service, during the trip itself? Presumably, at the time of the booking the focus of the customer is on price-service options relating to the schedule, the fare, and, possibly, the location of the seat, and less, for example, on features such as priority of boarding and options related to meals. Just prior to the trip and during the trip, a passenger may be willing to buy different products and services and from a different perspective, say experience. Kieron Branagan, in his thought leadership piece in Chapter 8, describes these purchase decisions in the framework of two wallets.

Figure 3.1 shows four building blocks relating to the use of a retailing platform. The first block relates to the need to have data-driven insights on customers – insights that are relevant. The availability of data and analytics can now help refine the segmentation process. Then come insights related to the needs of the segmented and targeted customers in terms of specific offerings. How do travelers shop and travel? What are their expectations, and how are these expectations changing? The development of such insights requires not only extensive databases but also tools for analyzing the data and making the insights actionable.

The existing data and analytics can be used to predict behavior, and prescriptive analytics can be used to make the right offer. The final recommendations can combine the schedule-related information and the ancillaries to make the personalized offer. For example, a recommendation could be to take a flight an hour earlier that will enable the customer to select the window seat without extra payment. Alternatively, take a flight an hour later and transport the bag for half the price. All offers can be generated in real time. Technology, such as machine-learning algorithms based on an individual's behavior and willingness to pay for the basic product – the seat – as well as related ancillaries can be leveraged.

It is not necessary to depend solely on surveys to get data. Profiling techniques can be used to identify customer behavior. Even when a person does not make a purchase on the website, there is still a lot of valuable data to be captured. More relevant information on customers can now be obtained with the use of emerging technologies, machine learning, and advanced algorithms to segment passengers and provide the services needed to develop relationships. Consider, next, how much time consumers spend on their mobile devices and the activities they are engaged in while on their mobile devices, such as streaming content and communicating with colleagues on social media. Consumers are looking for not just relevant content but also brands that provide relevant messages. Airlines can collect data that are more relevant from mobile apps and social media as well as the actual itineraries selected. For example, why did the traveler select a connection with an exceptionally long layover? Data on such anomalies needs to be captured, integrated, analyzed, stored, and shared. The making of the recommendation can also take into consideration the brand aspects. However, it is important to ensure that technology, for example, algorithms, is used to build trust, not destroy it.

The second block in Figure 3.1 relates to the goal of providing a differentiated experience to build a brand and loyalty. This block can address the needs for personalization but with a focus on the purpose of the trip. The object now is to build customer relationships to develop the brand and loyalty. The personalization aspect is to be able to recognize a customer as an individual, not as a passenger name record (PNR), and to treat each person as a unique traveler. Customers are looking for not just an experience but a differentiated experience, differentiated from other customers and differentiated from the services offered by competitors. In this area, it is necessary to recognize that the customer experience is based on the collection of interactions and engagements at all touch points.

As for brands and branding aspects, it is no longer sufficient to continue to rely on conventional wisdom relating to branding. The key question now is how consumers choose brands in the digital era, an era characterized by the always-on consumers and consumers looking for high-speed solutions (immediacy), while working in a mobile-first world. To succeed in the digital and the experience era, it is necessary to find new ways to deliver services that help customers to succeed in meeting their own needs. As such, the branding strategy will need to be not just to develop brands that consumers see as "different and relevant, but to *keep* being different and relevant."[4] The implication, therefore, is that if an airline wants to interact and stay engaged with its customers, then that involves customers developing a favorable relationship with the brand, and that in turn involves engagement for delivering experiential-based services to build trust. Consequently, a key requirement for branding is to establish a two-way engaging conversation with customers across all channels and through the formats preferred by customers, based on their behaviors. Keep in mind that customers are increasing their use of public social media platforms, and these communications can have a positive or negative impact on the brand of the service provider. Therefore, what is needed is a framework for two-way social media conversations.

With respect to loyalty, there are two options going forward. With the first option, an airline could reinvent its loyalty program by finding new ways to add value for customers and airlines.[5] This initiative, the development of mutual value, requires (1) aligning loyalty programs with brands and (2) the identification of nonconventional metrics to be used to measure loyalty, such as social sentiment.[6] To enable loyalty programs to generate mutual value, airlines need to find (1) new ways for customer engagement and rewards, (2) new ways to make customers feel more valued, and (3) new ways to transform customers into brand ambassadors. As mentioned in Chapter 2, blockchain technology shows a potential opportunity to transform loyalty programs to bring about step changes in value for customers. This option can become viable if an airline were to develop and operate a platform facilitating the brand to make loyalty more relevant by using the data airlines already have to get insights on the value desired by customers and to deliver that value. In fact, the loyalty programs can be used to capture valuable information to develop the brand. If an airline is willing to design its loyalty program with a greater focus on experience, customers are likely to be more willing not only to pay more for services, but they are more likely to provide information on their behavior to receive an enhanced experience. The information on behavior, in turn, can enable an airline to offer products, curated and based on personalization. The second option relating to loyalty is for an airline to engage third parties operating third-party based businesses that help customers fulfill their total mobility requirements on the basis of personalization, context, real time, and with 24/7/365 services and customer support.

The third building block in Figure 3.1 relates to the management of offers. Once customers have been segmented and targeted with respect to the differentiated experience needed, then personalized offers need to be developed and offered. The offer made should take into account that there are other opportunities for sale prior to departure. In other words, not all the profit needs to be optimized just through one sale at the beginning. Moreover, there are also opportunities for sales relating to other trips.

The offer will include products and services in four areas:

- the schedule and the fare;
- internal ancillary services relating to baggage, assigned seating, priority check-in and boarding, and onboard sales (food and beverages and in-flight entertainment);
- products and services related to travel but external to the airline, hotel accommodations, ground transportation, activities at destinations; and
- product bundling in real time and bundling of an airline's products and ancillaries, as well as those of related businesses.

If an airline is to become a sophisticated retailer, it needs to offer a full suite of services to meet customers' needs and almost limitless expectations. Focusing on the seat, which is a commodity product, even with the sale of seat-related services as well as the conventional travel-related products like hotel accommodations and rental cars, limits the value offered to customers because it limits the share of the wallet that can be captured. From this perspective, the value is in meeting the end-to-end needs of customers that may include various forms of ground transportation or a much higher level of integration within the travel ecosystem to provide a personalized offer. Consider the travel needs of a transatlantic passenger whose flight arrives in London at 7:00 AM but the hotel check-in is at 3:00 PM. What creative offers can be made other than the obvious one of paying for the hotel room for the night before an early morning arrival?

The fourth building block relates to the use of sophisticated tools to create price-service options to be included in the offers. As mentioned earlier, new tools and data are needed to create new strategies, not just dynamic pricing and dynamic inventory but also, even more fundamental, dynamic scheduling to optimize product offering and revenue at the same time while providing experience and building long-term relationships with customers. However, dynamic planning is a complex task. Take, for instance, fees charged for ancillaries. Generally, these fees are fixed – for example, for changing reservations, transporting baggage, having access to a lounge. In a data-driven world, these should be dynamic based on the customer and the situation, with fees determined by the value of the customer, the customer's complete itinerary, and offers made by competitors.

The creation of a dynamic offer requires coordination, resulting in an offer that is:

- personalized and context based;
- based with some information on the willingness to pay – the need to differentiate the customer who is simply looking for the best fare at the time of booking the airline seat vs. the customer who is looking for the best package at the time of booking;
- based on a reasonable understanding of the experience desired by the customer;
- embedded with personalized recommendations from trusted sources; and
- matched with the brand of the content-aggregating airline.

Airlines have been exploring different ways to conduct market research to identify the needs of different segments of customers and develop different products. One example was an early attempt at customization, with the introduction of branded fares. A second example was the development of premium economy cabins. The third example was the introduction of basic economy fares. As for dynamic pricing, in some ways, it is not a new strategy for airlines. They have been using "dynamic pricing" indirectly for years. Although prices stayed relatively fixed in various buckets, airlines controlled inventory dynamically. Now airlines are exploring technologies and strategies to have direct control over dynamic prices as well as inventory.

Leading airlines have begun to innovate and adapt to the retailing revolution underway. They are beginning to look outside the airline industry for inspiration based on the practices of trend-setting retailers. These perspectives can be helpful given that customer expectations are formed outside of the airline industry with the customer having had experience with the likes of Amazon, Alibaba, Netflix, WhatsApp, and Zara. These and other trend-setting retailers know that it is not sufficient to find out what customers buy and how, but how will the products purchased be used and to achieve what outcomes. An important trend now is merging in the physical and the digital worlds. Clothing stores can now install digital mirrors to help customers view images of how they would look in different clothes and, when combined, with different accessories. In addition, machines are being developed for shoe stores to create 3-D scans of a customer's feet to enable the sales staff to recommend the best pair of shoes. What can the merging of the physical and the digital worlds (digital mirrors and 3-D scans of feet) mean for an airline? According to one technology expert, an airline could show images of how a particular traveler would fit and move around in a specific seat in three dimensions and with a 360-degree view.

Next, the trend-setting retailers are using big data, analytics, and algorithms to understand customers' lives, which are changing dramatically. Take, for instance, shopping with robots and without bags. Stores can now provide carts (robots) to facilitate shopping to identify the location of selected items, keep track of the money spent as products are placed in the cart, make payments with credit cards, and have the products purchased transported to a customer's vehicle, or have the products delivered to a customer's selected address. Products can also be purchased using a smart mobile device in the hands of a customer, with the products loaded on a "virtual" cart. Leaving aside the value of the convenience of shopping for the customer, the key benefit to the store is the capability of the cart or robot to collect data on a customer's purchases as well as purchasing behavior. What might be some implications for airlines? Travelers could shop onboard an aircraft with their mobile devices and have the products delivered to their selected locations, especially purchases of duty-free items. Retailers are also reducing significantly the delivery time. Amazon, for example, is aiming for not only same-day delivery, but in the case of groceries, delivery within hours. On the airline side, as for fast delivery, items ordered onboard could easily be picked up as soon as the plane lands, depending on the stage length of the flight and the vendor selected.

Based on these insights, it is clear that airlines can do a lot more to find out how customers determine value, including not just price, but also meaningful and emotional experience, entertainment, and stimulation. Big data, technologies (machine learning and artificial intelligence), and analytics, such as journey analytics, are now becoming available to understand what outcomes various segments of customers want and how to connect and engage with various customers. Journey analytics can be used to explore not only the behavior of individual customers but also the behavior of clusters of consumers who are the best customers or how they can be made the best customers. These analytics can assist in the analyses of the behavior between research and shopping, for example, by looking at the behavior of online and off-line shoppers. Conventional data is not smooth. Online behavior can be analyzed by following the online breadcrumbs. Similarly, clusters of consumers can be analyzed to gain insights into their behavior as a group. Casinos used such techniques to analyze the behavior of "high rollers," for example, as a group, not as individuals. These technology-enabled insights will help airlines take bold steps to engage not only with customers but also with employees, to succeed in the value-driven retailing landscape.

Leading operations into the digital age

As mentioned in the beginning of this chapter, the commercial side of the airline business has received more attention for digital transformation relative to the operational side, which includes such areas as flight operations; maintenance, repair, and overhaul (MRO); and ground operations. Yet in all of these operational areas, the emerging technology ecosystem can:

- reduce operating costs by reducing delays and aircraft ground time;
- reduce unit operating costs by increasing labor productivity;
- reduce investment costs in spare parts and spare aircraft;
- improve customer experience;
- enable the generation of more revenue through an increase in the time available to use the aircraft; and
- improve employee experience to improve, in turn, customer experience.

These improvements can be achieved with the use of contemporary technologies, comprehensive information developed with the use of advanced analytics, and the establishment of a comprehensive data environment that provides 360-degree views of data and situations. In some ways, the operational groups in the aviation industry have always been leading users of technology and data. Consider some examples:

- For decades, NOTAMs (Notice to Airmen) have been enabling pilots to receive alerts of potential hazards.
- Likewise, ACARS (Aircraft Communications Addressing & Reporting Systems), a system developed by AIRINC, has been enabling the transmission of short messages between pilots and operators on the ground.
- EFB (electronic flight bags) have been in use for almost two decades, enabling pilots to preform flight management tasks much more efficiently by eliminating, or at least reducing, the amount of paper carried in the conventional flight bags – operating manuals, navigational charts, and so forth.
- On the airport side, the Airport Collaborative Decision Making (A-CDM) framework has been used by airports to track all aspects of their operations (including disruptions) to improve capacity planning and the utilization of resources – gates and slots, for example – through the increased predictability of events (for instance, the status and location of aircraft).
- In the cabin, flight attendants have been provided with electronic devices to upgrade services provided to passengers by recognizing individual passengers and their needs.

However, the operations sector can now achieve step changes in improvements with the new technology ecosystem and comprehensive data environments that not only have much more complete and inclusive data but effective ways to share and control data. Consider the value of an effective data environment to make informed decisions in the area of maintenance, repair, and overhaul (MRO). Sensors in modern aircraft are already generating vast quantities of data. However, new technologies can now provide the maintenance staff with a more holistic view of a situation. A comprehensive data environment would provide the data coming from sensors embedded in an aircraft engine that provide information in such areas as temperature, pressure, vibration, oil status, and airflow rate. In addition, the data would provide more value-adding information relating to, for example, performance degradation, to get a more holistic view of the situation so that corrective actions can be taken in a timely manner.

Along with a comprehensive data environment are now a set of advanced analytics to make informed decisions. Predictive analytics are already being used to get information on when certain components might fail. Moreover, from a tactical perspective, one question could be regarding when to perform maintenance prior to the upcoming failure. Prescriptive analytics can answer such a question about the ideal time to replace the part. Moreover, data and analytics can also improve vastly the first-time fix rates. Advanced analytics can also be used to undertake

part searches, and to identify patterns and ask questions. If data lead to the identification of a particular problem in a specific component in one engine, why did
it not show up in the data from the second engine? Following could be a question
from a strategic perspective. Based on the data and the use of analytics, can the
maintenance staff recommend a reduction in the number of spare parts or, even at
a higher level, the number of spare aircraft? Answers to such tactical and strategic
questions affect operating costs as well as investment costs. Predictive analytics
relating to the maintenance of aircraft engine are now expanding their horizon
and include aerostructures. As a result, informed decisions can now be made more
easily, decisions that have been a challenge in the past given the inadequacy of
the timely and integrated input from different departments, both within operations
from the commercial side and from other divisions within an airline and other
entities in the travel chain, such as airports and air traffic control. The potential
use of internal platforms (commercial and operations), based around effective
data environments – 360 degrees of the data – will lead to reductions in operating
and investment costs, increases in the revenue-generating capabilities of aircraft,
and improvements in customer and employee experience. Here are just six examples of the use of platforms:

- First, data relating to operations has traditionally been stored in multiple locations. However, within the digital context, operational data can be stored on
  a platform. One example of such a platform is under development by Lufthansa Technik (LHT), called AVIATAR. According to Lufthansa, this platform provides numerous apps that can facilitate the delivery of a wide range
  of services relating to maintenance, repair, and overhaul (MRO). Putting it in
  a different way, according to Lufthansa, it is "like iTunes or Amazon" within
  the MRO sector, and it can support airline customers in "real time and OEM
  independent."[7]
- A second example of a platform is an initiative developed by Airbus called
  Skywise, an operational open-aviation data platform that can be used by airlines to support their digital transformation in areas relating to the maintenance of aircraft. The Skywise platform enables the integration of data from
  numerous sources into a single secure source – cloud based – that users can
  access from a single point.
- A third example of the power of internal operational platforms is the development and use of "digital twins" by industrial companies such as General
  Electric. A digital twin – a virtual replica of a physical system or a component
  engine – has proven to be of tremendous value in monitoring the health of an
  aircraft. Staff on the ground can track and monitor how an engine is running
  during a flight.
- A fourth example would be businesses taking the "Internet of things" into the
  "Internet of outcomes."[8] The IoT technology leads to the creation of data. The
  Internet of outcomes enables businesses to use data-driven ways to optimize
  their operations in meeting their needs as well as the needs of their customers.

- Fifth, the operations of platforms are also being enhanced by the industrialization of additive manufacturing. This technology is now able to "print" components with quality and consistency.
- Sixth, airlines can work within the supply chain platforms, operated by MRO service providers to reduce costs, improve service levels, and focus on customer-centric challenges and opportunities. For more information, see Ben Boehm's thought leadership piece in Chapter 8.

One key benefit of a platform is the availability of integrated data. Consider an original equipment manufacturer (OEM) of an aircraft that integrates the aircraft design and aspects within the supply chain. Compare this situation to an OEM of an engine that has some control from the design to manufacturing phases. In both cases, the challenge is related to the integration of data as well as the control of data. Platforms can therefore play important roles not just in the integration of data and, to some extent, the control of data, but also the availability and use of analytics and the capability of diagnostics. One must also not overlook the value of platforms in the area of connectivity. For some insightful information on value-added services/solutions partners for airlines, see the thought leadership piece by Ben Boehm in Chapter 8.

Consider another area in operations – flight operations, which involves the management of flight crews, flight planning, and operations control centers, as well as cabin services. Digital transformation can move flight operations planning from reactive analysis to predictive analysis with the use of data mining, analytical techniques, situation modeling (and validation), and the advancements in satellite communications as well as Internet-related communications. Consider an example of reactive analysis. In the past, operations used data from standard services to establish static rules, for example, a certain amount of separation between aircraft and producing an alert if two aircraft began to converge on their approach to runways within a given amount of separation. In a dynamic and a proactive environment, separation can be reduced using data that has higher quality and data that is integrated, coupled with the use of advanced analysis (predictive) to improve the decision-making process. New digital tools are now available for flight optimization, with much more comprehensive considerations relating to navigation, fuel, labor contracts, crew duty rules, environmental regulations, and the changing nature of the capacity and costs of infrastructure. These new tools can also enable flight planning that is performance-based and dynamic while balancing much more efficiently and effectively different objectives relating to crews, passengers, and aircraft.

Consider another area – ground operations. This broad group includes (1) various aspects relating to the movement of aircraft in and out of gates, fueling, ramp services, cabin services, catering; (2) station operations, which includes baggage handling, baggage control, and security; and (3) cargo operations. Again, new technologies show the potential for substantial improvements. One example of a new technology would be blockchain to track assets and information. New tools are available to share flight data, relating to departures and surveillance, more efficiently among the three major entities – airlines, airports, and air traffic control. These technologies and tools have already begun to improve the management of aircraft departures and airport slots and gates. Moreover, the technology-enabled sharing of data will bring both agility and scale in operations. Consider a large number of questions raised during irregular operations (IRROPS) and the speed with which answers are required. The challenge in the past has been not just the large number of questions but the amount of engagement required in answering the questions. New technology has already begun to address this challenge.

The major development for leading airline operations into the digital age is the expected rate of increase in the e-enabled aircraft that are generating vast quantities of data. According to a Boeing study, only 3 percent of the commercial aircraft in 2015 were e-enabled. This number is predicted to increase to 70 percent in 2035.[9] This data will take to new levels the management of flights, the control of operations, the maintenance of aircraft, and the level of services provided to passengers. However, the critical success factor will still be the quality of the data environment. For example:

- Where will data be stored?
- What will be the reliability and integrity of the data?
- What technologies will be used to analyze the data to identify, for example, patterns and to deploy predictive and prescriptive analytics?
- Who will have access to the data?
- Who will own the data?

Bonding commercial and operational planning

A few far-thinking airlines have already begun to reevaluate at the basic product – a scheduled seat from Airport A to Airport B – to see how it could be enhanced to meet customers' broader needs. Based on the material presented in the previous chapter relating to the three major forces and the constraints, here are some examples of transformational strategies being considered:

- Simplify the shopping process that continues to be complex relative to innovations introduced by other business sectors. Airlines do recognize that both business and leisure travelers have been spending a considerable amount of time, not to mention experiencing frustrations, in the shopping process. The words used for advanced pricing policies are personalized pricing and dynamic pricing. Are they both the same, or are they different? There could be some challenges with personalized pricing, for example, from regulators. On the other hand, under discussion is the concept of "flexible" pricing, based not just on the seat but a package that contains other products. The variation would depend on not just the passenger (loyalty status, for example) but also product attributes such as advance booking, length of stay, and distribution channel. The offer could be facilitated with the use of AI coupled with machine learning instead of rules-based algorithms such as an X percent discount for a particular loyalty status.

- Adapt more effectively to customers' needs, which have been shifting from the need for just basic services to, first, the desire for experiences, and more recently, to the aspiration for personalized services and experiences. As a result, leading airlines have begun to broaden their focus from the management of operations, to networks, to revenue, and more recently, to experiences.
- Transform the conventional business processes to reduce costs substantially and offer lower fares in more fundamental ways than just through the introduction of lower-cost subsidiaries and the introduction of basic fares.
- Think fundamentally differently about airline services, instead of selling seats on scheduled flights between airport pairs, to find and offer solutions to consumers' total mobility problems.
- Deliberate on the challenges and opportunities relating to the development and introduction of new forms of air and ground transportation systems. Plan, for example, on the possibility of the small (10–15 seats) hybrid-electric airplanes operating in low-density short-haul markets. Such an airplane is under development by Zunum. How about a smaller (about 55 seats) supersonic aircraft designed and manufactured through the integration of existing airframe and engine technologies? It is under development by Boom Technologies. As mentioned earlier, Uber-type of flying taxis are currently being tested in Dubai and are scheduled to be tested in the US. The eVTOLs are being developed to cater to the needs of urban air mobility (UAM). Self-driving cars could transport passengers in thin, short-haul markets – passengers who are currently being transported by scheduled airlines using connecting services through major hub-and-spoke systems.

The transformational strategies described require, first, integrations of different sub-functions in the commercial space and the operational space. For example, one way to reduce costs is to reduce the planning cycle time from months to weeks. However, while the concept is appealing, its implementation calls for dynamic scheduling, a process that will require the overhaul of both the pricing and revenue management practices as well as the transformations of aircraft scheduling and crew scheduling processes. Second, in each of the two areas, commercial and operational, processes will need to be made much more dynamic, to acquire scale. Consider just one example. Most full-service airlines do work with passengers in their very top-tier levels to solve their mobility problems during regular and irregular operations. However, scale is needed to find solutions to the mobility problems of all customers. This requirement of scale calls for a strong bonding of the processes within commercial and operational areas.

There are four key requirements for effective bonding between the commercial and the operational areas. First, comprehensive and reliable data are needed to provide 360-degree views of customers in the commercial space and 360-degree views of situations in the operational space. Second, all sub-functions in each of the two major functions must work with the same data and with the same assumptions relating to short- and medium-term goals – relating, in turn, to revenues, costs, competitive positions, and so forth. Third, there needs to be a clear common understanding of what digital transformation is. Fourth, planning processes in each of the two major areas need to be much more dynamic.

Consider the third requirement regarding a common understanding of what digital transformation is. Although the words digitization and digit*al*ization are sometimes used interchangeably, are all divisions onboard with the meaning? From one perspective, digitization means converting information from an analog form into a digital form without changing the content and automating some conventional paper-based processes. Digit*al*ization, on the other hand, goes further and refers to the use of digital technologies (and digitized data) to change how business is conducted in some areas. For example, within a maintenance department of an airline, replacing the storage of information written on paper and kept in boxes to transferring the information into records in a computer would be digitizing the information. However, using analytics to create insights from the digitized information to manage more efficiently parts and components as well as to improve labor productivity would be referred to as digit*al*ization. Other examples of digit*al*ization would be:

1   the replacement or augmentation by an airline of its customer-contact centers with intelligent machines;
2   the collection of digital data coming from sensors embedded in an aircraft engine and using predictive analytics to predict when a part might fail and prescriptive analytics to determine when the part should be replaced; and
3   an airport using the digital data coming from sensors in a terminal to manage passenger traffic flows at different locations.

Based on this perspective, digit*al*ization is not about automating conventional processes encompassing tried-and-true methodologies. It is about identifying and implementing new ways to do things that produce more innovative solutions for customers on one side and airlines and airports on the other side – more agility, scale, and greater experience for employees, for instance. As such, digit*al*ization relates to the digital transformation of some specific processes within an airline or an airport relating to operations or customer services (and experience). Alternatively, digital transformation can relate to the management and operations of an entire organization and its capabilities, associating, for example, to business mindsets, business products, business strategies, business core competencies, and overall business models. From these perspectives, digital transformation must also include strategies related to the workforce, as discussed in the next section.

To survive and thrive in the hyper-competitive environment discussed in the first part of this chapter, planning in each of the two major functions needs to be much more integrated and dynamic. Take the standard divisions within the commercial department of an airline: network/fleet/schedule planning, pricing/revenue management, sales/distribution, and loyalty. The planning processes among these four divisions alone need to be made much more integrated and dynamic. The integrated aspect of network and schedule was discussed at some length in my previous book. The dynamic aspect of pricing was also mentioned in the same book.[10] The question now is much deeper than if an airline can reduce its schedule planning cycle from the traditional 12 months, with minor adjustments for seasonality, to two months. An even more important question would be if an airline should change its planning focus from capacity-driven demand or demand-driven capacity. While technology is clearly available, is the necessary data available? Going further, is there an integrated approach, and are the planning teams working with consistent assumptions? For example, what is the objective? Is it to maximize the revenue per seat, or revenue per customer, or even share of the wallet or is the objective to provide solutions to the mobility problems of customers? Dietmar Kirchner, in his thought leadership piece in Chapter 8, provides a different way of schedule planning, based on the experience from the air-cargo sector. In this sector, the likes of FedEx, scheduled capacity is based much more tactically on demand.

Prioritizing employee experience in the digital age

Just as customer experience is becoming a major focus on the marketing side, on the operations side the focus also needs to be on the employee experience and employee expectations. In fact, in digital transformation, employee experience and employee expectations are even more critical and must be embedded into the digital transformation process. If strategies, processes, and systems are becoming digital, then the employees need to get a digital orientation, too. Employees not only need to be comfortable with the use of data and different kinds of analytics, they also need to have access to better technology to see the information and use it to make the best recommendations to customers on the ground and in the aircraft. The priority now is to understand the multi-generational workforce expectations and needs and find ways to define experiences and measure experiences, particularly relating to digital employees. That raises the question as to who the digital employees are.

Within the context of digital transformation, digital workers are those who use digital technologies to become more productive in areas relating to business operations and customer services. A flight attendant equipped with a tablet and connected with real-time information located in different divisions of an airline, can provide passengers onboard with more than information relating to the status of connecting flights, how to get to the connecting gates, and the status of customers' baggage. The flight attendant can rebook passengers on flights based on their profiles. They can be given the information to recommend hotels and the passenger given the capability to book hotel rooms, if the inbound flight will not make the connection that is the last flight of the day.

Aircraft mechanics, using mobile devices and augmented reality, can become more productive, reducing significantly the downtime of an aircraft, not to mention bring an improvement in the first-time fix rates. For these systems and processes, data needs to be in place to facilitate interactions and engagement with employees while increasing transparency.[11] Employees are not just helping customers. They are also helping other employees at all levels, and they are helping partners. The employee involvement will be even more important when the IoT trend accelerates. In the final analysis, it is really people, enabled by technology, who are driving change. Just as technology is playing a role in customer experience, it can also play a role in employee experience. For example, people analytics can enable people to be connected. Artificial intelligence can be used to connect people with machines. As some experts say, it is "not human or machine" but "human and machine." Consequently, it is not only that customers may need human intervention in situations where machines cannot resolve an issue, but machines can also "learn" from the interactions of customers with employees.

The need to understand employee experience and employee expectations is becoming critical. While HR departments have had numerous tools to deal with standard issues of employee productivity and performance, attrition patterns, organizational compliance, and employee wellbeing, the focus is increasing in such areas as measuring skill gaps, network collaboration, and employee engagement. This is where people-related databases and people analytics come in. Just as on the commercial and operational sides, the challenge exists not so much in the existence of data but with respect to the quality and integrity of data and an understanding of its use. Machine-learning algorithms are playing a role, for example, in training people in not just generic sales but in revenue management, based on an understanding of behaviors and patterns and their changes. Consequently, in network and revenue management, it is the combination of human and intelligent technology working together to make better and faster decisions. Similarly, on the MRO side, artificial intelligence and machine-learning technologies are helping mechanics troubleshoot more rapidly and more effectively. Consider also the deployment of augmented reality, coupled with smart glasses, for a mechanic to "see" 3-D wiring diagrams interactively.

Just as there are customer experience management (CEM) platforms, there are also employee experience management (EEM) platforms. In addition, just as a CEM platform can help to increase customer engagement to develop strategies, an EEM platform can do the same for employees, not just to improve employee satisfaction or even to measure employee value, but also to enable employees to succeed. Now it is important to personalize employee experience. Technology can be used to transform employees by giving them access to data and other employees throughout the entire organization, and possibly even partners. This book suggests that platforms can provide holistic solutions to travelers' mobility problems. However, the use of platforms will require changes to systems and processes relating to core functions, changes in which employees have a major role to play. As such, there needs to be a link between business strategies (particularly when they involve digital transformation) and workforce strategies.

Notes

1 "Competing on Customer Service: An Interview with British Airways' Sir Colin Marshall," *Harvard Business Review*, November–December, 1995, pp. 100–18.

2 Deanna Ting, "Expedia's Hotel Boss on Becoming a Global Platform," *Skift Take*, July 25, 2018.
3 Samantha Shankman, "The Growth and Democratization of Flying Private," *Skift Take*, July 24, 2018.
4 John Gerzema, who helped develop Brand Asset Value while at Young & Rubicam, quoted in Allen Adamson and Joel Steckel, *Shift Ahead: How the Best Companies Stay Relevant in a Fast-Changing World* (New York: American Management Association, 2018), p. 7.
5 Evert R. De Boer, *Strategy in Airline Loyalty: Frequent Flyer Programs* (Cham, Switzerland: Palgrave Macmillan, 2018).
6 "A Wake-up Call for Sleepwalking Loyalty Programs," *A Global Benchmarking Survey* by EAN (Expedia's Affiliate Network) and Points. Travel Loyalty Report, 2018, p. 6.
7 "Lufthansa Technik Sets New Sales Record: Focusing on Digitization and Internationalization," *Aviation Maintenance*, April/May 2018, p. 6.
8 Lee Ann Shay, "Inter of Outcomes," *AviationWeek & Space Technology*, MRO Section, April 9–22, 2018, pp. MRO12–16.
9 "2017 Services Market Outlook," Boeing Commercial Airplanes, 2017, p. 13.
10 Nawal K. Taneja, *21st Century Airlines: Connecting the Dots* (London: Routledge, 2018), chapters 3 and 4.
11 Jacob Morgan. *The Employee Experience Advantage: How to Win the War for Talent by Giving Employees the Workspaces They Want, the Tools They Need, and a Culture They Can Celebrate* (Hoboken, NJ: John Wiley, 2017); Tracy Maylett and Matthew Wride, *The Employee Experience: How to Attract Talent, Retain Top Performers, and Drive Results* (Hoboken, NJ: John Wiley, 2017).

4 Designing intelligent engagement platforms

This chapter lays out not only the reasons for utilizing platforms but also some ways to transition the business from a conventional operating framework to one based on platforms in general and intelligent engagement platforms in particular. Platforms, per se, are not a new concept in the aviation industry, even though the systems developed and deployed by the industry were not called platforms. In addition to their own systems, airlines have also been using a broad spectrum of platforms developed by different businesses to address their specific business needs. Some of these platforms have been developed by businesses that are related more to travel, such as Expedia. Some are related less to travel – for example, platforms developed by technology companies such as Google, retailers such as Amazon, and social media app developers such as WeChat. However, to meet the total mobility needs of travelers, airlines need more than the use of their own traditional operations-centric platforms and the existing, value-adding but independent and unconnected platforms developed by third parties. What is needed are intelligent engagement platforms that are customer solution-centric and customer experience-centric to enable customers to make informed decisions about their needs and for airlines to make decisions on how to adapt to the needs of customers while growing and generating sustainable profits.

Re-platforming the airline business

Surprisingly, the aviation industry is not new to the use of platforms, even though the systems they developed were not called "platforms" at the time of their development. To their credit, airlines already have an excellent knowledge of working with their own systems as well as numerous ad hoc platforms developed by third parties. Here are just nine examples of systems that, in contemporary jargon, might be called platforms.

- IATA, established in 1945, developed and operated the inter-line and the bank billing and settlement plan system platforms. The inter-line system was developed for airlines worldwide to transport passengers on each other's networks using standard rules and conditions. The billing and settlement plans were efficient ways to facilitate the sale, remittance, and reporting processes relating to ticket sales made by the IATA Accredited Passenger Sales Agents. The plan also provided financial control to airlines and improved their cash flows. This system had huge benefits for travelers, as they could fly literally anywhere in the world on one ticket, no matter which airline they used, as all tickets were endorsable on all IATA carriers.

- Comprehensive systems for real-time communications were developed and operated by SITA. The company, founded in 1949, was the first aviation business to develop a platform to handle worldwide communications within the aviation industry.

- Early versions of the computer reservation systems (also known as central reservation systems) were developed by airlines to store and retrieve information relating to passenger reservations. American Airlines launched its famous SABRE (Semi-Automatic Business Research Environment) system in 1960, which within a few years resulted in it being "the largest civil data processing system in the world." Subsequently, such systems were used by travel agents and global distribution systems.

- Texas International Airlines, based in the US, is reported to have developed the first modern frequent flyer program that tracked the miles traveled by passengers and provided them with some rewards. However, it was American Airlines that, in 1981, introduced a new frequent flyer program that began to offer special fares to its frequent travelers. Subsequently, these innovative loyalty program platforms began to be used by a broad spectrum of providers of financial services (banks and credit card companies) and a wide array of retailers.

- The Airline Tariff Publishing Company (ATPCO), founded in 1975, took over the operations of the Air Traffic Conference of America (founded in 1945), which published passenger fares. The ATPCO started to operate a platform that enabled the collection and distribution of fare data and fare-related content (for example, rules relating to the transportation of baggage) worldwide. This information was reliable, standardized, and organized in a format that could be used easily and efficiently by airlines (providers of the initial data) and users such as global distribution systems (GDSs) and travel agents.

- Around the mid-1980s, network carriers developed network platforms that enabled regional airlines to feed the larger network carriers at their hub-and-spoke systems. These affiliate airlines operating under the brands of the major airlines provided cost-effective service to major airlines to expand their hubs while providing reasonable frequencies for travelers to and from smaller cities.

- Two major airlines, Northwest and KLM, formed an alliance in 1989, a platform that allowed the two airlines to extend their networks, benefitting both airlines and their customers. However, the KLM-Northwest alliance set the stage during the coming decade for the formation of three major platform-based global alliances – Star, oneworld, and Skyteam – enabling alliance member airlines to cooperate in different marketing and operational areas.

- Aeroxchange, founded in 2000 by a number of airlines from around the world, developed an electronic telecommunications platform to facilitate operations in the aviation supply chain on matters relating to repairs and inventory pooling of parts and components. This platform systematized the exchange of information and documents among the trading partners and third parties relating to the purchase and sale of maintenance-related goods and services while increasing the timeliness and accuracy of information. Technological standards like Airinc and Spec 2000 were also developed jointly to ease air-to-ground communication or share spare parts.

- Major GDSs have been facilitating the coordination of flight schedules, seat availability, pricing, and reservations for decades. Prior to the entry of these B2B e-commerce businesses, travel agents spent large amounts of time identifying and pricing itineraries and making reservations.
- TripAdvisor, an online user-generated content business founded in 2000, is a platform that provides reviews of travel-related businesses, such as hotels, restaurants, and tourist attractions. Given that TripAdvisor acquired, in 2014, Viator, a platform in itself, being an online curator of local tours and activities, the TripAdvisor platform is now also able to sell tours.

Besides their own systems, historical and current, airlines also make use of, to various degrees, platforms developed by related businesses. These platforms are independent and were developed by businesses to meet their own specialized needs. Here are just nine examples of such independent systems or platforms.

- Online travel agencies (OTAs) began to emerge in the mid-90s, beginning with Microsoft Expedia Services. Later the OTAs developed their own platforms that facilitated travel while working with the GDSs.
- A wide variety of metasearch engine platforms now exist to help travelers find travel specific deals such as low fares and the best time to buy airline tickets. Just four examples are Kayak, Booking.com, Momondo, and Skyscanner.
- People communicate with one another using a number of well-known social media messaging platforms. Examples include WhatsApp, Messenger, and WeChat.
- On the technical side of the airline business, MROs have their own platforms. Chapter 3 mentioned an initiative of Lufthansa Technik to develop a big data analytic platform with the capability to determine when a component should be replaced.
- Airports have their own platforms. Just one example is the Private Suite, operating at Los Angeles Airport, in which customers pay an annual membership fee, along with a per-visit charge, for facilitating travel through the airport.
- Well-known technology companies developed their own platforms to enter the travel vertical. For example, Google Flights, an online flight booking service, was launched in 2011. In the future, this platform could easily become a one-stop service for online travel. In addition to the existing customer-centric features, it is now adding a capability to "predict" flight delays.
- A number of platforms exist to provide aviation business intelligence, data, and tools to the aviation community. Two examples of companies with such databases and platforms are diio and OAG.

- A broad spectrum of credit card companies utilize platforms working with airlines, exemplified by the issuance of co-branded airline credit cards. Depending on the co-branded card, the benefits can go beyond just travel.
- A number of platforms exist to provide various levels of advice relating to travel. Routehappy offers information on different aspects of seats, legroom, and seat width, for example. Tripit keeps online the information on an individual's complex itinerary by collecting information forwarded by an individual relating to booking confirmations. Rome2Rio offers a door-to-door search engine on a broad spectrum of areas relating to a planned trip.

Finally, there are platforms in the marketplace developed by third parties to help a wide array of businesses meet their specialized needs. One example of such a platform that could be used by the airline industry enables users to log on to access data on individuals that provided various levels of information to a broad spectrum of businesses participating on the platform. One such example is VER-IMI, a company based in Berlin. The business name claims to have a combination of the words "verify" and "me." The data is secure and relates to the identity of individuals with control exercised by an individual. According to the information available on the company's website, examples of participating partners include Allianz, Daimler, Deutsche Bank, and Lufthansa.[1]

The early types of internal systems (platforms) enabled airlines to deal with the complexity and constraints of the industry while providing safe, efficient, and increasingly affordable forms of air travel. However, within the airline sector, while some older generations of systems are still operational, they are no longer capable of transforming planning at the dynamic and integrated levels, either in marketing or operations, as discussed in Chapter 3, let alone improving either customer experience or employee experience. These limitations are understandable since older generations of systems were not designed to provide flexibility for airlines and to focus deeply on customer service, let alone customer and employee experience, relative to contemporary standards. From the beginning, they were designed to overcome the complexity of logistics that caused airlines to focus more on operations than on marketing. This line of thinking was reasonable at the time since the airline industry worldwide was heavily regulated (until about the end of the 1970s), preventing managements from developing and implementing traditional marketing strategies relating to, for example, price-service options. Even after the airline industry was deregulated (although in steps), management focus, with the exception of a few airlines, continued to be high on the logistics of operations relative to the marketing side of the business. More recently, however, a few top-tier airlines, having "almost mastered" the logistics of their operations, have begun to devote more attention to contemporary marketing challenges and opportunities (discussed in Chapter 3), even though complexity continues to exist and, in some cases, has even increased. Hence there is a need for re-platforming the aviation business.

Consider, as background, some tipping points. Travel by consumers in emerging markets is about to become higher than in developed markets, as pointed out in Chapter 2. Online bookings are about to cross over the bookings made offline.

More shoppers are likely to be communicating with chatbots than humans. Capacity offered by low-cost carriers worldwide is increasing significantly, especially in heavily traveled international markets. High-value passengers could accept traveling on nonstop flights approaching 20 hours, bypassing congested hubs. OTAs are becoming involved in the business-to-business (B2B) business. New travel marketers are emerging and could get involved more deeply with intermediaries such as Google and metasearch players. New travel marketers could enable search not only for services provided by low-cost carriers but for all carriers worldwide (over and above those members of IATA) in their metasearch programs. A large percentage of travelers are still, at least, searching on Google, if not booking travel. The media is quoting a 2017 survey by OAG that reports 44 percent of travelers would prefer to book their travel with Amazon. In addition, "62 percent of consumers would be comfortable booking directly with Google Flights."[2] What do these trends mean for access to consumers, consumer acquisition costs, intermodal travel, packaging, and pricing (dynamic and personalized)?

Based on these developments, airlines have been exploring and implementing some customer-centric and even a few experience-centric marketing initiatives. The bundled product has been unbundled and the physical product has begun to be integrated with some digital elements, such as the mobile capability to shop and book, the availability of digital boarding passes, and the availability of a limited level of personalization. Some full-service airlines also created lower-cost divisions and started to offer fares that matched the fares offered by lower-cost airlines to appeal to the price-sensitive market. Air France went even further and designed its low-fare division, Joon, launched in December 2017, to appeal to millennials by introducing some digital features such as streaming-based entertainment. Moreover, Joon could be used as a platform for testing new ideas relating to networks, schedules, or products. More recently, a few airlines have even looked at the basic product – a scheduled seat from Airport A to Airport B – to see how it could be enhanced – to try to meet the end-to-end journey needs of different segments of travelers. This last development is the beginning of the thought leadership relating to the mobility-as-a-service concept.

New-generation intelligent engagement platforms

Going forward, the new-generation intelligent engagement platforms are needed to enable airlines to work around their conventional and new complexities while helping travelers meet their total mobility needs. Specifically, such platforms can assist in the following areas.

- Enable airlines to accommodate the projected growth in the demand for air travel (as discussed in Chapter 2), not just coming from growth of economies and disposable incomes, especially of people living in developing regions, but also because air travel is becoming more and more an integral part of people's lives. Airlines can accommodate the projected growth in travel despite the increasing limitations of the conventional infrastructure – capacities of major airports and air traffic control systems, for example.

- Provide scale to enable airlines to meet the needs of all passengers, not just those within the top-tier status or those traveling at much higher fares in premium cabins. It is possible to offer even lower price-service options to meet the needs of large segments of people who are not traveling or are traveling very little. In developed regions, for example, the US, major carriers generate about 50 percent of their revenue from about 15 to 20 percent of their customers. The other 80–85 percent of passengers travel infrequently, only once or so a year, making it difficult for airlines to understand the needs of these infrequent customers. Platforms can enable airlines to collect, interpret, and share data, data that either does not exist or resides in multiple fragmented silo systems.

- Provide agility for airlines to keep up with technology that is moving at a fast rate and that is enabling consumers to expect much higher levels of customer service and experience. New types of consumer-related technologies have been entering into the lives of consumers, broadening consumers' access to travel options before, during, and after travel. However, some travelers are frustrated by having to use multiple apps on their mobile devices, and they will be drawn to the services provided by the operators of comprehensive consumer-centric and experience-centric travel platforms to meet their total mobility needs. Customers want greater control of their travel – whether it is relating to shopping, or in-flight services relating to an environment to work, be entertained, or just rest, or a change of plans relating to normal or irregular operations. Customers want user-friendly identity-related services and ways to make payments for such services much more conveniently.

- Provide solutions to the total mobility problems of customers on a personalized basis and with a seamless and consistent experience. This feature includes the provision of situation-based solutions in the end-to-end journeys, for example, shopping and pre-flight, in-flight, and post-flight activities as well as activities at destinations.

- Provide data to develop a much higher level of understanding of customers. This understanding can facilitate the sale of all components of an end-to-end trip, coupled with a higher degree of personalization and with a higher level of experience, through engagement with travelers throughout the journey and at all touch points. These touch points encompass the trip-planning phase (research and booking), the airport processing phase (check-in and boarding), and the in-flight phase (in-flight entertainment and online shopping), as well as arrival at the destination phase (baggage and information on ground transportation).

- Provide experience to employees, too. Good employee experience, as discussed in Chapter 3, will increase their satisfaction, improve their interactions with customers, improve employee productivity, and create an environment for innovation. Engagement platforms will enable businesses to listen to the voice of their employees.

To summarize, consumers are looking for:

1   convenience – shopping, with choice, on-demand, online, context based, seamless, experience-based, and on an end-to-end basis;
2   transparency – clear and complete details on the prices charged and services provided;
3   control – during regular and irregular operations, in real time, through automated systems and or through human engagement; and
4   support – monitoring the trip with the use of super PNRs.

On the side of airlines, they are looking for/to:

1   ways to compete more effectively in a marketplace in which the product is becoming commoditized and where loyalty to a given service provider is becoming questionable;
2   effective ways to remain relevant and grow with sustainable profits;
3   develop and market much more value-adding price-service options through collaboration;
4   generate new incremental revenue through the sale of ancillary mobility-related products and services; and
5   establish two-way feedback systems with existing and potential collaborative suppliers based on customer engagement throughout the customer journey and ongoing analyses of marketplace information.

Consequently, it is the availability of strategic and tactical partnerships on a platform that will help consumers reduce their pain points and airlines to produce the intelligent aggregation of intermodal travel services for customers to receive the personalized experience that they are seeking. As such, there is much value in flexible platforms that (1) provide an effective interface between customers and service providers and (2) derive mutual value from the interface. However, the design of the mutual value-adding interface calls for a much higher level of knowledge of customers, knowledge that can be gathered with the use of intelligent engagement platforms. For some excellent insights on the role for platforms in the hyper-personalization era, see the thought leadership piece by Antonio Figueiredo in Chapter 8.

An intelligent engagement platform framework

Figure 4.1 displays one framework of an intelligent engagement platform that is a technology- and innovation-driven business. It integrates numerous ad hoc and independent platforms as well as apps to create new value for consumers and for strategic partners offering travel-related services.

The platform is intelligent because, using cloud-computing capabilities, it enables the collection, integration, and sharing of data – data that has insights and insights that are actionable. It is an engagement platform because it can integrate

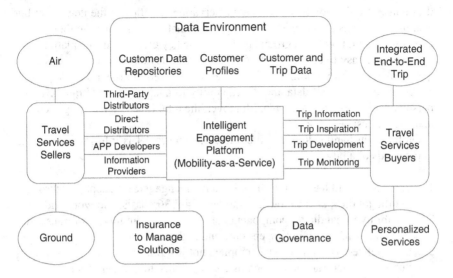

Figure 4.1 Intelligent Engagement Platform Framework

existing independent platforms to find personalized solutions for travelers based on travel on different modes of transportation depending on specific journeys, the physical and the experiential needs of travelers, and travelers' willingness to pay. It can even regroup travelers based on their needs and their willingness to pay, based in turn on the price-service options available. However, it not only engages all entities proactively, but it also engages them at the right time and at the right touch point. The platform is agile in that it adapts to real-time situations and changes in the customer base. It is also upgradable in that it adapts to new technologies, new functionalities, and changes in the industry structure. It is scalable in that not only it meets the needs of all customers, but it covers all touch points.

The main point is that they can provide customers who are interested in buying not just different components of travel but finding solutions to their mobility problems without leaving the platform. Working with an intelligent engagement platform will help, since a consumer can have and understand only a limited number of different apps on the mobile device or work with a limited number of different websites. In addition to the mobile technology, intelligent engagement platforms will also have three other technologies embedded in the platform – social, voice, and artificial intelligence (machine learning)[3] – enabling the system to remember what the customer asked during the previous visit and to make personalized offers that are relevant. This aspect may be even more important during "bleisure" trips (combining business and leisure trips). Think about the value that an intelligent engagement platform can provide where different sellers can add value for a business traveler who wants to stay an extra day to see some local attraction and or participate in a particular event such as a concert or a sporting event. This desire may require not only additional reservations relating to the new event but also modifications to the existing reservations relating to at least the three major components: air, hotel, and ground mobility. The key elements of the platform are to be simple, easy to use, and provide timely and relevant answers to a traveler's questions relating to mobility by having access not only to other service providers but also to relevant data and the capability to analyze the data quickly, on a personalized basis, and at a scale. Moreover, the total itinerary will be placed and managed in a super PNR.

On the right-hand side of the framework in Figure 4.1 is information relating to the needs of a buyer.

1   convenient and hassle-free shopping and an engagement capability throughout the journey, at each touch point, on a 24/7/365 basis, and worldwide;
2   capability to handle all components of trips – different modes of transportation and different activities, en route and at destinations;
3   personalized trips that can be complex, not just relating to the itinerary itself but also ad hoc functions, such as the capability to order meals prior to the flight, the desire to "dine-on demand," or the desire to use personal in-flight entertainment systems on board; and
4   capability to use a traveler's loyalty points, with a 24/7/365 access worldwide, for almost any product or service: ground transportation, tickets for shows and sporting events, meals at special restaurants, or even participation in activities during a planned or unplanned layover.

Next, the platform would enable real-time integration among the suppliers of different services within the chain – for example, an airline, a hotel, and a car-rental company – to collaborate effectively to improve customer experience. In the super PNR, the hotel could learn from the airline reservation about the time that a passenger could be checking in at the hotel. If the arrival was expected to be very early in the morning, the hotel could make a room available for an early check-in with additional charges based on real-time costs of getting a room ready. Similarly, a car-rental company could find out from the airline reservation a reasonably accurate time of arrival of the passenger and have a driver deliver the rental car right to the curbside.

On the left-hand side of the framework in Figure 4.1 is the information on the services available from travel-related businesses such as airlines, hotels, car-rental companies, and a broad spectrum of facilities at destinations. In between are numerous independent platforms operated by sellers of travel-related services (such as airlines and hotels), distributors (such as GDSs and OTAs), and information providers (such as TripAdvisor and Kayak). The intelligent engagement platform integrates the services provided by all relevant platforms. It is the availability of strategic and tactical partnerships on a platform that will help airlines (and airports, discussed in the previous chapter) to produce the intelligent aggregation of intermodal travel services for customers to receive the personalized experience that they are seeking. On the part of consumers, they do not want infinite choices. It is confusing and emotionally stressful. They want just a few relevant choices. On the part of airlines, they can extend their reach. Ryanair, for example, aspires to be the "Amazon of Travel" to drive more revenue. This aspiration is possible because the airline already gets a very high percentage of web traffic, and it could sell more travel-related products/services. However, with the use of the type of a platform, envisioned in Figure 4.1, Ryanair could (1) start selling sophisticated ancillaries and (2) possibly even sell tickets on full-service carriers. However, without the use of a sophisticated platform, it would be a challenge for any airline, let alone a low-cost-carrier, to become a solution provider to customers' total mobility needs.

The platform is not just selling airline seats or hotel rooms, but it is solving travelers' problems. Airlines and hotels are not set up to be ultra-sophisticated retailers. The brand will be the platform, not the airline, the hotel, or even the airport. Consider a broad spectrum of services at destination services, media streaming on mobile devices, personalized services based on physical location, and location-based notifications. Consider also the role of self-service technologies in all the phases of travel – booking (shopping), check-in, baggage check-in, dwell time, boarding, onboard, and baggage claim. Consider the value of seamless connections from curb-to-curb, enabled by the Internet of things and with integration among passengers, airlines, and airports. All these considerations are possible with the use of platforms.

One key component of the framework, shown at the top in Figure 4.1, is the management of data. Not only is data required to match customers' needs (based on their profiles) with the products and services available from different suppliers, but the platform also addresses the sources of data. Figure 4.2 shows that data can come from internal sources at an airline or external sources. Moreover, in the future, new forms of technology, such as the Internet of things, can provide additional sources of data. Technologies embedded in the platform will be able to track passenger habits before, during, and after the flight. For example, the

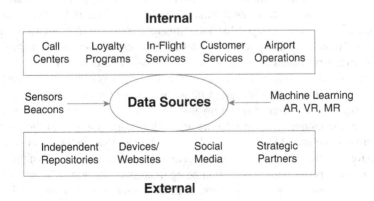

Figure 4.2 Data Sources

platform system can track, gather, and analyze information while the passenger is in-flight, enjoying a curated entertainment service.

Data can come from individuals directly or from different suppliers (respecting the privacy of data), or from specialized repositories. For example, the operator of an intelligent engagement platform should be able to get data on a specific traveler from the traveler directly, from the airline, or from the hotel. One example of a repository would be VERIMI, mentioned earlier in this chapter, an entity that has data given by users and data that can only be released by users to order services from the Internet "stores." In addition, technology is enabling the collection of more data as more and more passengers are booking online, as well as the fact that technology is available (from the use of apps) that can facilitate the collection of relevant data at different touch points or at stressful points. Think about what passengers are viewing on their screens. What are they doing in social media? The platform operator, or an independent platform, can set up an effective listening feature in the platform while being mindful of consumers' concern for privacy, the regulations of which vary worldwide.

Within the data environment is an important aspect – data governance – providing rules and standards for working on the platform and sharing data, which is now, in some ways, a currency. Data verification is another feature included within data governance. Moreover, the data governance aspect will also address the issue of data privacy (General Data Protection Regulations) and cyber security as well as the availability of data backups against technology-related disruptions. Platform developers and operators would have identified effective ways to acquire relevant data, to store it securely, to synthesize it, and to mine it in order to provide location- and situation-based services and solutions to customers' personalized requirements.

Airlines, particularly full-service carriers, offer a wide array of products and services. However, they relate mostly to selling seats on their own networks and those of their alliance partners. As such, the focus continues to be on products (network, schedules, prices, and cabin services) and not on outcomes or solutions to mobility problems desired by customers. Customers, for example, need to be at specific locations *other than airports* at specific times in order to attend a meeting, a wedding, or to board a cruise ship. Being informed that the flight has been canceled or even delayed for a significant amount of time due to the very late arrival of another flight, to the unavailability of crew, to insufficient crew rest time, does not provide a solution to the consequential mobility problem facing a customer. Yet most airlines continue to focus on products rather than outcomes. Some are even focused on processes rather than products. In addition, most airlines continue to use conventional methods to measure success: on-time performance for the month, average load factor for the month, the size of the positive gap between the actual load factor and the break-even load factor for the month, and so forth. Where does customer satisfaction come in the evaluation of the business, and how is customer satisfaction being measured? Imagine if a shopper for air travel was asked to give ratings and comments after every itinerary booked.

There are two other important components displayed in the intelligent engagement platform framework in Figure 4.1. First is the management of the customer order and its financial settlement among different suppliers of services. Unlike a conventional PNR, which just contains information on a passenger's itinerary, in the mobility-as-a-service order, there will be multiple suppliers of services requiring ways to settle payments using a variety of payment systems. The platform will now be developing super PNRs. In addition, there could be an insurance component that deals with not only the means to provide a refund for money paid for a product or service not delivered but also to be handling the additional cost of providing a solution. Suppose that a ticketing airline delays its flight, affecting significantly the plans of a traveler who is traveling on a restricted fare. Then the insurance will cover the additional cost of making a reservation on any competitor still flying, regardless of the fare for a reservation made at the last minute. This is similar to different forms of insurance travelers can buy now. However, the framework, in Figure 4.1, will cover all aspects of the insurance, relating to travel, health, and unforeseen events.

The other important component relates to the existence of an open-source environment that enables different app developers to introduce their value-adding apps. Open-source platform thinking calls for leveraging the synergistic strengths and core competencies of strategic independent platform partners in the travel chain and related businesses, including innovative startups, without totally disrupting the conventional processes and systems of different partners. The objective of the intelligent engagement platform is to improve the content from the viewpoint of the end-to-end journey within the framework of context and real time. Moreover, the platform would also enable the entry of new collaborators: innovative app developers. These apps would provide information in critical areas such as contextual-based events and their management, data management, and connectivity among contextual-based suppliers. An obvious app would enable real-time information on a wider spectrum of transportation modes.

Consider an app that informs a passenger on a delayed flight the names of restaurants near the gate that meet the interest of the passenger. The app could even suggest various sightseeing activities within or near the airport based on the expected delay in the departure of the flight and activities of interest to a passenger. In addition, based on the potential connection among different passengers on the delayed flight and using information gathered from social networks, the app could even suggest that passengers with common interests visit potential sights as a group. The app could enable multiple forms of payments. Another aspect of the service provided by an app could be not just the connectivity in real time to context-based suppliers but also insightful feedback to suppliers to adjust their offers. Moreover, the platform framework will provide a capability not just to access information and services by users but also for users to provide feedback on the services received and potential areas for improvement.

Intelligent engagement platform frameworks of the type in Figure 4.1 have a value now and in the future with the use of new technologies as well as the introduction of new forms of transportation. Startups, in particular, are coming up with significant new ideas leading to enhanced services and enhanced experience. Consider blockchain technology, which started with an application in the financial sector. It now shows numerous applications in different areas of the travel sector, ranging from airline loyalty programs to airline maintenance programs. The use of AI will produce services with a higher level of personalization and experience. Platforms can help airlines capitalize on new technologies through strategic partnerships with new forms of transportation. There will be self-driven cars, small electric-powered regional aircraft, helicopter services provided by the likes of Uber, a new generation of small supersonic aircraft, and ultra-fast ground transportation systems along the lines envisioned by the developers of the Hyperloop. These transportation systems not only will offer different price-service options, but they will also impact significantly existing service providers in the travel chain: airlines in their short-haul operations and airports relating to parking facilities and charges, and airport slots used by the operators of feeder services.

Most importantly, trips consist of more than just reservations for seats between airports. An intelligent engagement platform can enable an airline to sell all components of an end-to-end trip with a higher degree of personalization and experience level. However, the design of end-to-end trips calls for a much higher level of knowledge of customers that can be gathered by intelligent engagement platforms. The first important function of the intelligent engagement platform is to generate customized offers to a client based on the profile of the customer. This profile is constantly updated over time based on ongoing experience. Once the offer has been accepted, the second important function of the intelligent engagement platform is to have independent platforms to monitor the trip from start to finish 24/7/365 and worldwide. In case of disruptions or requested changes, the trip is modified and placed in an active file. In terms of monitoring services, the monitoring platform, incorporated into the intelligent engagement platforms, can have different tiers for membership: silver, gold, and diamond, for example. The difference in the membership level comes in the way of support. All members get services to provide integrated itineraries. In the silver level the support may in the form of texts to answer questions and offer solutions. The gold level support might be in the form of AI-powered digital assistants that can be connected to persons for complicated issues. The diamond level support might be in the form of live agents who will always have the up-to-date personal information available, even when the agents responding are different. They will always have real-time information available to find real-time solutions to travelers' needs.

Building blocks

Based on the success of other businesses, it appears that a business needs to become a customer-driven business, not just a customer-aware business. That means that the business must be driven by insights, not driven by data. Based on the experience of other platform businesses and businesses working within the framework, there appear to be three important levers – vision for the business, enabling technologies, and design thinking that calls for defining and focusing on customer and employee experiences and their expectations in the digital era. Using these three levers, not just the airline sector but also the airport sector can move forward to compete in the digital age by attracting higher-margin traffic, achieving agility in terms of time-to-market, and building brands and loyalty through the development of higher levels of customer and employee experience. However, the operation of these three levers requires a change in corporate culture for innovating both from within (through engagement with employees, for instance) and outside of the organization, a culture that is just beginning to surface in the airline sector. Clearly, airline businesses engage internally (with employees in numerous functional divisions) and with external organizations, like airports, to improve airlines' conventional processes. In reality, things are different. How many airlines provide their call centers with convenient access to their internal systems and the data that employees need to solve a caller's problem? Where are the interfaces through which strategic partners in the travel chain can engage affectively to enable deeper collaboration and to increase the speed of innovation through timely and fresh ideas? The challenge for service providers is to decide if the value for each provider (airlines, airports, distributors, and so forth) lies in having the data, owning the data, or sharing the data.

First lever – vision

In general, while customer centricity is certainly being discussed by managements at all levels, it is operations centricity that is being practiced, for the most part. While a few airlines have begun to think about customer centricity and have even developed some initiatives that deal with the challenges faced by customers, the initiatives have tended to be incremental and ad hoc in nature – small and specific improvements to websites, improvement in the booking capability on mobile devices, delivery of boarding passes on mobile devices, small improvements in the self-check-in processes, capability to print baggage labels and drop-off at self-service stations, faster receipt of information on the flight status, and so forth. These are all steps in the right direction. However, selling outcomes rather than products calls for a different vision, such as to:

- provide mobility solutions relating to the end-to-end journeys;
- create value by delivering seamless traveler experience while achieving operational excellence; and
- transform major processes, leading to convenience and transparency.

The development of just these three features calls for a different vision. Consider the need for transparency in itineraries involving code-shared flights. Transparency involves not only specificity relating to the price and service offered by each partner but also a clarification of the responsibilities of the marketing airlines and the operating airlines, especially in the handling of irregular operations. Transparency is now more important because customers' expectations are increasing and because customers now have more choices. Consequently, airlines need to deliver not just broad levels of personalization but personalization that is contextually based and includes the need for flexibility and empathy depending on the context.

It is more than just providing fast information about the status of a flight. Consider the situation when the last flight of the day is canceled and the passenger is on her own to find a hotel room in the middle of the night, along with 300 other passengers, then needs to pay for a hotel room.

Based on multi-industry insights, some airlines have begun to think more broadly about service than just about the development of schedules between airports and the associated fares. For example, as discussed in Chapter 3, some airlines are now aspiring to become sophisticated retailers and offer experience, not just products. However, they need to go further and think in terms of providing solutions to total mobility problems – the totality of the journey, with changes being facilitated on a contextual basis and in as close to real time as possible. This kind of a vision calls for a much higher level of customer engagement and a deeper search for employee talents and empowerment of employees who sell mobility solutions, not mobility products. Challenges, therefore, relate not just to the acquisition and implementation of technology to improve back-office operations but also to the capitalization of business opportunities in the front office, enabled by technologies, with a focus on human skills and collaboration within the ecosystem.

It is a change in the mindset that is needed to understand what the business is today and how to change the business to create new value for customers and new sources of revenue for airlines, using technology as an enabler. Unfortunately, senior executives are tied emotionally to the business models they have built and with which they are comfortable. Thinking about helping customers solve their problems and achieve their goals requires different mindsets. What is the customer trying to achieve, and what is the role that an airline can play in helping the customer to achieve an outcome? This kind of thinking forces an airline to think outside of the boundaries of its own business and its comfort zone.

Consider a change in vision in the auto industry. Automakers are clearly reevaluating their business models, recognizing that many people no longer want to buy cars but instead are looking for on-demand mobility, including the availability of self-driving vehicles. Managements are beginning to rethink legacy visions and mindsets relating to legacy processes and products. Daimler-Benz is clearly leading the charge in this area by focusing not only on on-demand mobility through the deployment of platforms but also working with cities that are becoming smart cities, using their own platforms. Tesla is another example of an auto company with a different vision and a mindset. It is not just building cars with a different propulsion system – batteries – but its vision is to become a platform-based software company that creates mutual value – value for customers and value for itself.

Second lever – technologies

Relating to the second lever, technology, the key ingredient for succeeding in digital transformation is the generation and movement of information across functions within an airline and across partners in the travel chain to connect customers, employees, and partners. Consider the deployment of enabling technologies – AI (including virtual assistants), blockchain, sensors, and in-flight connectivity, just to name four. Airlines must rethink their design thinking to capitalize on the opportunity to digitalize conventional processes. Consider SITA's robotic vehicles facilitating the check-in of bags at curbside or within the airport terminals, or soon the availability of One Identity for processing passengers through airports, activities that may require the proof of identities as many as six times. In addition, let us not overlook the roles of chatbots deploying intelligent technologies while human beings handle the more complex issues with machine learning, through AI, from the solutions provided by human beings. Consequently, the design aspect must now balance the role of machines and human beings. Let us also not forget that there is still the consideration of empathy in providing solutions to travel-related challenges.

Platforms will deploy different technologies, AI, for example, to develop and distribute content differently.[4] Airlines, in addition to the use of such technologies, can also use a wide array of analytics to compete more effectively in the development of competitive products that currently tend to be similar in features and prices.[5] Technology-enabled platforms can also be analyzed to bring about massive improvements in the value provided to passengers, over and above lower prices, and to airlines with information relating to potential extensions of the core business. Clearly, platform operators, or information specialists working on the intelligent engagement platform, will have extremely valuable information on what different consumers are looking for and what they are willing to pay, based not just on their shopping behavior relating to airline tickets but also relating to products and services provided by other sellers in the value chain. The value of such a feedback loop cannot be underestimated.

Investments in technology to build such a customer solution-centric and customer experience-centric platform would not be very high. First, technology costs may, in fact, be coming down due to the increase in the capabilities of the cloud and mobile technologies. Second, the platform developer would simply integrate the functionalities and services of mostly independent but existing platforms. One critical success factor would simply be the number of subscribers, as a critical mass needs to exist to make the platform viable to get it started. For airlines, they would need to develop internal engagement platforms to work around the conventional silo systems to produce solutions to mobility problems on a personalized and contextual basis. Internal platforms can, for example, reach into different silos and access the information needed on a passenger from different departments within an airline (marketing, sales, reservations, loyalty programs, etc.) and collate the information into a single 360-degree view of a passenger on a personalized and contextual basis. The external platform operator would engage with internal engagement platforms operated by suppliers of different travel-related services (airlines, hotels, ground transportation companies, etc.) and integrate services to offer a complete solution to meet the needs of a customer at each touch point. Moreover, external independent platform operators can identify for service providers new opportunities for the generation of ancillary revenue streams, while improving customer experience.

Third lever – disciplined design

Taking customer experience and employee experience to new levels by itself calls for a rethinking of the role of disciplined design, the third lever. Consider the access to mobile services worldwide provided by telecommunication companies through arrangements with service providers worldwide and the establishment of user-friendly interfaces. A customer of one telecommunication service provider in one country can have instant access to telecommunication services of other providers worldwide. For airlines, it means working on carefully designed platforms to make services available within, not only in the omni-channel space but also at all touch points involving all strategic alliance partners, and on a contextual and personalized basis.

There are six basic reasons for disciplined design thinking.

1   Customers are getting experiences that are more desirable from other business sectors, in some areas of retail and hospitality, for example. Customers desire and are receiving increasingly personalized and contextual-based services. Customers also want a better experience at all touch points, and those touch points are increasing. Moreover, each touch point has its own complexities. Think about the beginning of a trip when different consumers need different formats of information relating to inspiration.

2   Design thinking is much more than incremental changes to existing processes and systems, such as self-service check-in kiosks and boarding passes on mobile devices. As such, the design phase calls for strong input from experts in user experience, input that is not inward-focused but is outward-focused. This input can come from employees, customers, and partners. If customer experience is an important consideration in the design process, then it must be seen from customers' eyes. Moreover, customers seem to be looking for empathy – an understanding of customers' true needs and emotions. According to some experts, more innovative ideas can come from the crowd than from corporate research labs.[6]

3   Design thinking must take into account the fact that customers are becoming increasingly connected – not just with a broad spectrum of producers and sellers but also among themselves through social networks – in their evaluation and purchase decisions. As such, airlines must think of new ways of connecting with customers through customers' own channels and customers' own devices.

4   Design thinking needs to relate to the totality of problems, old or new. The ongoing hassles relating to the processing of passengers at airports requires, for instance, the provision of airline-airport-integrated solutions. At the very least, travelers must be given "one version of the truth" relating to information on the status of operations, based on the situation.

5   Design thinking must also take into consideration not only all forms of existing air and ground transportation services but also the emergence of new forms of air and ground transportations systems. Examples include small

hybrid-electric aircraft that would operate in thin short-haul regional markets and small supersonic aircraft being built on existing technologies, on the airside, and driver-less vehicles, on the groundside. Moreover, the introduction of an Uber type of flying air taxis will call for not just airline-airport but also ground-integrated solutions.

6   Given that some airports are likely to go through major changes in their business models, they, too, need to rethink the role of design. Think about how driver-less cars and Uber cars could reduce the revenue generated through parking and car-rental facilities and how biometrics, enabling passengers to pass through airports relatively fast, could reduce the need for a huge number of shops. Then there is the possibility of some new airports with hub-and-spoke systems, developed at strategic locations and built around the use of next-generation narrow-body equipment with ultra-long ranges. Such facilities used by low-cost carriers would call for very different airport systems and facilities to require very low costs to develop and offer low fares that "drive" demand.

Take just one example of the need to rethink design thinking relating to how mobile is now not just a channel of choice for travelers but to how it is now a lifestyle, with impact from the inspiration stage to interactions at all touch points before, during, and post-travel. In the digital space, consumers are looking for a higher level of mobile capability on the ground and in the aircraft, frictionless interactions, and personalized services. A key requirement within the digital space, therefore, is the need to adapt to the "mobile-first experience" and to engage with consumers in real time and with relevant information at all touch points. The reason for real-time engagement with customers is to provide personalized services in which preferences go well beyond straightforward desires, such as an aisle seat or a nonstop flight. Other product features within the digital space may include the availability of voice search and virtual assistants.

Travelers get recommendations from social media before travel and provide their reviews after travel. They are looking for an experience that is personalized, context based, and consistent. The inspiration stage calls for insights on people's preferences based on, for example, their browsing behavior. Disciplined design, therefore, means acquiring and leveraging real-time data, particularly behavioral data, and data coming from all sources, including social media. Think about some insights derived from prevailing platforms operated by Amazon, Facebook, and Google. Examples include (1) developing profiles on all customers, (2) capturing changing consumer behavior, (3) accessing consumers at scale, (4) undertaking personalized engagements, and (5) monetizing the relationship with customers. Also, as mentioned earlier in the chapter, is an example of a new type of platform, developed by a European business entity, VERIMI, that works with multiple business sectors and offers a user-friendly platform for services relating to user identity and payments.

Undoubtedly, major digital transformation initiatives can involve a large risk unless planned with extreme care. For example, while measurements in cost reductions are relatively straightforward, measurements of improvements in customer and employee experience, not to mention achievement of scale and the creation of strategic competitive advantage, are much more difficult. Implementation becomes even more complex if it involves partners, like airports, and government agencies relating to security and immigration and the acquisition and development of human talent. There is also the concern of making sure that passengers, crew, and aircraft do not get affected negatively. Realizing these concerns for risk, it is understandable that airlines start the design process slowly, take small steps, and use the fail-fast concept.

Rethinking design thinking

Both platform developers and operators as well as travel service providers need to rethink design thinking. In both cases, the focus is on mobility-as-a-service and customer experience – the emerging battleground for businesses.

Related to the platform

Platforms can be designed to offer mobility-as-a-service, given that they represent not only the interface between sellers and buyers but also the points where value and profits are for both platform operators as well as service providers. However, they need to be designed strategically, and that means that design thinking needs rethinking,[7] since the focus now is on the totality of services to provide mobility solutions. There are requirements to get such solutions. The first requirement is to use services provided by third-party developers and operators of customer-centric platforms. Relating to this requirement, a critical success factor is the willingness on the part of service providers like airlines to trust the operator of platforms to share information and the platform operator to protect the confidentiality of the information provided by service providers. The benefit for service providers, like airlines, is the development and delivery of services that go well beyond their own basic products. The second requirement for airlines is the need to bond marketing and operations (a subject discussed in Chapter 3) using internal platforms. The third requirement for an airline is to have some control over what products and services are offered through third-party platforms and how they are integrated. Platforms will enable an airline to become a contributor to mobility solutions rather than simply be a marketer of seats between airports. It is the contribution to the generation of solutions to mobility requirements that will generate new levels of customer and employee experience, higher margins, and new streams of revenue, not to mention the development and maintenance of much higher levels of loyalty to the brand.

The design team needs to look at the entire end-to-end journey from two perspectives. One aspect of end-to-end thinking relates to the three stages, starting from pre-travel (inspiration and shopping), to during travel (airport processing and in-flight), to post-travel (reviews sharing travel experience). The second perspective is to look at travel from the point of origin to the final destination, involving different modes of transportation. In both cases, there is the potential of new entrants with a consumer orientation and "datafication" capability to improve the end-to-end experience for both the business traveler and the leisure traveler.

Who could be the new potential entrants to totally change the travel landscape?

They are likely to be visionary startups that would think about customers' needs before customers do. Recall the development of products that met consumers' unstated or, at least, their future needs:

- the development of the first portable (pocket) transistor radio;
- the development by Sony of the Walkman, the portable audio cassette player;
- the development of an embedded camera in a mobile phone by Sanyo to allow people to take photos with their mobile phones;
- the capability provided by Netflix to use technology to allow people to stream movies and watch them through their chosen devices;
- the inclusion of Siri by Apple in its iPhone to be an intelligent personal assistant to answer questions while on the move; and
- the development of smart speakers with artificial intelligence – Amazon's Echo and Google's Home.

The inspiration for such innovations comes from visionaries. Steve Jobs, chairman, CEO, and co-founder of Apple, is reported to have said, (1) "It is not the customers' job to know what they want," and (2) "You've got to start with the customer experience and work back toward the technology – not the other way around." To repeat, one insight for platform developers and operators is that customers want travel-generated outcomes, not travel products, per se. Theodore Levitt, a professor at Harvard Business School, told his students, "People don't want quarter-inch drills – they want quarter-inch holes." This concept of consumers wanting outcomes instead of products is also supported by Peter Drucker, educator, author, and a management consultant, who wrote more than five decades ago, "The customer rarely buys what the company thinks it sells him." In our case, the object is to "sell consumer-desired outcomes" rather than air travel products. Technology can help, but it will be the visionary new entrants within the air travel industry – working with customer-centric startups – who will use digital technologies as well as customer-centric platforms designed to produce solutions to consumers' global mobility requirements on a contextual and personalized basis.

Based on the above points, the first aspect of the design phase is to have strong input from experts in user experience that is not inward-focused but outward-focused. This input can come from employees, customers, and partners. The second area relates to the potential synergistic capability of collaborators to work together to co-create value in the price-service options where the total value is greater than the sum of its parts. This aspect calls for the identification of key passenger trends with a focus on customer values – values defined by customers, not service providers, and customers' expectations of experiences now in the on-demand and sharing economies. Relating to value, consider an example from Apple on how customers viewed value in a different business. Research in Motion

(RIM) produced its smartphone, called the BlackBerry. It was a global success for people who wanted an easy but sophisticated system for making phone calls and sending emails with the use of a "real" keyboard. Nevertheless, it was the value perceived by consumers in Apple's iPhone that was a game changer. So, what was that value? It was the ability of the user to view the iPhone as a personal computer on the move, with connections to the Internet and the availability of numerous customer-centric and experience-centric apps to make people's lives easier.

Related to internal airline products and services

Let us examine the value for rethinking design thinking in two areas of the airline business, customer-contact centers and cabin configurations and services.

Customer-contact centers

In the past, customer-contact centers, even though they have been considered to be cost-generating centers rather than revenue-generating centers, have played an important role in resolving travelers' problems during regular and irregular operations. However, there is now an opportunity to transform the customer-contact center channel from one that has been a cost center to one that even goes beyond being a revenue-generating center. The vision can be to transform the customer-contact center into an experience center that shapes customer experience, leading to the enhancement of the brand and the enhancement of customer loyalty. In today's digital world, encompassing new forms of communications, web chats, mobile apps, and social media, consumers expect responses 24/7/365, worldwide, and in a consistent framework. However, the transformation of customer-contact centers to become experience centers requires not just a replacement of the legacy technologies and legacy systems, or even the installation of automated call-answering systems either to replace live agents, or to support live agents, or even to replace live agents with chatbots. It calls for changes in an airline's organizational structure and corporate culture to enable agents to be able to work smarter. Technologies, data, and analytics can be added to support live agents to not only offer meaningful and contextual-based recommendations but also for agents be able to make "predictions" in some areas. The systems need to have simple and intuitive designs with dashboards with the right buttons at the right locations and with interactive dynamics to increase usability and customer satisfaction. The simplicity and the intuitiveness of the design is important, given that agents, with 20+ years of experience, are working next to recently-trained agents.

Let us first start with some typical pain points that customers encounter relating to the operation of conventional customer-contact centers. A customer learns that the customer-contact center is not open 24/7/365. A customer is made to wait a long time before the call is answered due to the high volume of calls, particularly during irregular operations, the very time when customers need fast responses. Then the customer is told that the agent on the phone works for the marketing airline and not the operating airline. The customer must, therefore, call the operating airline to get the problem resolved. However, the customer-contact center of the operating airline is closed at the time. The customer is referred to the airline's website even when the customer informs the agent that the website is not providing an answer to the specific question of the customer.

In order to become experience centers, customer-contact center agents need to have access not only to a 360-degree view of the customer but an end-to-end view of the customer's journey. What good is telling the customer that she is now rebooked on the next day's flight across the Atlantic if the agent could simply look into the full reservation and see that the passenger was, in fact, returning the next day? The passenger is informed that the agent cannot rebook the passenger on the next flight due to the restricted ticket that the passenger is holding on the flight that has been canceled, or that the flight was canceled due to reasons beyond the control of the airline and that the airline has no responsibility to even help the customer find hotel accommodations, let alone pay for the accommodations. Imagine the reaction of the customer if an agent was to help a customer on behalf of a partner airline. Imagine the impact on the brand of the airline. This initiative would require an airline evolving from product centricity not just to service centricity but to experience centricity. It will also change the role of the customer-contact center from operating in the back-office framework to one in the front-office framework.

Next, agents in customer-contact centers need to have access to contemporary data systems and centralized data warehouses. Even updated versions of the existing passenger service systems do not allow the data to be "sensed" and analytics to suggest actions. As for data, it can sit in as many as 4–5 dozen locations or silos. Consequently, digital strategies cannot be implemented on unintegrated data. Going further, live agents can be supported by advanced chatbots that are AI-powered and are voice-based digital travel assistants. Customers will accept voice support and self-service options up to a point, but they expect human intervention if their problems are not solved – hybrid AI. However, human intervention is needed, as chatbots currently are not able to track a customer's end-to-end journey, or if chatbots appear to be having conversational difficulties. Nevertheless, the use of a hybrid AI-human combination has the potential to reduce operating costs and offer personalized experiences. Moreover, while not today, chatbots will soon be able to provide not only seamless and personalized service, but, given the improvements in artificial intelligence, also be empathetic like live agents. They will also be able to respond to questions not just with the use of conversational language and in an everyday context but also answer questions posed in multiple languages. Finally, the transference from a chatbot to a human person will not require the customer to repeat the description of the situation.

There are, however, three major challenges facing the transformation of customer-contact centers to experience centers. The first challenge relates to the consistency of the goals of the business. Is the goal to reduce costs, or optimize revenue, or develop the brand and build loyalty? Is the goal to maximize ancillary revenue sales or develop a brand? Should prices vary by channel? Are the goals of distribution of the team consistent with those of the pricing team? Is the purpose trying to go direct to save distribution costs or get close to customers to gather data, and then not only control data, but monetize it? Is the goal of the agent to up-sell and cross-sell or to solve the problems and concerns of the passenger? Is the goal to work to compete with alliance partners or cooperate with them? Is the goal of agents to enhance customer acquisition and retention based on personalized solutions or minimize the time spent with each customer? Is the goal to minimize customer-contact time with low-fare and infrequent travelers and to focus on high-fare and/or frequent travelers?

The second challenge is how to evaluate the performance of a customer-contact center agent in making a sale or solving a customer's problem. Is the goal to minimize the time spent with a customer or to improve the customer's booking experience? What is the value of agents providing feedback that could lead to additional sales and marketing opportunities? Data can be a challenge and an opportunity. It is a challenge if an agent does not have it and is not getting it from the relevant departments. It is an opportunity to filter data from a broad spectrum of sources and interactions and to provide filtered data to many departments. What is the value of that filtered data? Much data can come from customers themselves while agents are solving their problems. What is the value of that data?

The third challenge relates to the compensation made to customers calling with complaints. How does the agent decide when the complaint is legitimate and when the customer is playing a game to make financial gains? It is relatively easy to allow the agent to give money to the customer making a complaint in the form of money that can be spent on purchasing travel on the airline. However, how much money should an agent offer for different types of complaints? This challenge cannot be solved until agents are being armed with data. For example, data can be used to determine if gamification is being played where certain customers have developed plans to extract money from an airline on a regular basis, and the airline is not in a position to verify the claims and to relate the recurrent claims to individual customers.

Cabin configurations and services

It is hard to provide personalization in some areas, for example, personalizing the seat from a physical point of view. At the least, it will be very costly. However, it is possible to design the cabin configuration to provide more flexibility. Personalization can relate to location, layout, and comfort of the seat and the related conveniences such as in-flight entertainment services, lighting, and temperature control options. Flexibility can also relate to the conversion of space to provide special areas for family-related activities, work-related activities, and socialization. New design can include the consideration of a number of nonconventional seat layouts, for example, seats located at different heights and middle seat located slightly behind the window and aisle seats. In the economy class, there is a limit to the physical aspects of personalization, but it is possible to explore some options relating to the physical design and some psychological aspects. Step-changing innovations lie in the area of the seat design for the economy-class cabins. One example is a seat that not only folds and unfolds in different directions to enable a passenger to adapt the seat to her body but also makes movement of passengers easier in the cabin. For example, the horizontal part of each of the three seats could fold up and the three seats as a block could move forward to stack up behind the row in front and enable passengers to have more room to walk around. Recall also the innovative "Skycouch" introduced by Air New Zealand in its economy-class cabins. In this concept, a row of economy-class seats could be easily converted into a couch after takeoff. As for the psychological aspects, the design could explore some features of virtual reality. For example, a passenger could be watching a movie in the aircraft cabin but psychologically feel that she is present elsewhere.

Inside the aircraft, many areas of the cabin can be redesigned. Three key areas are wireless in-flight connectivity, cabin space for passengers and their baggage, and the overall atmosphere. Wireless connectivity relates not just to a passenger's ability to use her own mobile devices to stream her desired entertainment and to be able to control the built-in entertainment of the aircraft but also to order food and shop for duty-free products, not to mention shop a wide array of stores online. Next, LED lighting is an example of the attempt to change the overall atmosphere. Relating to the cabin experience, for some customers, media could play a major role in consumer's choice of an airline based on peer recommendations.

The key challenge facing designers is the tradeoff between comfort and experience and cabin profitability. How can cabin profitability be computed? Is there money being left on the table? Seating configuration within economy-class cabins is already generating ancillary revenues based on seat location, for example. But how can seats be priced by location in real time, not even taking into consideration the cabin mix? Many factors enter into the equation to maximize the revenue for the fixed real estate – level of revenue generated from premium cabins, load factors, upgrades for loyalty programs, new revenue generated from upgrades, certification costs for providing flexibility for converting the cabin space or cabin mix – first, business, premium economy, economy, and possibly, even, higher-density economy.

Although airlines clearly want to satisfy their high-value customers, designers are developing the ultra-premium offerings, such as showers, suites, and double beds, that are priced at much higher levels, more to develop and promote brands than to generate compensatory revenues. Even in the area of top-of-line in-flight entertainment systems (IFE), the question remains as to how many business travelers select an airline based on the IFE vs. flight schedules and membership in the loyalty programs. In any case, an increasing number of passengers have their own mobile devices on which they can load their preferred content. Moreover, are high-value customers, say business travelers, simply looking for fast and reliable Wi-Fi to increase the productivity of their time? But then designers ask if the focus is on just business travelers, or all travelers, and on digital customers, or on all generations of customers. Moreover, should designers consider the installation of screens with higher quality (HD, 1080 pixels, or even higher, for example) and larger screen size (15 inch, for example)? Besides the additional costs of such items, there is also the question of whether airlines will also be willing to pay higher amounts to the studios for content to be delivered in higher resolution – content that passengers are beginning to get on their mobile devices. Also, there is the question of the adequacy of the power available on aircraft for mobile devices; they could require more power in the future if many passengers started to bring their own devices.

The emphasis on design thinking makes sense, because customers are becoming increasingly connected – not just with a broad spectrum of producers and sellers but also among themselves through social networks – in the evaluation and purchase decisions. As for the mobile channel, mobile is now not a channel of choice for travelers but is now a lifestyle, with impact from the inspiration stage to interactions at all touch points during and post-travel. Travelers get recommendations from social media before travel and provide their reviews after travel. They are looking for experience that is personalized, context based, and consistent. The inspiration stage calls for insights on people's preferences based on, for example, their browsing behavior. Designing, therefore, means acquiring and leveraging real-time data, particularly behavioral data. Moreover, the need for rethinking design thinking is also based on the availability of incredible amounts of information and analytics to identify and fulfill customer needs with respect to outcomes desired by customers.

Operational considerations

Once airlines start to operate within a carefully designed intelligent engagement platform framework, different airlines can strategize their actual and potential business models at different points on a platform continuum. For example:

- At one end of the continuum, there could be airlines that become an ACMI (aircraft, crew, maintenance, and insurance) provider for other airlines or airline systems, giving up all of their marketing functions.
- Next, there could be airlines simply fighting for their survival, using their prevailing business models and the earlier generations of mostly operational (with limited marketing capabilities) legacy technology systems and processes and prevailing hub-and-spoke as well as revenue management systems.
- A little further along the continuum could be airlines thinking about incremental improvements in services provided, for example, better information on the status of flights, a slightly higher level of mobile-device capabilities, and the initiatives to go directly to consumers instead of accessing passengers through distributors.
- Further along the continuum could be conventional airlines that want to become different airlines. Examples include full-service airlines that have created not just low-cost subsidiaries (for example, IAG and Air France-KLM), but also subsidiaries that provide platforms for other airlines who hold Air Operator's Certificates to provide services for the platform carrier. Examples of such platform operators include Lufthansa and Qantas and their divisions, Eurowings and Jetstar, respectively.

- Further out on the continuum could be airlines beginning to think about going beyond the core business and selling a much broader spectrum of services, hoping to become the "Amazon of the Airline Industry." Ryanair is one example of an airline planning to work on its own newer generation of a retailing platform.
- Even further along the continuum could be some large conventional airlines with multiple hubs that could start to experiment to become "virtual" airlines by offering to transport passengers from Airport A to Airport B without, at the time of bookings, identifying the exact routing via any of their hubs. Examples could be airlines with multiple hubs such as the International Airlines Group (IAG) and the Lufthansa Group in Europe and American, Delta, and United in the US.
- Next, an airline could offer off-site facilities for processing passengers. Jazeera Airways is providing its Perks Fly check-in and bag drop-off facility across the Amiri Terminal at Kuwait International Airport. Passengers can drive to and check-in in a designated parking zone, where a valet agent handles the passenger's car and a shuttle takes the passenger to the terminal.
- Next, there could be some airlines that want to exploit the retailing revolution, deriving their inspiration from leading retailers such as Amazon (relating to shopping and delivery) and Zara (relating to fast-design cycles). Lufthansa already launched, in 2017, its AirlineCheckin.com to enable passengers to check in on more than 100 airlines.
- Even further on the continuum could be airlines, in collaboration with airports, looking at not only biometric identity for boarding, tracking technologies for baggage, and chatbots for customer service and experience but also effective coordination with other forms of transportation to enable the booking process for end-to-end journeys.

There is no question that airline business models of many full-service airlines have been changing, but mostly to deal with the lower-price services offered by newer generations of airlines, such as low-cost carriers, ultra-low-cost carriers, or hybrids. What is missing is the potential entry of newer-generation airlines, or even "virtual" travel companies, with business models designed to offer outcomes and solutions to mobility problems. This is the line of thinking where intelligent engagement platforms come in with an unprecedented capability to make connections among buyers and among sellers, leveraging digital technologies and integration within different ecosystems. The beauty of the intelligent engagement platform system is that airlines can work with their own customized versions of platforms, developed from the integration of other platforms, to meet their own business needs. Consequently, while some airlines have been investing in incremental innovations, managements must now start thinking about disruptive innovations by working differently and taking on not more but less risk.

There is no need for an airline to develop its own intelligent engagement system from the ground up, given that the airline business is already complicated. It is capital intensive, given the cost of airplanes. It is information intensive, given the need for vast quantities of information that flow among a vast number of entities outside of an airline and between various departments within an airline. Merging the physical assets of an airline (airplanes and maintenance facilities, for example) and its digital assets (information and relationships, for example) is already an enormous challenge. In addition, from some perspectives, airlines are risk averse. They work within much shorter-term frameworks, have disjointed technology systems, have little experience of working within the asset-light space, and have less information on truly emerging technology. Consider the last point. How much knowledge do airlines have on the role of artificial intelligence in the management of their revenues and the capability to receive information on travel requests from "chatbots" and to communicate effectively to "chatbots," even for the flight-related offers, let alone collaborative offers? Consequently, airlines can work with a generalized intelligent engagement system, but that has yet to be customized to meet the business model of the airline.

Notes

1 www.verimi.com
2 www.tnooz.com/article/amazon-of-travel-oag-travel-bookings/and www.tnooz.com/article/flights-passenger-experience-oag/.
3 Some writers prefer the use of the term machine learning rather than AI in that the technology embedded in, say, a chatbot may enable the algorithm to be enhanced without the need for the system to be reprogrammed.
4 Deborah Bothun and David Lancefield, "AI Is Already Entertaining You," *Strategy + Business*, pwc|Strategy &, Summer 2017, pp. 36–45.
5 Thomas H. Davenport and Jeanne G. Harris, *Competing on Analytics: The New Science of Winning* (Boston, MA: Harvard Business Review Press, 2017).
6 Andrew McAfee and Erik Brynjolfsson, *Harnessing Our Digital Future: Machine, Platform, Crowd* (New York: W. W. Norton & Company, 2017).
7 Martin Kupp, Jamie Anderson and Jörg Reckhenrich, "Why Design Thinking in Business Needs a Rethink," *MIT Sloan Management Review*, Fall 2017, Vol. 59, No. 1, pp. 42–5.

5 Airports creating contemporary value propositions

Just as airlines need to change their value propositions with agility and flexibility to adapt to the changing marketplace dynamics, airports also need to rethink their conventional value propositions. As with airlines, airports also need to find new ways to deal with the two sets of opposing forces. For example, airports are looking at new ways to expand their capacity while airlines are looking at ways not only to expand their operations at airports but to expand at lower airport charges and better customer experience. Moreover, just as airlines work with a large number of internal and external complexities, airports face an even more multifaceted challenge. Airports have to deal with even more constraints to expand capacities. Moreover, value propositions of airports are more complex, as they relate not only to their customers (airlines with different business models, a broad spectrum of retailers, and so forth) but also to the ultimate customers (passengers) as well as their neighborhoods, for which they are both a blessing providing convenient long-distance mobility and a curse, creating environmental problems. This chapter discusses four major challenges facing airports, followed by a discussion of some potential strategies for the transformation of their business models – a challenge in itself, given the symbiotic relationship between airlines and airports. The final section presents two scenarios of future developments that could bring about revolutionary changes in the business models of airports, the development of new strategically located technology-enabled secondary hub-and-spoke systems, and the emergence of platform-enabled intermodal hubs that address efficiency aspects for airports and experiential-based end-to-end journeys for travelers.

Major challenges facing airports

There are four major challenges facing airports. First, many forecasts show that demand will exceed the available capacity. In many parts of the world, it is a challenge just to expand capacity of existing airports, while maintaining operational excellence, let alone build new airports. There are only about half a dozen major airports under development around the world. Second, the business models of airlines are changing. Low-cost carriers are growing their networks as well as their products and services. In terms of products, they are flying more in international markets, and some even in intercontinental markets, and, in some cases, with premium-cabin configurations. The third challenge relates to the increasing expectations of travelers for experience-based and personalized services for their end-to-end journeys. This calls not only for travel on integrated modes of transportation but also for the provision of experience that is consistent at each touch point. The fourth challenge, public's increasing concern for the protection of the environment, relates to both aircraft noise and carbon dioxide emissions. The concern for the environment will increase due to the expected growth in the demand for air travel and the ongoing challenge of migrating to more sustainable aviation fuels to lower footprints of carbon and noise emissions. Although technology can help airports to manage these challenges, the broader question is if management can overcome their cultural and organizational constraints to work in fundamentally different ways.

Demand-capacity gap

Chapter 2 discussed IATA's detailed report, *Future of the Airline Industry 2035*, in which researchers aggregated numerous forces into four different scenarios for the global airline industry in 2035 to help airlines plan their strategies with respect to both opportunities and challenges.[1] In 2018, Eurocontrol published its report, *European Aviation in 2040*, in which it described the challenges facing traffic growth in Europe.[2] This report also developed four scenarios of the future between now and 2040. For this chapter, let us assume that passenger traffic will continue to grow in line with the middle two scenarios discussed in the IATA report and the middle two scenarios discussed in the Eurocontrol report. Consequently, the question then is not if passenger traffic will continue to grow but what the rate of growth will be. Consider the data shown in Figure 2.4 in Chapter 2. In light of the expected redistribution of traffic in the top ten markets, Indonesia's rank is forecast to change from number 10 to number 4. This change is the result of the growth in traffic that, in turn, will require substantial expansion in airport facilities, a fourth terminal, and a third runway at the existing Jakarta's Soekarno-Hatta International Airport, or the development of an airport at a new location.

Even under the moderate scenarios developed by IATA (going out to 2035) and Eurocontrol (going out to 2040), meeting the growth in demand by airlines and their passengers would be quite a challenge for airports and the related infrastructure. Consider, for example, an inference presented in the Eurocontrol report. Within the context of the *Regulation and Growth* scenario, there would be 1.5 million more flights than airports will be able to accommodate, implying that 160 million passengers might not be able to fly.[3] This demand-capacity gap would exist despite the plans and costs to increase airport capacity. With respect to costs of expansion, one estimate shows that between 2017 and 2021, about $1 trillion will be invested in the expansion of existing and the development of new airports. Moreover, over $2 trillion will be invested in improving the airport structure globally through 2030.[4] Yet despite these investments to expand the capacity of existing airports and to develop new airports, it appears that the capacity of major airports worldwide will still not be able to keep up with the growth in passenger demand. There are already about 200 slot-constrained airports now. Going forward, consider just one example of insufficient capacity. London Heathrow Airport is operating at capacity right now. According to the Eurocontrol report, in 2040, there would be 16 "Heathrow-like" airports in Europe within the framework of the mid-range scenario and 28 "Heathrow-like" airports within the context of high-growth scenario.

Expansion plans of airports vary by region. On a worldwide basis, there are only about a half-dozen mega-airports under development or under consideration around the world (located in Addis Ababa, Beijing, Dubai, Istanbul, and Mexico City), each with a planned capacity of more than 100 million passengers per year. In Asia, particularly in China and India, there are a number of new airports of varying sizes under construction. India, which has about 100 airports now, plans to build another 100 in the next 15–20 years, about two-thirds in areas that currently do not have airports and about one-third that will be designated as secondary airports. In North America, the expansion initiatives are generally related to the expansion of terminals, except Denver International Airport, which is also looking into adding one or two more runaways to its existing six runways. On a global basis, there are a few major airports with plans to add a new runway. Two examples include the Hong Kong International Airport, scheduled to have a third runway by 2023, and London's Heathrow Airport, scheduled to have a third runway by 2025.

The constraints to increasing capacity are in many areas – environmental and regulatory compliance requirements, lack of space, sources of funding, and the methods to recover charges for expenditures relating to expansion, just to name four. On the last point, consider the questions relating to how London's Heathrow Airport will recover the money to build the third runway or Singapore's Changi Airport to recover the expenses relating to the new Terminal 4 building. It is true that new facilities would enable existing carriers to expand services and new carriers to add services. For example, the third runway at Heathrow Airport would enable a carrier such as easyJet to obtain slots at Heathrow to serve numerous airports in Europe. EasyJet claims that it would be able to offer fares that are about 30 percent lower than the fares available currently on competitors.[5] However, would such additional operations be able to absorb the enormous investment costs? This would be an important question if the plans are to enable an increase in domestic operations, currently at about 15 percent of the total operations. Estimates for the new Northwest runway, along with new terminal buildings and compensation for various parties, are reported to be about £14 billion. One solution to manage flight delays is not only to develop a strategic relationship among airlines, airports, and air traffic management service providers but also to use the platform framework suggested in the previous chapter.

Structural changes within the airline industry

The relationship between the business models of airlines and airports has always been delicate. However, while there have been conflicts and differences between the two business models, going forward the partnership needs to be strategic to adapt to the dramatically changing and uncertain marketplace to create a win-win situation by improving connectivity for passengers and goods. Consequently, if airlines are changing their business models dramatically, as discussed in the previous chapters, then airports need to reexamine their own business models to reduce the gap between airlines' and airports' business models. Consider just one aspect. Just as competition is increasing among airlines, it is also increasing among airports. For example, the older generation of full-service airlines based in Europe faced stiff competition when full-service airlines based in the Persian Gulf region entered the marketplace. However, major hubs in the Persian Gulf region also produced significant competition for the major hubs in Europe. Going forward, a similar trend is taking place regarding airlines based in China and the airport hubs in China.

Consider one specific example of a structural change in the business models of airlines and the impact on airports. Bangkok's Don Mueang Airport was closed in 2006. It was replaced by the Bangkok Suvarnabhumi Airport. However, Don Mueang was reopened in 2007 when the government decided to put in place a two-airport policy, with Don Mueang designated to cater mostly to the needs of low-cost carriers. The domestic market in Thailand more than doubled between 2012 and 2017, resulting from the growth of the low-cost carrier activity at Don Mueang airport. Low-cost carriers based at Don Mueang Airport stimulated the market with lower fares that were attractive to the growing middle class. In 2017, Don Mueang Airport, now a low-cost airport, handled almost 40 million passengers, a number that is about the same as ten years ago when it was Bangkok's main airport. Now the low-cost carriers are expanding in international markets to and from Don Mueang. Major carriers serving Don Mueang now include Thai AirAsia, Nok Air, Lion Air, Thai AirAsia X, Nok Scoot, and AirAsia. Bangkok Suvarnabhumi Airport now also caters to low-cost carriers, but mostly to the foreign low-cost carriers (for example, VietJet Air), while Don Mueang caters mostly to the domestic (Thailand-based) low-cost carriers.

Some low-cost carriers that previously focused on point-to-point operations are beginning to offer connecting services. Within this group, a few are even promoting self-transfer services. As for full-service carriers, some have developed low-cost subsidiaries, as in Europe, while some have introduced ultra-low-fare products in their main cabins, as in the US. On another front, some full-service airlines and low-cost airlines are now willing to feed traffic to each other. Singapore Changi Airport's Terminal 4 handles full-service airlines (such as Cathay Pacific, Korean Air, and Vietnam Airlines) as well as low-cost carriers (such as AirAsia, Spring Airlines, and VietJet Air). Similarly, the initiatives of the London Gatwick Airport are facilitating connections between full-service and low-cost airlines, including the development of self-made connections. London Gatwick Airport launched its new product, GatwickConnect, in 2015 to enable passengers to self-connect through the airport on a wide array of non-inter-lining flights operated by different airlines. Couple this development with easyJet's announcement to inter-line with short-haul carriers (such as Loganair to Scotland) and long-haul carriers (such as Norwegian and WestJet). Consequently, there is a convergence in the models of low-cost and full-cost airlines. On another front, while the Persian Gulf-based airlines are continuing to grow, full-service carriers based in China have begun to expand at a fast rate. On the other hand, there is market consolidation, especially in North America and Europe.

There are two other structural changes underway with significant potential impact on the business models of airports. Aircraft manufacturers are already developing single-aisle aircraft to operate in ultra-long-haul markets (with ranges approaching 4,500 nautical miles with a full payload of passengers and cargo). Besides their long ranges, these aircraft also have seat-mile costs approaching the level of the traditional wide-body aircraft, depending on stage length and cabin configuration. These aircraft are enabling smaller airports, located at strategic points around the globe, to develop relevant facilities to accommodate both the expected growth in traffic and the traffic diverted from congested and or high-cost airports. Consider the smaller airports located on the East Coast of the US and in Ireland that have been able to attract the attention of low-cost carriers to offer transatlantic service to and from their airports. Consequently, while low-cost carriers may only have about 5 percent of the capacity across the North Atlantic, it could increase significantly. In a different part of the world, consider the new planned airport in Vietnam, Long Thanh International Airport. While the first phase is expected to handle just under 20 million passengers per year, the final phase could increase the capacity to just under 100 million passengers per year.

Second, while there has already been a significant amount of consolidation in the global airline industry, the process is not over yet. In the US, about 75 percent of the domestic market is transported by four major carriers – American, Delta, Southwest, and United. In Europe, consolidation has taken a different route in recent years. In some cases, consolidation came via mergers and acquisition, as in the case of Aer Lingus. In other cases, it came via the insolvency proceedings route, as in the case of, Air Berlin, Malev, and Monarch Airlines. Further consolidation can be expected given that there are a few small airlines that may not be able to compete either with the major full-service airlines or the low-cost carriers.

Customer experience

Requirements for service and experience continue to increase, given an increase in stress levels and in customer intolerance. Customers expect improvements in travel before the trip, during the trip, and after the trip. During the trip, at the airport, typical problem areas that passenger see relate to signage, security lines, aircraft boarding areas, making connections, walking time at major airports, and delivery of baggage for travel in general, and for passengers traveling in international markets, the immigration process at arriving airports. Besides the length of time taken at these touch points, passengers question the need to present identification documents at multiple locations at an airport. Passengers also desire either less number of touch points or points where they can serve themselves. While these concerns are valid, let us look at the situation from an airport's side. First, many passengers travel very infrequently, for example, once a year. Second, because these passengers travel so infrequently, they have low- to no-tier status in airline frequent flyer programs. Third, some passengers spend very little time at airports. Fourth, the passenger mix is changing, with not only more leisure travelers but also passengers from a much broader number of countries, representing different cultures and different language needs. Fifth, the average expenditure-per-customer is most likely decreasing given the increase in the percentage of passengers traveling on lower fares and on low-cost airlines. Sixth, there is a large volume of free-flowing, isolated and separated, information in the ecosystem. Consequently, airports face a major challenge in providing a personalized experience, partly because dramatic improvements in customer experience call for significant increases in investments and partly because most airports do not even know their customers. How could they? A major airport such as London Heathrow handles about 80 million passengers per year. On any day, there could be 200,000 passengers passing through this airport. And yet customers have high expectations. Wanting accurate information in real time is not a problem. Wanting more control during their trips is a challenge. If flights are delayed or canceled, some passengers now even want airports to have facilities for video and teleconferencing. In fact, according to some passengers, airports should become "hubs" for videoconferencing, in general.

Airports, of course, are beginning to become customer-centric by leveraging data, technologies, and analytics. Airports are using multiple facial-recognition technologies and sensors to monitor passengers (for the purpose of security, safety, navigation, and transmissions of timely information) and their flows (to maximize operational efficiencies). And since traffic is shifting to the East, airports are preparing for the need for more languages and ways to fulfill cultural needs. Airports are also trying to improve the experience in a wide array of areas, ranging from the implementation of technologies to assist visually-impaired passengers to reducing the length of lines at duty-free shops or exploring ways to eliminate lines altogether. Finally, some mega-airports under development are focusing on the experience for passengers in terms of longer distances to walk for both local and connecting passengers. Dubai World Central – Al Maktoum International Airport – is planning, for example, to use technologies and innovative designs to minimize the walking distances for passengers.

While customers want more value, the challenge is to define value. Airlines and airports may not even be clear on what value is now and how to measure it, let alone the strong evidence that value is shifting rapidly. For example, some passengers are listing "transformative travel experience" high on their list of needs.[6] How can this value be defined, and how can it be measured and tracked? Yet airports are listening, and some are now offering, for example, dedicated spaces for yoga for travelers to reduce their stress. Going forward, just as with airlines, technologies discussed in Chapter 2 can help develop much more contemporary value propositions for airlines and their passengers.

Environment

Local communities' concerns for noise and air quality are increasing at an alarming rate. Consider just one case to see the length of time it takes an airport to get its expansion plan approved. The UK government's Airport Commission began studying the third runway at London's Heathrow Airport in September 2012. The project was expected to provide an additional 700 operations per day. Then, even though the government accepted the recommendation of the Airport Commission for the third runway in 2017, it will not be completed until 2025. The arguments for the third runway related to reducing aircraft and passenger delays, increasing the possibility of lower fares resulting from an increase in competition, and maintaining UK's hub connectivity status in the world. With respect to the last point, for example, whereas London Heathrow Airport had maintained the status of No. 2 in terms of connectivity in 2008 and in 2017, it slipped to No. 3 in 2018. Frankfurt Airport, which had been No. 3 in 2008 and 2017, moved up to No. 1.[7] It took almost 20 years to develop Terminal 5 at London Heathrow from the initial discussion to its completion. The Northwest runway project could take just as long.

Despite the efforts of aircraft manufacturers to introduce quieter aircraft and the airports' efforts to efforts to soundproof and buy buildings near airports, airports and airlines continue to deal with operational flight control initiatives. Typical curfews relate to operations between the hours of 23:00 and 06:00. Currently, Frankfurt Airport, for example, has restrictions that go from 23:00 to 05:00, whereas London Heathrow's restrictions go from 23:00 to 07:00. If the environmental concerns continue to climb, limiting the capability of airports to expand, or if the costs to expand continue to escalate at a high rate, the only solution may be to limit aircraft movements, either through caps or through market-price charges.

As for emissions, although airports are moving rapidly in implementing initiatives relating to emissions generated on the ground, the concern for emissions generated in the air could result in the introduction of restrictions and market-based incentives. Challenges relating to transitioning to alternative aviation fuels relate to "production economics, engineering processes, industry partnerships, certification, and financing."[8] In recent years, another challenge is emerging, the rise of water from climate change. This is a serious challenge for low-lying airports. According to the data reported in the media, almost one-quarter of the world's 100 busiest airports are less than ten meters above sea level. And 12 are less than five meters above sea level. This list includes such busy airports as New York and San Francisco in the US, Rome in Europe, and Shanghai in China. There is no question, airports are committed to sustainable development – reduction in greenhouse gases (CO_2 emissions) – and the community aspects are particularly important in the case of inner-urban airports. Take, for example, Hamburg in Germany, an airport with serious initiatives in the areas of noise, CO_2 emissions, and public transport, not just for passengers but also employees. Just as one example, Hamburg Airport promoted the use of bikes for employees to come to work, and the airport provides facilities such as bike-rack spaces, for pumping air in the tires, and bike repair services during certain times of the year.

While air travel worldwide accounts for approximately 3 percent of the greenhouse gas emissions, the concern is about the increase in this percentage, as a result of the expected growth in air travel. On the positive side, advancements in electric propulsions have the potential to change the facilities required at airports. Currently, the focus of electric aircraft has been in the areas of urban air mobility (UAM) air taxis. Some proposals relate to the use of advanced-technology batteries. Other electric vertical-takeoff-and-landing (eVTOL) vehicles propose to use hybrid-electric systems. The developments in small regional aircraft relate also to hybrid-electric systems. Airports would need to build enabling infrastructure to accommodate UAM. However, electric propulsion would reduce the concerns relating to noise and emissions.

Business model transformation

In looking for new airport business models, managements are going through age-old questions like the following.

- Who are an airport's customers, and how does an airport make money serving these customers at the lowest costs while remaining competitive?
- How can an airport maximize the use of its assets within the framework of high-fixed costs and low-marginal costs?
- How does an airport resolve the conflicting requirements of its customers? Some low-cost carriers claim that some airports are building, compared to their needs, unnecessarily large facilities, resulting in unnecessarily higher charges.
- Should a highly congested airport use its limited capacity to serve only full-service airlines?
- How can value be created from an airport's resources (accessibility, destinations served, reliability of operations, intermodal services, around-the-clock operations, and more)?
- How can customer relationships be managed? Should an airport focus on its most valuable customers or the airport's valuable customers' customers?
- How can an airport get closer to the population it serves and learn about the challenges and opportunities facing the different communities with different characteristics of catchment areas?
- Should management become more entrepreneurial and develop a tighter bonding between different functions, as discussed in Chapter 3?
- Should and can management practice the fail-fast type of experiments?
- Should large airports try to create a "wow experience" for passengers or focus on reducing customers' frustrations?
- How does an airport attract the right partners – airlines, service providers, retail, etc.? Even within the airline sector, is it full-service airlines, low-cost airlines, ultra-low-cost airlines, or hybrid airlines?
- Assuming land is available, should it be used for expansion of aeronautical facilities, terminals, runways, etc., or for developing non-aviation commercial activities?

- Should airports, with congested terminals, build off-site processing, check-in for passengers, and drop-off for bags?
- What are the important characteristics of the catchment area---size, affluence, diversity, and global reach?
- What is the optimal method for determining charges relating to revenue streams, airline fees, passenger charges, concessionaire contributions from service providers, subsidies, and so forth? Should the airport use the "dual-till" model vs. "single-till" vs. the "hybrid-till?"
- How can an airport build flexibility into its business model to leverage ongoing improvement in technologies and innovation processes, relating, for example, to the design of a terminal?
- How can management introduce agility in its planning processes, given multi-year planning horizons and investments, not to mention the capital and labor intensities of the airport business?

These questions are hardly new, and airport managements have struggled with answers for decades. However, answers may be more readily available with the use of platforms, with not just airlines and communities, but all other stakeholders – car-rental agencies, parking operators, retailers, etc. First, platforms enable the integration of very large quantities of data. Think about it. Almost everything at a major airport encompasses connectivity. A major global airport can have 200,000 passengers passing through its airport. Think about the number of employees, which could exceed 50,000 if one includes the employees of couple of hundred businesses operating at a major airport. Through an analysis of this vast quantity of data, a platform framework can now enable an airport to meet the divergent needs of its customers, different types of airlines, for example, and the mix of their customers – business, leisure, premium leisure, "bleisure," and so forth. What is important to which customer: the number of destinations served, type of retail stores, time required to check in, lower connecting times, time required to go through security, customer experience, self-control facilities, access to different modes of transportation, and so forth? Some of these issues have been hard to address due to the lack of data, for example, on how customers' habits are changing. Now, airports are beginning to find new sources of data and leverage their fresh talent and innovative ideas from employees. Regarding retail, customers want airports to meet their physical and digital needs. But what are digital needs? Airports need to promote route development – a difficult challenge in the path of consolidation in the airline industry. Passengers need not only a wide network but also a choice of airlines. Again, platforms can help in the making of these decisions, not just because of their integrative features but also their ability to generate data. In the final analysis, since airlines are managing their yield, why should airports not do the same? They can with the use of platforms.

In addition, while the major challenges facing airports are not new, the complexity of each challenge has been increasing. It is getting harder and harder to expand capacity. The investment costs are increasing. The structure of the airline industry is becoming more complex and more uncertain. Environmental constraints are becoming a bigger challenge. Consequently, airports need to develop a different mindset not just to adapt to challenges while capitalizing on new opportunities but also to decide on a priority of issues. Consider just one basic question. Is it better to build more capacity or manage demand through establishing caps (say on operations) or through economic measures (congestion pricing)?

With the questions raised in the list above, the decision on the sources of revenues is now particularly important. How much of the revenues should be generated from aeronautical services (landing fees, rents from terminal space, etc.) and how much from non-aeronautical services (retail, parking, etc.)? According to the data available from the Airports Council International, based on 900 airports worldwide, almost 60 percent of the revenue came from aeronautical sources.[9] With a change in the mix of traffic, the issue is becoming much more complex. In many developing regions, for example, not only is the revenue coming from low-cost airlines less, but also the revenue-per-traveler from airport expenditures is lower, especially at airports that serve primarily domestic traffic. This also brings in government's intervention. Does the government favor the single-till, dual-till, or hybrid-till model? In the hybrid-till model, a certain percent of the non-aeronautical revenues is used to cross-subsidize the charges for aeronautical services. In the single-till model, all non-aeronautical revenues are used to subsidize the aeronautical charges. There is no subsidy in the dual-till model. The single-till model will produce the lowest cost per passenger, and the dual-till model will maximize the revenue for the airport. The hybrid-till model might be better for airports needing large amounts of investments for expansion. However, if the goal is to increase the revenue generated from non-aeronautical sources, then there is a need to develop strategic relationships with retailers. In the final analysis, the goal is presumably to balance the needs of airlines, airports, and local communities.

Platforms can now help airports change their business models to adapt to the four major challenges. Here is a rationale.

- Platforms are not only efficient ways to deliver better services to passengers but also excellent ways to collect and synthesize data.
- Platforms are an efficient way to share data among airlines, airports, government agencies (especially air traffic control), and providers of ground transportation services.
- Airports play a central role in integrating the services provided by different modes of transportation, not just relating to existing modes (such as airlines, trains, busses, etc.), but also new forms of transportation coming in the future (flying taxis, self-driving cars, Hyperloop, small hybrid-electric aircraft, small SSTs, drones, and more). Airports will be at the center of the attention in bring about mobility-as-a-service.
- Platforms will also be better ways for major airports to compete with secondary airports. Traffic at secondary airports will grow fast due to congestion at major airports, the availability of airplanes with attractive payload-range characteristics, and the expansion of low-cost carriers (LCCs) and ultra-low-cost carriers (ULCCs).

Consider the first two points about collecting the data and sharing the data. An airport could easily develop a platform that, at the very least, allows much better coordination with airlines on one side and air traffic management systems on the other side. This platform will enable the generation of one source of information that can be used by all parties, including ground handling companies and airport security groups. This platform can also be integrated into the intelligent engagement platform discussed in the previous chapter. Consider the last point about a potential increase in competition between major airports and secondary airports. Secondary airports will not only serve point-to-point markets but also develop a reasonable size of hub-and-spoke systems. They will offer better economics to airlines and provide higher levels of experience. See the first scenario in the next section.

Just as with airlines, different airports can work at different points on the continuum.

- At one point could be an airport like Singapore's Changi Airport, which will be opening its $1.7 billion Jewel Changi Airport Facility to make the airport not just a global hub (in terms of global connectivity) but also a destination.
- At a different location could be an airport like the London City Airport, which is trying to simply expand its extremely limited capacity by adding a few aircraft parking stands and a parallel taxiway.
- At another location could be Ürümqi, China, which is already developing into a hub-and-spoke system for China Southern, with flights from multiple locations in the Western part of China connecting with flights connecting to as diverse regions as Central Asia, the Middle East, and Europe.
- At a very different point on the continuum would be an airport planning not for short lines for check-in, security clearance, and border control, but for no lines at all.
- At another location could be a small airport that has the potential to grow with the help of a strategic partner. Consider Ljubljana Airport in Slovenia, which has an excellent potential to grow, partly because it is under the wings of the Fraport AG group, partly because of its location (serving the Balkan region), and partly because of the local economy. Fraport has already rebranded the airport as Fraport Slovenija.
- For another airport, strategic partners could be different, for example, the economic division of a small country, and its tourism authority. Consider Keflavik Airport. Tourism is an important component of Iceland's economy, and Keflavik Airport is a vital part in the development of tourism. Keflavik could easily become a significant size of hub-and-spoke system, further connecting North America and Europe. Four large carriers based in North America are now serving Keflavik Airport – Air Canada, American, Delta, and United. While services from Keflavik are currently between North America and Europe, services could easily be expanded to Asia. Traffic will increase much more with an increase in the use of wide-body aircraft as well as the expansion of the terminal.

- At another point could be an airport that provides special buses at locations where passengers are deplaning planes to take those passengers who want to go straight to car-rental locations. Why should this group of passengers be required to walk through the entire terminal just to board buses that will drive them to car-rental locations, some near the terminal and some a number of miles from the terminal? Arrangements could also be made for their baggage to be delivered at a common location for all car-rental companies.
- Going further out, a major airport under development needs to think about its position in the expanding global marketplace. The Istanbul New Airport opened on October 29, 2018, offering an initial capacity of 90 million passengers per year, with the capacity to grow to 200 passengers per year. The synergy between Turkish Airlines and the new airport is clear. The airline, which is expected to transport almost 75 million passengers in 2018, is planning to carry about 120 million passengers per year in five years.[10]
- Some airports are developing off-site facilities to reduce congestion in terminals. Taiwan Taoyuan International Airport has established a check-in facility at the Taipei Main Station downtown that offers a direct rail link to the airport.

The key point is that just as platforms can facilitate the development of a tight bond between airlines' commercial and operations spaces, platforms can achieve similar results between airports' different planning divisions – hub and network, retail, operations, and parking, for example. Different airports can work on platforms while working at different locations on the continuum, ranging from those trying to increase capacity using conventional strategies (more runways and more terminals) to those exploring new sources of revenues from different retailers once the use of (1) biometrics starts to move passengers rapidly through airports and (2) self-driving cars begin to reduce the need for a large number of parking spaces at airports. Platforms can also add value in the evaluation of potential strategies to explore different privatization options for new sources of funds and different planning frameworks, with impact on speed and flexibility. However, plenty of space exists on the platform continuum for airlines and airports that may consider addressing passengers' global mobility and personal requirements. And, given the changes coming from the use of technologies (driver-less cars and biometrics, for example), one question could relate to the new use for the additional space available in the parking garages and retail stores. One strategy for an airport could be to identify high-value customers – for example, airlines who in turn are also looking for their high-value customers – and establish special tracks for them. The space available, enabled by the use of these technologies, can also be used to develop attractive relaxation facilities for travelers, as well as entertainment for them. Vancouver International Airport is planning to build ten remote aircraft stands in the space becoming available from the reduction of 2000 parking spaces.[11]

Scenarios

Just as leading airlines are developing a set of scenarios going out 5–10 years, some leading airports are doing the same. Only airports are going out much farther and developing scenarios for the next 20+ years. The need for the development of scenarios is more critical now than in the past. Airlines are developing new strategies, and the models of airports need to consider the changing models of airlines. Airlines are now exploring new potential strategies relating to networks – mergers and acquisitions (M&A), alliances, and virtual operations, just to name three The first would have major impacts on smaller airports based on the results of M&A activity in the US – the impact on Cincinnati, Ohio, when Delta merged with Northwest, for example. What could be the outcomes if Finnair, LOT Polish, and SAS were to be combined in some manner with the three existing major Euros? Similarly, even an initial phase of virtual operations could produce a major challenge for the hub and network planning division of airports. Consider the implications for an airport if IAG were to implement a small change in its booking pattern. Allow a passenger to select an approximate time of departure and arrival between her point of origin, say Zurich, and destination, say Los Angeles. The passenger could, say, request departure sometime in the morning of a certain day and arrival sometime in the evening of a certain day. The airline group could then decide the exact routing and provide the information to the passenger closer to the day of departure – two British Airways flights with a connection through London Heathrow, or two Iberia flights with a connection through Madrid, or two Aer Lingus flights with a connection through Dublin. The group could also select different alliance partners at different connecting hubs. Such decisions are currently made at the time the booking is made. With virtual operations, the decision could be made by the airline even a couple of hours prior to the departure.

Consider just two scenarios for airports where the operating entities make technologies the centerpiece of their commercial and operational strategies. In both scenarios, technologies will cover broad areas of information and communications on the one side and vehicles, ground and air on the other side.

Secondary airports

Secondary hub-and-spoke airports set up at strategic locations around the world and manage to achieve economies of scale. Examples could include the western part of China (Ürümqi, for example), the center of India (Hyderabad, for example), the northwestern part of Africa (Casablanca, Morocco, for example), the northern part of South America (Medellín, Colombia, for example), and the mid-Atlantic region (Keflavik, for example). From the new secondary hub-and-spoke airports, airlines operate advanced narrow-body aircraft with nonstop ranges up to 5,000 statute miles, representing flight times up to ten hours. One might recall that passengers did fly long-haul distances in narrow-body aircraft such as the Boeing 707–320B and the Douglas DC-8–62, aircraft with a range of almost 6,000 statute miles, and a capacity of about 150 seats, in a mixed-class layout. The network of the hub-and-spoke systems will be expanded enormously by airlines by leveraging the low unit seat-mile costs and the long range of the new narrow-body aircraft.

In the US, some small but strategically located airports could be privatized and expand their facilities to relieve congestion at nearby major airports. In the greater

New York region, Stewart International Newburgh has already made it through the FAA's Airport Privatization Pilot Program (APPP). Now, an amazingly strategic airport, Westchester County Airport (KHPN) in White Plains, could follow the privatization plan. It is located about 30 miles from the center of Manhattan and is close to Fairfield, Connecticut. This location makes it very convenient for the well-to-do residents in the New York metropolitan area. In his thought leadership piece in Chapter 8, Bernard Thiboutot shares some ideas on the future of so-called "secondary" airports.

On the groundside, much less space will be needed for marking parking facilities, given the entry of driver-less cars, and terminal space would be optimized for satisfying the needs of two basic groups of passengers. One group would be the fast track for those who want to board their aircraft as quickly as possible and have no desire to visit any retail stores. They would already have checked in prior to arrival at the airport and move through security fast, with preclearance information embedded into the systems, coupled with the use of on-location biometric technology. The other group would be passengers who travel infrequently and want to take advantage of the opportunity to visit the airport and move through it at a leisurely pace, enjoying the services of different retail and food facilities.

These new secondary hub-and-spoke airports would leverage the latest technology being developed, for example, within the framework of the New Experience Travel Technologies (NEXTT) initiative being developed by IATA and the Airports Council International (ACI)[12] as well as SITA's experimentation with Leo, the baggage robot, and Kate, the moveable robotic check-in kiosk. They would deploy sensors, biometric scanners, automated check-in kiosks, automated bag-drop locations or moving robots, and high-tech security and border control systems. Digital assistants available would have the capability of conversing in multiple languages.

Artificial intelligence (including machine learning) and big data would be used to advance and improve on-time departures – the accuracy of the off-block time. Improvement in the prediction of off-block times will increase the capacity of the airport, especially during disruptions, and improve customer experience. Couple this with the technology to be able to "see," in real time, where passengers are on their way to the boarding area to improve decisions regarding whether to hold the plane back for late arriving passengers, or close the flight and depart, or even provide seats to passengers on the wait list. Similarly, informed decisions can be made as to wait or not for a connecting bag when the gate agent can "see" the location of the bag. Ground handlers would "see" the location (along with the PNR of the passenger) of the bag in the hold, if it needs to be removed because of a non-show passenger. The IoT will help, for example, showing the time when a particular bag was loaded.

Technology will be used to identify and track passengers at airports and predict their movements and flows. As the Internet of things (IoT) paradigm comes into maturity, airports and airlines can benefit from shared information on real-time terminal processes that improve the predictability of operations and disruptions. Sensor systems and data platforms are currently being developed, which provide an accurate picture of the passenger flow movement patterns, including lines, bottlenecks and dwell times, which can be used to project future transit times and profiling of the passengers using the airport facility. This opens up a myriad of new applications, including coordinated airport-airline delay management, bottleneck prediction and resolution in security checkpoints, and targeted retail offering. This information will improve passenger experience and the efficiency of operations conducted at airports to relieve congestions at such locations as security clearance. The identification of passengers will come from a variety of sources, such as hand-held devices by passengers, networks of cameras and beacons located at airports, and locations where boarding passes have been scanned. Technology will be used to not only determine the location of each passenger (check-in area, security clearance area, shopping area, etc.) but the track of the passenger. It would then be possible, for example, to predict the movement pattern. This information will be used to assist a passenger, for example, with an exact navigational path to a specific gate (with an estimated time of arrival the gate). Information on passenger location, movement, and predicted time of arrival will be used by the staff at the security clearance area to improve the processing time by dynamically changing the number of staff. From the commercial side, such information would be used to provide dynamic retail-related offers to passengers.

Intermodal transportation hubs

Intermodal transportation hubs are already on the scene. Consider, for example, the Hongqiao Transportation Hub. The Hongqiao Transportation Hub is a large multi-modal transportation hub located in the western part of Shanghai, China. It connects the area's second international airport (Shanghai Hongqiao International Airport), both high-speed and the traditional intercity rail lines, and the area's metro system, as well as taxis. The hub links the various road networks that serve the Yangtze River Delta region, which has a population of about 130 million and a GDP of about $2 trillion. This example already shows the feasibility of a people-oriented integrated transportation system that could be developed further to improve customers' travel experience in the areas of baggage delivery, walking distances, and fare integration.[13]

The next generation of intermodal transportation hubs would offer multi-modal services using various types of air vehicles and ground transportation systems. On the airside would be conventional subsonic aircraft, second-generation small supersonic transports, hybrid-to-electric regional aircraft, eVTOL, and flying cars, leaving aside, for now, personal jet jackets and drones. On the groundside would be conventional trains (local and intercity) and the Hyperloop for intercity and inter-airport travel. Airport platform-coordinated facilities would provide not only seamless and frictionless door-to-door travel, but with a high level of technology-enabled personalization. Consider, for example:

• while being driven to the airport, be told by a voice that due to the traffic ahead, it is highly unlikely that the passenger will make the flight, and ask if the machine should look into the availability of the next flight;

- through a scanned image, be shown the location of an empty space in the parking garage and the probability that it will remain empty in the next X minutes;
- mobile devices automatically speaking the expected departure time for the flight and the number of minutes to the gate from the current location, based on real-time information and information with real-time translation capabilities;
- technology for geolocation of passengers and to provide intelligent navigational capability;
- technology for in-wallet scanning of travel documents and coordinated facial recognition;
- transportation information for local areas and airport attractions, including augmented reality videos of local sites; and
- interfaces to enable travelers' mobile devices to communicate (through a person or voice) with other systems at any point at the airport (kiosks, for example), to obtain seamless service.

The mobility-as-a-service platform will address the increasing expectations of travelers for experience-based personalized services relating to the end-to-end journey. This requirement calls not only for travel on integrated modes of transportation but also the provision of experience that is consistent at each touch point.

As demand for air travel continues to grow, leading airports are not only identifying ways to operate much more efficiently, given the capacity constraints around the world, they are also exploring smart ways to use technology to increase capacity, reduce operating costs, and improve customer service. At the same time, customers expect a much higher level of experience with their travel through airports. Both aspects (increase in operational efficiency as well as customer experience) call for the acquisition of more data and the use of analytics to obtain insights for tracking customers and airport resources. The data can come from diverse sources, such as the behavior of passengers using self-check-in facilities to the use of Wi-Fi throughout the airport to the use of social networks. The acquisition of this data and its analysis to identify the right service for the right traveler will be facilitated by the use of platforms. On the customer side, platforms will enable not only the collection of the personalized travel components of a trip but also the provision of 24/7/365 support to manage the trip. On the airport side, internal platforms will enable the development of initiatives for holistic solutions, as opposed to incremental improvements in such areas as the efficient use of individual facilities and staff.

Notes

1 "Future of the Airline Industry 2035," IATA, Geneva, Switzerland, 2017.
2 "European Aviation in 2040: Challenges of Growth," Eurocontrol, 2018, Edition 2.
3 "European Aviation in 2040: Challenges of Growth," Eurocontrol, 2018, Edition 2, p. 3.
4 "Current Market Outlook: 2017–2036," Boeing Commercial Airplanes, March 2018, p. 9.
5 Lewis Harper, "Disruptive Thinking," *Flight Airline Business*, September 2018, pp. 24–9.
6 "Rise of Transformative Travel: Shifting Toward Meaning, Purpose, and Personal Fulfillment," A Skift Report, 2018.

7 "Airports Council International: Airport Industry Connectivity Report 2018," June 19, 2018, p. 5. Analysis based on SEO's NetScan connectivity methodology.
8 U.S. Department of Energy, "Alternative Aviation Fuels: Overview of Challenges, Opportunities, and Next Steps," Energy Efficiency & Renewable Energy, March 2017, p. 3.
9 Sean Broderick, "Airports Try Direct Approach to Problem-Solving," *AviationWeek & Space Technology*, September 3–16, 2018, p. 44.
10 Alan Dron, "MEGA-HUB," *Air Transport World*, September 2018, pp. 17–18.
11 Sean Broderick, op. cit., p. 45.
12 Graham Newton, "NEXTT Steps in Travel Vision," *Airlines* (a publication of IATA), 2018–1, pp. 41–3.
13 Linna Li and Becky P. Y. Loo, "Towards People-Centered Integrated Transport: A Case Study of Shanghai Hongqiao Comprehensive Transport Hub," *ELSEVIER, Cities*, 2016, Vol. 58, pp. 50–8.

6 A platform scenario: dynamically integrated travel

Based on the deployment of the *mobility-as-a-service* concept (MaaS), being experimented by *smart cities* around the world, this chapter presents a hypothetical scenario of a travel-based platform, along the lines discussed in Figure 4.1 in Chapter 4. The platform is an open-based system that offers dynamically integrated and personalized travel through strong collaboration within the travel value chain. The ubiquity of information has already enabled the opportunity to integrate various aspects of travel on a personalized basis. Moreover, the MaaS process has already proven that it can offer more choice and efficiency, plus it is user friendly. One only needs to look at the proven application of the MaaS concept in urban transportation in Helsinki, Finland. This city is successfully pursuing its goal to make the ownership of a personal car obsolete and replace it with MaaS. This encompasses trip planning and ride hailing easily, along with the booking, ticketing, and paying process, which is not only easy but also seamless. Mobility service options in Helsinki vary from an all-inclusive charge per month to pay-per-rides and encompass all forms of ground transportation: train, bus, minivan, taxi, rental car, and bike sharing.

In the scenario in this chapter, the intelligent engagement platform takes the MaaS concept much further. The platform has been developed and is being operated by a far-thinking, brand-named global airline. A small group of entrepreneurial-minded, deep-seated, and radically innovative thinkers managed to convince the airline's board to take a risk and go beyond the airline's core competency to develop the platform. The effort took a lot of analysis of other potential developers, as described in the first part of the chapter, as well as the challenges and opportunities facing the airline to support the development, totally from customers' perspectives, of its own platform. The group also managed to convince the chief digital officer of the airline to get some internal platforms developed within its commercial and operations divisions. Then the chief digital officer of the independent business running the platform managed to get the two airline divisions, commercial and operations, to be bonded along the lines suggested in Chapter 4. The chief digital officer then managed to integrate its internal platforms with those available from related businesses worldwide to form its intelligent engagement platform. Throughout the development and operations of the platform, the independent airline group experimented with numerous conventional and platform-based strategies and managed to finally close the gap between its conventional legacy systems and the innovative new systems. The final platform, while still evolving, offers a broad spectrum of travel-related services to meet the needs of an equally broad spectrum of travelers. The range of travelers extends from those on very strict travel budgets to those traveling on businesses in which the itineraries keep changing, to those looking to travel within a wide array of VIP styles.

This chapter provides, first, some challenges and opportunities faced by the chief digital officers of the airline and the independent innovative group in developing the intelligent engagement platform. Next, the chapter discusses the different types of customers likely to use the platform and the different types of services available through the platform. Some of these services have already been available on different types of excellent but unlinked platforms and apps. The final section shows an example of a service that is currently not available in any comprehensive manner, namely the 24/7/365 support of customers' itineraries in real time.

Development of challenges and opportunities

The challenge

In developing its intelligent engagement platform, our small radically innovative group within the airline faced numerous challenges. The foremost challenge was to change management's mindset in two areas. First, just like many of its competitors, the airline had been offering the same basic commodity product: scheduled seats between airports, albeit with changes relating only to new markets, new planes, new schedules, and new prices. Moreover, there was a constant struggle to find new ways to sell the same basic product and services. The innovative group kept reminding management of the statement by Abraham Maslow, a prominent psychologist, who said, "I suppose it is tempting, if the only tool you have is a hammer, to treat everything as if it were a nail." Second, the group convinced the airline's chief digital officer that while she was working on digitalizing numerous processes within the airline, there was a need for a MaaS platform. However, the design of such a platform had to be built based upon customers' perspectives. Even more importantly, the innovative group could envision that if the airline did not develop such a platform, it would be developed by one of five other groups within the travel chain. They considered the following five possibilities.

First, the platform could have been developed by one of the mega-online travel companies. More than its size, an OTA would be one that was well financed, branded, focused, motivated, and acquisition-minded. It could provide consumers, through embedded metasearch engines, information on all components of the trip. The OTA-developed platform would offer greater choice with localization-based personalization. The main feature of the OTA-developed platform would relate not just to the breadth of suppliers but also to the depth of the search in real time, a fast response time, and the capability to make the booking efficiently.

Second, one of the major global GDSs could develop the platform, given that GDSs have always been service-platform businesses. The GDS could re-platform its conventional business to work not only with a more diversified group of suppliers of products and services but also with different business arrangements with different suppliers, relating to the sharing of data, degrees of collaboration, access to content, pricing arrangements, and so forth. The strength of a global GDS-developed platform is that it knows and has worked with the complexity of the airline business, understands the challenges and opportunities relating to distribution, has access to data, and comprehends the limitation of existing technology systems. Moreover, the GDS has already been exploring the use of new technologies to renovate the passenger service systems.

Third, a platform could also be developed within the hospitality sector. AccorHotels (a hospitality and leisure business) has already been developing its strategy to compete in the new environment where not only the likes of Amazon and Google could penetrate the travel sector but where Airbnb has already become a dominant player. In the middle of 2018, AccorHotels had already started to explore the possibility of acquiring equity in Air France-KLM, possibly acquiring the equity share held by the French government. This would not only have strengthened the relationship between two large players in the travel sector but also have developed a platform to improve customer experience. AccorHotels had already been expanding in the hospitality area, for example, by participating in the "home sharing" area. Our airline independent innovative group was concerned that AccorHotels could not only provide Air France-KLM a strategy to work out its labor-management relationship but also provide a more focused vision to take advantage of the travel synergy between the two businesses (membership in the loyalty programs, increase in the databases, better control in the distribution space, and so forth). Our innovative group recognized the history of airlines owning hotels. In the early 1970s, United Airlines owned Westin Hotels and Air France owned the Le Meridien (both of which are now owned by Marriott). In the case of Air France, its partner KLM and AccorHotels had experience in developing digital strategies and could easily push the frontiers in innovation, relating, for example, to new ways of managing revenue. Besides AccorHotels, another strong player, such as the InterContinental Hotel Group (IHG) or Marriott International, could also develop the platform. Hotels recognize, for example, that customers want more than just rooms for the night, and even want more than good experiences. For this reason, Marriott invested in PlacePass and Marriott Moments, metasearch platforms for product services more than rooms, plus the flexibility to adapt to changing customer needs.

Fourth, a platform could be developed by one of the major new technology businesses that collect all kinds of data by monitoring customers' activities. The innovative group was concerned that these information powerhouses could end up deciding who gets what information. The group was also concerned about the potential control and, therefore, market power that these technology companies could exercise in the airline distribution space. Google, for example, tends to attract consumers looking for travel at the very early stages of their trip planning. Google also makes a significant amount of money from bookings made online through its system, but by offering consumers choice and value. These newer generations of potential technology business distributors do have access to consumers, their locations, and insights on them through a broad spectrum of data. The question raised was whether control that should be with customers could end up with distributors, not service suppliers. However, the group realized that the key point is who provides value-adding information (organized information on content) to the consumer with respect to ease, relevancy, and meaningful options, for example. From this perspective, suppliers and distributors could collaborate in a way that the basic information provided by a supplier, like an airline (schedule, fare, seat configuration, meals, in-flight entertainment, baggage policies, and so forth), could be organized, supplemented with other information, and then displayed in more insightful ways and in different channels.

Fifth, a platform could be developed by an asset-light mobility business that has expertise in technology, data collection and analysis techniques, and CRM capabilities, with access to cloud storage and computing. Such a new marketing distributor would also have global brand recognition and a brand-name portfolio to provide total solutions for travelers' global mobility requirements while protecting consumers' privacy and providing better value propositions through shopping and payment technologies. These new travel marketers would not be saddled with the concern of travel service suppliers of the control exercised by the marketer, either over data or over customers. On the customers' side, the new marketers would also be careful of the concern for hyper-personalization. While they would be aware of the requirement of large amounts of personal data needed by the platform, they would also be aware of consumers' concerns for privacy. Moreover, the new marketers would not undertake hyper-personalization to offer "gimmicky" features. Instead, they would provide truly relevant content while taking out friction at key touch points such as shopping and check-in. As such, consumers would appreciate the degree and type of situation-based personalization offered by the new marketers.

In light of the potential threat of customer solution-centric and experience-centric platforms being developed by non-airline organizations, this group decided to list some internal specific concerns relating to platforms to proceed further in developing its own platform with total commitment to customer centricity. Following is a summary of the some specific concerns, requirements, and questions raised by the innovative group.

1 If airlines have vast quantities of data on their passengers, then why are customer satisfaction levels relatively low? How can an airline make the experience better for everyone, not just an airline's high-value customers?
2 Data needs to be collected, but even more importantly, it needs to be shared, and that means it needs to be treated like currency. One entity provides a certain amount and type of data, and the other provides a different type and amount of data. How does one determine the value of data provided by each entity?
3 The bundling of services needs to involve much more than the collection of products and services of the airline or even traditional partners such as hotels

and car-rental companies. However, this requirement calls for a comprehensive knowledge of each customer's needs.

4   Should the platform developed have the capability to find customers or enable customers to find the platform? Should the process be interactive?

5   The platform will display all products and services on the platform, not just the products on the airline's own shelves, like fare bundles. How will the airline platform operator relate to interactive distribution? How will the platform enable sellers to offer dynamically packaged products and services? How will the platform extend the reach – not just hotels and rental cars, but different options for urban transportation?

6   How do the platform developer and operator keep up with the changing requirements? For example, now the digital data strategies need to be fully GDPR (General Data Protection Regulation) compliant.

7   How can smart data and personalization technologies help the airline think about mobility of people on the ground and in the air in a new dimension?

8   The challenge is not just to arrange an intermodal itinerary but also to follow it in real time and on a personalized basis.

9   Personalization is a challenge in itself. However, it becomes complex when it means different things to different people at different times. When every element of the trip is working just fine, then being greeted by a flight attendant by name is pleasant. But when almost everything has gone wrong before a passenger boards the flight, then there might be many more important things than being greeted by name.

10   One key is to provide consumers with one-click capability to be able to compare alternative price-service options instead of having consumers go to the websites of multiple service providers.

11   What happens when consumers have their personal digital assistants who identify the products and services desired based on the personal information provided by the human user?

12   Would consumers like to have self-service control on the platform and work with different suppliers regarding the content desired?

13   How will the independent airline group operating the platform become a trusted mobility advisor?

14   How will the platform operator take care of all challenges? For example, how will Wi-Fi in different countries be connected, and when, where, and how will money be exchanged?

15   Finally, how will the platform offer advice, ranging from the availability of medical help to tickets for performing events in local areas? Would the platform provide human-assisted information?

The opportunity

While the independent airline innovative group was well aware of all the challenges discussed here, the group also knew of a few key benefits of the platform for the airline.

1   It is the development and operations of a MaaS that will provide the airline with a competitive advantage, not the continuation of the airline's traditional business models.
2   The new technology-based platform would be a new tool for the airline to go beyond its core products and offer MaaS to meet travelers' mobility requirements. Consumers will pay a premium if they see value. According to a PricewaterhouseCoopers (PwC) survey, for instance, passengers will pay, for example, 10 percent extra for an airline ticket for a great customer experience.[1]
3   The platform will have the capability to create a coordinated set of products and services (from horizontal and vertical partners – current and future) to meet the total mobility needs of customers while simplifying the travel process and providing a consistent experience in real time. The vital part is the exchange of data. However, whereas individual service providers may not be willing to share data among themselves, they might be willing to do so with the platform operator.
4   While MaaS is a limited concept today, based on the experience of cities like Helsinki and companies like Uber, it will expand very rapidly with the proliferation of such technologies as artificial intelligence. Consider what artificial intelligence has already achieved in the development of self-driving cars. Compare this situation to what is now possible in the media space. Consumers can get almost any content, almost anywhere, almost on any device, and in almost real time. Moreover, MaaS has the potential to provide not only an incredible improvement in convenience and experience but possibly lower prices.
5   Given that the chief digital officer of the airline's independent group has already bonded the commercial and the operations divisions, the airline can sell more of its own capacity by dynamically creating itineraries for travelers.
6   Finally, and most importantly, the airline might be able to make more money from the operation of the platform than from flying aircraft!

Since the key requirement of the platform is to aggregate content from a growing number of sources and then to personalize it, the innovative group decided to explore the personalization concept in more detail, but from customers' perspectives. The point is to separate those consumers, for example, who want to be greeted by their names and have the capability to select their meals and their in-flight entertainment from those who want to be presented with only a few relevant intermodal travel options, based not just on behavioral but also on emotional needs. The latter would have solutions provided during the trip relating to events planned and unplanned. The main point is to engage with people at the right touch point to offer solutions.

Figure 6.1 shows three important pillars of personalization to be offered by the intelligent engagement platform developed by our airline: content, experience, and support. The starting point is some information on "why" this person is traveling, relating to context, time, place, and situation.

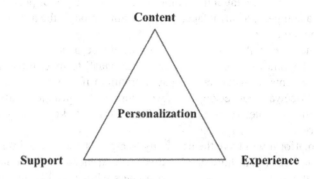

Figure 6.1 Three Pillars of Personalized Services

Personalization

As the title of Antonio Figueiredo's thought leadership piece says, "hyper-personalization is the new oil." Airlines, full service and low cost, are trying to leverage technologies and data to personalize the services offered to their customers to enhance customer experience and strengthen brand loyalty. This section provides some background on three basic pillars of personalization: content, experience, and support.

Content

The platform available from this airline's independent group went through a disciplined design process to make it customer solution-centric and experience-centric for travelers to improve their everyday lives, for example, their time constraints, in a fast-paced world with global unrest. For business travelers the constraints also related, for example, to the compliance of travel arrangements with their company rules. Consider a typical corporate business traveler. Currently, most businesses use business travel management companies that do the ticketing/sales for the basic travel-related components: air, hotel, and rental car, for example. The inventory generally resides in a GDS. Once the booking has been made and downloaded to the traveler's smartphone, there is no "ongoing coverage in real time" unless the traveler calls and submits a request for changes to the booking. In case of changes to flights, tickets have to be canceled and new tickets issued. Additional requests today, like transportation to the home airport, lodging in an Airbnb-recommended location, the use of a car-sharing vehicle for ground transportation, hiring a business jet in cases of an urgency, handling of a visa application, reserving a restaurant for a business meal, and providing digital maps for the destination area are not covered within the framework of the business travel company, at least, not at scale. Moreover, all expenses not booked through the business management company's system have to be handled manually for the expense report, whereas the platform being discussed integrates all travel-related services and is able to separate two accounts (business related and personal expenditures). Using a platform, a travel management company can help the corporation manage its travel costs while improving the experience of a traveler by offering flexibility and choice.

For the airline management, the platform is providing the capability to make informed decisions. In addition, it provides management the ability to achieve agility, flexibility, scale, and scope that is already leading to product differentiation, resulting in brand loyalty. However, the key point is that the newly developed platform provides mobility solutions for all segments of the airline's customer base. It is sometimes said in the media that the airline business cannot be "Uberized," meaning that a customer cannot "just hail an airplane." Why not? Think about this scenario that was handled by an app in the platform. A group of three senior executives was traveling to attend a very important business meeting. The incoming flight was late and the travelers would not have made the connecting flight for the short-end of the trip. This platform arranged a charter flight, having found out that the customers did not find the costs to be prohibitive. In any case, a customer can certainly "hail a seat" in a MaaS by simply asking, "Can anyone get me to Times Square in New York at the lowest possible price, but within 12 hours?"

The platform handles the needs of all customers. High-end travelers are looking not just for experience, physical, digital, and emotional, without stress, but for personal fulfillment on a contextual basis. Think of the complexity involved when an app in the platform recommended a safari tour in Africa to meet the individual needs of travelers. In these cases, an important role was played by apps developed by startups and embedded in the platform. An app is also available to provide a 360-degree virtual reality video of the tour. On the platform are startups that take a single complex travel-related problem, study it extensively, and then find a solution. How about even the needs of general but different groups like visitors from China vs. Europe vs. North America? How about families interested in packaged tours? Today, many families organize their vacation trips via tour operators who provide air transportation, ground transfer at the destination, hotel accommodation, and side tours. The content, as well as its integration, was normally handled through off-line agencies. The younger generation, being more flexible and digital, seems to prefer to do self-organized trips by using all sorts of apps and mobile devices to find content, navigation, and communication. Certainly, they would appreciate a platform that integrates all those functions and provides an additional range of options (outside of a tour operator's content). Examples include the chance to share a van taking the family to the home airport, to have 24/7 access to advice (for instance, a once-weekly appointment with a representative of the tour operator), to reschedule the itinerary, to shop for delivery at the hotel or at home, and to have access to all sorts of entertainment, in line with the family's favorite suppliers at home. In some situations, 24/7 advice can be important. Consider a traveler getting information from a colleague through social media when the colleague happens to be only 50 miles away. The platform will find a way to connect the two people through some form of transportation.

How about meeting the needs of customers on tight travel budgets? Today, budget travelers need to book flights early and hotels late to get inexpensive deals. Using the platform they can submit a request to travel to a designated destination within a time window of, say, 48 hours, not being concerned with spending 50 percent more time traveling than the minimum travel time defined by the fastest public routing on a given route. The request is stored in the platform's system until the time that the platform operator learns of the information that after an airline has allocated the seats for its prime travelers, the airline is still seeking passengers to fill-up the short-term demand. At that time, the budget traveler is assigned to a given flight number, which might even be changed at the last minute in the case of an overbooking, as long as the flexibility and speed parameters of the customer are still met. The platform also provides last-minute hotel rooms and it organizes ad hoc ride-sharing services to and from the airport.

This platform enables the coordination of the services provided by no-frills airlines on one side and the needs of customers with various levels of budgets to find flights on the other side, by no-frills or full-service airlines that may have seats available at discounted prices. For customers, the platform offers convenience related to shopping (including dynamic packaging), traveling, and changing travel plans, with significant flexibility. The platform also integrates with other specialized platforms offering budget-related services to meet the needs of such customers. On the supplier side, a number of low-cost carriers are going after business travelers and want to feed traffic to full-service carriers. The platform integrates and orchestrates the use of a suite of technologies and apps and content providers to offer solutions to the mobility requirements of travelers at the lower ends of the pyramid by matching them with the relevant service providers.

Prior to the development of the platform, the airline tried to differentiate itself on price and or product quality in the areas of network, aircraft, frequency, and the loyalty program. Now the platform is finally able to differentiate the airline by enabling it to engage with its customers through meaningful interactions at the right touch points. However, given the increasing focus on digital customers, an increasing segment of the population, the innovative group went into some detail to gain insights on some common attributes of digital customers. Here are some examples that the innovative group designers discovered:

1   A customer who is totally connected on virtually a 24/7 basis, has access to a vast quantity of data and uses digital channels – the Internet, mobile devices, and social media – to search for competitive products and services, to engage with different providers of products and services, and to complete the transactions for acquiring the desired products and services.

2   A consumer who tends to be a purchaser of "in the moment" situations and on an "on-demand" basis, but with a heavy focus on content – what she is buying and why.

3   A customer who is looking not just for an experience but for a digital experience, both on the ground and during the flight. On the ground, it means the availability of situation- and location-based solutions and self-controlled

capabilities to find solutions, accompanied by a human touch when necessary. In the aircraft, it means high-speed and high-quality in-flight connectivity for activities relating to work, shopping, and entertainment.

4   A customer who is distrustful of traditional advertising campaigns, especially company-produced campaigns and company-purchased media.

5   A customer who is much more likely to rely on recommendations coming from trusted sources, colleagues or trusted sources within her social media network, and share experience through social media.

6   A customer who is likely to be much more vocal through social media, relating to both positive and negative experiences.

7   A younger-generation customer who tends to be more resourceful in finding ways to get the information needed, as she is hyperconnected anyway. She works with brief texts, sending and receiving information.

The platform designers focused heavily on the needs of these customers. According to the IATA 2017 Global Passenger Survey, for example, the newer-generation of travelers want more control during their travel journeys, such as the ability to track their baggage and stay connected on board aircraft.[2] On the other hand, as indicated in the surveys conducted by PricewaterhouseCoopers, when it comes to experience, what matters most to older generations surveyed holds true for the younger generations, too. In the final analysis, the platform designers decided that the key to the platform design was getting the basics right: efficiency, convenience, ease of payment, knowledgeable help, and friendly service.[3] In addition, another insight developed by the platform designer was related to the role of human touch to create "real connections by making technology feel more human." As such, it meant that the platform had to have the capability to identify service providers who had armed their employees with the capabilities to provide higher levels of customer experiences. The platform was also designed to recognize and differentiate situations, such as when human intervention is needed and when high-tech solutions are appropriate. From this point of view, the platform can differentiate between the needs of different generations, given the differences as to how the following groups search, shop, and travel:

- Mature/Silents (1927–1945)
- Baby Boomers (1946–1964)
- Generation X (1965–1980)
- Generation Y/Millennials (1981–2000)
- Generation Z (2001–)

However, there are differences within each segment. There are customers traveling for the experience of being someplace: a leisure destination, for example. Other customers want to engage with people, such as those during business meetings. They are both looking for experience, but of a different type. Then there are segments categorized as "bleisure," those who are planning to conduct business and be on vacation and, as such, they are looking for different experiences on the same trip. In addition, within each segment, the platform is able to identify customers who are in frequent flyer programs and those who have not joined a frequent flyer program, and those who travel infrequently. The platform can provide some level of personalization to an infrequent traveler who is on the website of the airline without knowing that the service will be organized through the framework of the platform. It is all about identifying an individual based on different interactions and the use of technology in the pattern recognition space.

Next, there is the role of self-service. The self-service aspect relates not just to the younger generation but also to frequent travelers. When things go wrong, these segments want to be able to take care of their own needs: booking the next flight, for example. The fulfillment of these needs calls for not only a high level of automation, enabled by the platform, but also simplicity built into the design of the service provided. The idea behind the self-service capability is to allow the passenger to choose the service features to meet her needs and for her to have some control over the experience. The platform also recognizes that there are travelers who like to engage with others through social media, whether it is getting recommendations or sharing insights.

Experience

As an increasing amount of discussion in the industry now relates to customer experience and expectations, the innovative group was well aware of a simple but basic point that customer experience must be viewed from customers' perspectives. The point is how consumers, not service providers, define, measure, and track customer experience. Consumers in other business sectors, for example, seem to be asking sellers to spend more time understanding consumers' lives and the importance of empathy for consumers.[4] Moreover, customers' perspectives must now be explored within the context of both the physical space and the digital space as well as within the social media environment. In addition, experience is now extremely important as prices converge. And the platform recognizes that experience can be enhanced with the use of embedded apps to navigate through airports, track bags, and make payments or with chatbots to conduct voice search and interaction, provide information on the best time to make a booking, provide information relating to an irregular operation, and facilitate the rebooking process. Customers already have experience with the use of chatbots, given the proliferation of such devices as Amazon's Alexa, Apple's Siri, and Google's Home.

The platform developers looked into business entities that measure customer satisfaction. One group is the American Customer Satisfaction Index, which measures the Customer Satisfaction Index for airlines. This group has created a list of 12 categories in which airline customer satisfaction can be measured. The list includes categories such as the ease of making reservations and checking in for flights and the breadth of schedules. During the year 2018, the category receiving the highest ranking was the ease of the check-in process. The category receiving the lowest ranking was seat comfort.[5] It is interesting that according to the American Customer Satisfaction Index, in 2017, airlines scored 75 out of 100, high, but still in the "bottom 1/3 of the more than 40 sectors."

The platform operator makes the buyer aware of detailed information such as this to enable the passenger to make an informed decision. Moreover, the platform was designed to take into consideration the voice of the customer at each touch point (inspiration, shopping, booking, pre-travel, day of travel, and post-travel) and its impact on customer satisfaction. The challenge in the design process was how to measure the voice of the customer, and one method considered was the use of the Net Promoter Score concept. However, the platform pays attention to what the service provider promised and what was delivered. And the platform personalizes the offer with respect not just to the product, price, and channel, but also to context. It is the presentation of the offer on a contextual basis at each touch point that will improve the perception of the brand. This is what digital transformation means – improving customer experience with emerging technologies and apps. Some examples are electronic boarding, electronic bag tag, self-bag, and self-drop off.

Personalization goes even further, relating, for example, to passengers who want to watch movies on their own devices vs. those who are quite satisfied by watching on the screens in the seat backs. Relating to in-flight connectivity, there are passengers who want access to the Internet for browsing and those who want to communicate through emails and text messages. Then there are passengers who are more concerned about the uncertainty regarding the time at security lines, about the unreliability of information about flight status, and baggage delivery.

An embedded app in the platform recognizes passengers and knows about their needs and preferences to communicate solutions to their mobility problems in real time. The shopping offer, for example, considers not only the input from a passenger's past purchase history. Take, for instance, a passenger who always orders a vegetarian meal on intercontinental flights but forgets to mention this requirement at the time of booking the trip. The app recognizes the lack of this information and asks if this request is still valid. The offer should also consider the passenger's communications on her social network (subject to privacy concerns), the passenger's bias toward selected online reviews, as well as the passenger's postings. The app also understands that customers demand more but is able to determine if they are willing to pay more. The app also knows that some passengers want to be in control of what is happening at every touch point. They consider their time extremely valuable. Finally, the app takes into account that people's attention span is measured in seconds, not minutes, and, as such, the offer needs to reflect this characteristic of the digital environment.

In another embedded app, information is available on the exact location of a passenger after arrival at an airport. The passenger is then provided with real-time information on the location of the gate and the way to get there as well as the locations of relevant places such as airport lounges. In-flight, the passenger is informed not just on the status of the checked baggage as well as connecting flights but also solutions to problems, information such as the connection at the arriving airport will be tight, but an agent will meet all the passengers affected and escort them to the connecting gate, while informing the gate agent of the expected time of arrival at the gate.

It is evident that tectonic shifts are taking place in consumer expectations. These changes in expectations have been and continue to be set by user experiences in other business sectors where consumers interact more frequently and extensively than they do with travel service providers. While airlines can point to the complexity of buying a travel itinerary compared to buying a book, for example, the significant difference in the consumer experience in dealing with airlines and other leading retailers has been narrowed by this platform, which has minimized the gaps in the mobility chain. In fact, the intelligent engagement platform has an embedded customer experience management (CEM) component with features that have:

- access to sources of real-time data and ways to extract data;
- different types of analytics and algorithms to identify actionable insights relating to customer behavior, preferences, and expectations; and
- ways to operationalize the information to offer personalized services relating to the provision of contextual-based solutions to mobility problems.

The data could be held with any vendor (an airline, a hotel, a car-rental company) or a third party, such as a GDS, a metasearch engine, or a social network. The customer experience management component even handles the critical areas relating to onboard passenger experience:

- cabin configurations;
- onboard connectivity;
- in-flight entertainment; and
- meals and beverages.

Consequently, the platform operator is able to provide a much higher level of in-flight entertainment that is fast and is a reliable Wi-Fi system facilitating the engagement of travelers with the outside world. New systems are enabling airlines to convert their proactive in-flight systems from cost centers to revenue centers by making them an in-flight pro-engagement system. However, an embedded app on the platform arranges for specific movies to be streamed to a customer's preferred device, with a capability for the customer to continue to watch the show after deplaning on her own device or start watching before enplaning the aircraft and continue to watch the program. Charges can be based on loyalty status of the traveler within the platform, and content can be based on what has been viewed in the past. The app even places a bookmark where the passenger stopped watching the movie and can continue watching on the next flight. In addition, the app makes recommendations based on the length of the flight, the route, and customers likes and dislikes.

The question about the use of the platform is not about its ability to meet the desire of customers for experience that is flawless, seamless, and personalized in real time but to determine the willingness of travelers to pay for such experience and for the ability of travel service providers to scale the production of such an experience based on the customers' willingness to pay. Passengers traveling in first class with purchased tickets and in the highest levels of loyalty programs of the top-brand full-service global airlines are getting such an experience already. On the other hand, infrequent passengers traveling at the lowest fares, say at the recently introduced basic economy fares, cannot expect a similar experience during regular or irregular operations. However, data, technology, and apps are being leveraged in the platform to achieve improvements for all passengers in all areas, such as the time spent during the shopping process, the transparency of the price-service options purchased, the status of flights, and options available in the event of irregular operations.

The platform is particularly good at handling the pain points of travelers relating to the shopping process. The designers of the platform took into consideration the information in one report that indicated that consumers visited up to 38 websites to find the information and compare prices before making an airline reservation.[6] Another report stated that 44 percent of online shoppers searching for optional ancillary products and services, for example, the location of seats and the amount of legroom, believed that the shopping process needed to be improved. Distribution needs to become "active." For example, the mobile challenge calls for "the need for distribution systems to interact with speech and voice recognition software."[7] The design also embedded fare prediction apps. Consider Hopper, an app that helps shoppers identify the ideal time to make a booking with an airline or a hotel. Obviously the websites of suppliers, airlines or hotels, are interested in getting shoppers to buy right away. However, such apps are of interest primarily to leisure, price-sensitive shoppers. The developers of such apps obviously charge a fee, but the platform can provide connections to different apps: those, for example, that forecast seven days in advance vs. those that work in real-time. The platform can help shoppers decide not just on price but also on the destination. The platform is also attractive to the markets and shoppers of tours, which have traditionally been handled by off-line businesses. Moreover, the platform can finally develop and offer dynamically-packaged non-commoditized tours, especially those with an emphasis on experience and cultural connections, and the ability to make payments digitally seamlessly.

Support

The platform includes services provided by artificial intelligence and human-supported concierges available 24/7/365 around the world, not to push products or promotions but to offer solutions to mobility problems or requirements as they appear. Within this context, the platform enables service providers to find applications of their expertise that go beyond their core businesses.[8] In addition to connectivity, the platform also ensures the generation and communication of up-to-date information on travel and related services, not to mention the availability for user-friendly shopping and seamless integrated travel. An AI-based entity also works with the blurring of the lines between business and leisure travel ("bleisure").

Some airlines have already started to coordinate itineraries with a limited number of modes of transportation. A passenger can book a trip on Lufthansa to go from Cologne to Beijing via Frankfurt. The first leg, Cologne-Frankfurt, could be on a high-speed train that takes just under an hour. The passenger can leave the luggage at a location near the point of disembarkation and walk to the boarding gate of the connecting flight while passing through different points, such as security. However, the platform now allows connections on many different modes of transportation. The interesting part is that whereas airlines and airports may have found ways to share data relating to customers during their journeys, the platform now provides the framework for the relevant data to be shared. For example, the data could relate to more ground transportation options for the traveler. The sharing of data facilitated by the platform can enhance personal experience. Think about a passenger who is being met by a driver of a limousine service at the airport. The driver could be standing at the baggage claim area holding a plaque with the passenger's name for a long time, not knowing that the flight was delayed, that the flight landed at a different gate, or that the passenger was reaccommodated on a different flight. The use of this platform reduces the frustration for both the passenger and the driver.

Consider the next level of integration, a trip from Columbus, Ohio, in the US to Seljalandsfoss, Iceland. The website of Rome2Rio showed, on Friday August 10, 2018, numerous options, with trip journeys ranging from 14 hours and 36 minutes to 18 hours and 47 minutes and with prices ranging from US$380 to $1,429. The very first leg involved a bus trip to the Columbus Airport costing US$3–5 with hourly service. The second leg of the trip could be on a number of different airlines between Columbus and Reykjavik Keflavik Nas Airport, with five options that include a single stop at airports in the US and Canada and two options that require two stops. Flight times ranged from 7 hours and 45 minutes to 14 hours and 5 minutes. The third leg, from Reykjavik Keflavik Nas Airport to Reykjavik, involved a bus trip of about 45 minutes, costing between US$26 and $51. The final leg, from Reykjavik to Seljalandsfoss, involved another bus trip of 2 hours and 40 minutes and costs between US$35 and $50.

Such apps and websites already exist and provide detailed information for planning trips. However, the platform goes further and has embedded apps that enable the trip to be followed in real time. These embedded apps are required when a change needs to be made either because of unplanned disruptions affecting a customer or due to a change in the plans of a customer. Think about the capability of the Google Maps app. It provides users with an ability to plan routes (by walking, bicycling, driving, or taking public transportation) with real-time traffic conditions. The system uses geospatial data and algorithms to analyze traffic in real time. The application also provides maps relating to the journey. It is with the use of these types of embedded apps that the platform supports customers with after-sale services on a personalized and flexible basis to enhance customer satisfaction and experience at all touch points in the itinerary. This level of support is possible because the platform was designed to be open and scalable to offer solutions to mobility problems and not just unlinked products.

Notes

1 "Experience Is Everything: Here's How to Get It Right," A Paper by PwC, 2018, p. 10.
2 IATA, Global Passenger Survey, 2017.
3 "Experience Is Everything: Here's How to Get It Right," A Paper by PwC, 2018, p. 6.
4 Michael Dart and Robin Lewis, *Retail's Seismic Shift: How to Shift Faster, Respond Better, and Win Customer Loyalty* (New York: St. Martin's Press 2017), Chapter 8.
5 "ACSI Travel Report 2018," American Customer Satisfaction Index, April 24, 2018, p. 4.
6 "A Digital Airline Commercial Platform: Reimagine Retailing," Sabre, 2018, p. 2.
7 Henry H. Harteveldt, "The Future of Airline Distribution – 2016–2021," IATA. Executive Summary, Atmosphere Research Group, 2016.
8 Erwin Danneels and Federico Frattini, "Finding Applications for Technologies Beyond the Core Business," *MIT Sloan Management Review*, Spring 2018, Vol. 59, No. 3, pp. 73–8.

7 Staying ahead of the transformation wave

At the time of the preparation of the manuscript of this book, in mid-2018, political commentators were discussing four powerful potential forces that could change all businesses: "populism, protectionism, religious extremism, and nativism." Relating specifically to the aviation industry, two reports containing forecasts of the aviation activity, *Future of the Airline Industry 2035* and *European Aviation in 2040*, provide four potential scenarios, each in the contexts of geopolitics and data environments (an IATA report)[1] and the perspective of Europe, inward vs. outward and adaptable vs. less adaptable (a Eurocontrol report).[2] Depending on the direction of these higher-level forces on a global level, the aviation industry could be impacted in favorable or unfavorable ways. However, placing extreme scenarios on one side, this concluding chapter provides a perspective, based on a narrower viewpoint of the two sets of forces discussed in this book, as to what is on the horizon for the aviation industry and how to stay ahead of the transformation curve.

As indicated in the previous chapters, the airline business will most likely go through a step change, shifting from an evolutionary to a revolutionary mode. This supposition is based on the assumption that the airline business is facing two opposing sets of forces, the likely resolution of which will create a seismic change. The first set of three forces includes disruptive market dynamics, explosive growth in demand, and a proliferation of enabling innovative technologies. This set of forces will produce substantial growth in travel, facilitated by a broader spectrum of price-service options. At one end of the spectrum there will be even lower-cost products and services, resulting from the development of advanced aircraft, the newer generation of planning systems, and with products distributed by newer channels. At the other end of the spectrum, there will be high-end products and services enabled by the introduction of advanced aircraft, such as flying taxis and advanced supersonic jets. In addition, developments in numerous technologies will reshape the industry. Examples include blockchain and new software capabilities such as artificial intelligence that will deliver everything from personalization, to better customer experience, to more comprehensive searches. On the other hand, while there is a potential for strong growth enabled by the favorable forces described, the forces of complexity and regulations are conspiring to limit the effectiveness of change by the existing players. As such, the forces of complexity and regulations will be a massive restraint for existing players, saddled with self-defeating complexities created by the tyranny of the installed base of technologies. New players will still be constrained by regulations because regulators are normally falling behind the market to meet the needs of customers and the suppliers of travel-related services. However, new players will not be burdened with conventional complexities to the same degree as existing players.

Accordingly, these two sets of forces are requiring airlines to manage in two domains and plan on two major axes – one axis representing marketing and the other representing operations. The marketing axis has to address the needs of the market, which are growing faster than ever and in different directions simultaneously. Therefore, working on the marketing axis calls for the continuous introduction of new products and services that are offered on a personalized basis. And airlines need new marketing and retailing platforms to operate on the marketing axis. One insightful example of a marketing platform is given by Soumit Nandi in his thought leadership piece in the next chapter. Another example of a perceptive retailing platform is provided by Kieron Branagan in his thought leadership piece, also in the next chapter. Consider the marketing axis on which management needs to transform its business processes to practice demand-driven marketing. Think about the conventional process. The industry continues to operate from the perspective of providing supply and then marketing to see how to fill up the seats. However, explosive changes in marketing technologies can now create an opportunity to plan on demand-driven platforms, a move from a product-centric world to a mobility-centric world for both the business-to-consumer (B2C) and business-to-business (B2B) segments. This transformation is needed in the emerging world, where the industrial sectors are moving toward rent-reducing forms of travel in the MaaS framework, encompassing new air and ground vehicles. Chuck Evans provides an excellent description of the upcoming advanced air vehicles, for example, eVTOLs, in his thought leadership piece in the next chapter. Getting some insights from a different industry, Ian Czaja, in his thought leadership piece in the next chapter, provides a parallel between the airline industry and the insurance industry, and how to move from operational excellence to strategic leadership.

Consider now the operations axis, where the battle is to become the most efficient and the most flexible low-cost producer and where management wants to achieve operational excellence. Up until now, the industry has operated with long lead time planning horizons and fixed capacity and low flexibility. However, the volatile changes discussed in this book call for a more demand-driven capacity planning that is flexible and efficient. This planning environment requires much shorter planning horizons and a much better coordination of resources, probably much more decentralized in terms of both existing and new providers. Dietmar Kirchner, in his thought leadership piece in the next chapter, provides value-adding insights in how the passenger airline sector can benefit from the business practices of the cargo airline sector. Consider also the thought leadership piece by Bryan Terry, in the next chapter, on capacity utilization and asset maximization by using data to make operational and efficiency gains. He provides an excellent example of the Formula 1 concept to develop smart operations by combining hardware and software to bridge the "physical-to-digital" divide.

Planning strategically in both domains requires management to bond the commercial and operational functions and numerous sub-functions within each of the two domains. Such a bonding process requires each subgroup to work with one data set where the data is corroborated, cleansed, integrated, and continuously updated in real time. On the commercial side are at least five major sub-functions: network/fleet/schedule planning, pricing and revenue management, sales and distribution, customer experience, and loyalty. On the operations side are at least three major functions: flight operations, ground operations, and maintenance, repair, and overhaul. The object is to make the airline digital, with a strong bond in the two domains. The bonded process will enable management to adapt to the extremely challenging business environment and to develop innovative solutions that produce mutual value for customers and the airline's employees and shareholders. Take, for example, Ben Boehm's concept, in his thought leadership piece in the next chapter, of working strategically with partnering MRO service providers to reduce, if not eliminate, non-value drains on resources.

The irony is that the aviation business sectors – airlines, airports, and aircraft manufacturers – already have vast quantities of data that, if placed in effective data environments, can be used much more effectively to optimize internal operations. In fact, the data can even be monetized.[3] Moreover, it is the creation of internal data platforms that will break down the internal silo systems, enabling marketing to bond with operations to focus on (1) customer and employee experiences and their expectations and (2) competitors, existing and potential – airlines as well as new travel marketers. And the internal data platforms will enable management to move away from the dependency on the legacy systems, and from the fixation on conventional streams of ancillary revenue and focus beyond the core products to the broader concept of mobility-as-a-service (MaaS). Examples of prevailing revenue streams include baggage fees, reservation change fees for airlines, and airport parking and concessionaire-related fees for airports. However, there are much higher-value opportunities for new streams of ancillary revenue from the development of MaaS for airlines and creating destination facilities by airports. But these new revenue streams require the availability of a single view of each customer to provide offers that take into consideration the total needs and preferences of each customer and the value of each customer to the airline, current value as well as lifetime value. Similar thinking applies for airports in considering the needs of airline passengers as well as residents of the neighboring communities.

Planning along these two axes, marketing and operations, and managing successfully in the two domains, marketing innovation and operational excellence, brings into focus the major challenge, which is, in turn, also an opportunity. This challenge/opportunity is to provide mobility-as-a-service to meet the end-to-end journey needs of travelers while providing consistent customer service and seamless experience. This challenge/opportunity calls for the need to switch from flight/product/operations-centricity to customer/solutions/experience-centricity and to extend the "core boundaries" of the business by either developing or working on intelligent engagement platforms. Such platforms could be developed by entrepreneurial-minded but independent groups within pioneering airlines, as discussed in a scenario in the previous chapter. Or they could be developed by new travel marketers, technology businesses that provide relevant customer experience in travel shopping, arranging, guiding, and booking through mobile devices today, and wearable clothing as well as digital assistants tomorrow. Keep in mind that the core competencies of these businesses lie in the areas of data, analytics, customer relationship management, and the provision of "software-as-a-service." Artificial intelligence will play an important role to (1) curate a personalized product with the capability to make meaningful and relevant predictions and recommendations, (2) deliver it with consistent and seamless experience, and (3) provide support at every point throughout the end-to-end trip. Dietmar Kirchner provides excellent insights into what passenger airlines can learn from the experience of cargo carriers and how the concept of "personal logistics" can support the concept of "mobility-as-a-service."

Consider the last point in light of the mission of some technology companies to "empower people to achieve more." Some pioneering technology businesses could become the new travel marketers and provide services to meet the stated and the *unstated* needs of travelers to make their lives easier. Airlines that do not take seriously the potential market entry of new travel marketers might think about the advice of Bill Gates, the principal founder of Microsoft: "We always overestimate the change that will occur in the next two years and under estimate the change that will occur in the next ten. Don't let yourself be lulled into inaction." What will be the behaviors, the attitudes, and the expectations in the next ten years of the current generation of millennials? Since life expectancy continues to increase, what will be the expectations of the older generations – the Baby Boomers (born between 1946 and 1964) or even the Silent Generation (born between 1925 and 1945)?[4] Even more important is the question about the expectations of different generations of consumers in emerging markets, especially in Asia.

However, the MaaS challenge/opportunity brings into focus two additional challenges/opportunities: (1) faster response time and (2) de-complexing the business. The first challenge/opportunity – faster response time – calls for the capability to dynamically match supply and demand. This requirement, in turn, calls for the need to develop a good understanding of how the digital environment is different from the traditional business environment. In the digital environment, the speed of change is much higher, necessitating a much faster response time. The uncertainty in the business landscape is also much higher, requiring not only a willingness to experiment and iterate but, more important, requiring the need to scale the business. The challenge and the opportunity are to focus much more on business transformation than on developing digital strategies.

Consider this challenge/opportunity relating to the digital environment. While managements do understand different aspects of the digital environment, the real challenge is to focus much more on business transformation than on developing digital strategies. The value of digital technologies is not simply to digitize some functions, namely convert information from an analog form into a digital form without changing the content – in other words, simply automating some conventional paper-based and labor-intensive processes. The value is in digit*al*ization that goes further and refers to the use of digital technologies (and the digitized data) to change how the business is conducted. Data will still be required – in fact, in larger quantities – to capitalize on such technologies as artificial intelligence and augmented reality. For example, the use of 3-D environments requires much more data. However, even if more data is available, there are questions relating to data interpretation, data location, data storage, and the costs related to big data and its use.

In the digital environment, successful businesses started with a vision on what the business strategy should be. Next came the digital transformation strategy, followed by the workforce strategy, and followed, in turn, by the organization structure strategy. Moreover, the successful businesses made their process sequence circular and continuous, as opposed to top down. In addition, the process was made proactive rather than reactive. Moreover, the engagement of the workforce was particularly necessary, as it is not just about the use of technology to improve operations: it is also about the need to change processes to get the most out of technology. These businesses saw great value in conducting a collaborative and concerted strategy design involving technology, business goals, and workforce. From their experience, employees could not be simply the end users of the technologies selected and implemented. Digital transformation needed to be not just customer-led but also employee-supported. There was a question, for example, as to how artificial intelligence would support the workforce in changing the processes – in the case of airlines, in the areas of operations control centers and customer-contact centers, for instance. For airlines, the technology-enabled support will be particularly important in the operations control center area, where there are normally many different events and critical data coming from different sources. The machine-learning process will depend on the degree of structure in each event. Therefore, technology can augment and support employees.

As for the organizational structure, there is a need to clarify the roles of the chief information officer, the chief technology officer, the chief digital officer, and the chief customer officer. The chief digital officer is responsible for the design and strategic digitalization of business strategies. The chief information and the chief technology officers deal mostly within the technology space – emerging technologies, infrastructure, and data quality and integrity. The chief digital officer is more of an integrator of business strategies and their implementation across the enterprise, keeping in mind organizational challenges as well as opportunities. The critical success factor is to try to get the business executives to be asking the right question in the first place before trying to find the best solution. For example, the question is not about how to optimize the ten-year fleet plan, but does the airline even need to plan ten years ahead in the emerging business environment? Next, the question is not about the optimal annual schedule, but whether the airline should even produce a schedule one year in advance, even with the knowledge that it can be changed incrementally to adapt to the needs of seasonality. Although digital transformation calls for the use of new technologies, more importantly, it calls for changes in business processes. As such, it is the chief digital officer who manages the changes in the processes. On the other hand, it is the chief customer officer who is the champion of the customer by breaking down the internal organizational silos to develop customer centricity, particularly important in the digital era for developing and managing physical and digital products and services.

The second challenge/opportunity is to de-complex the airline business to navigate strategically within two domains, operational excellence and marketing innovation, to manage the expected growth and change in the traffic mix by using technology intelligently and, even more importantly, without adding further complexity. State-of-the-art technologies can play a major role in reducing the existing level of complexity, not increasing it, to meet the changing needs of customers and the business. The reduction in complexities can be used to exploit potential opportunities in two areas: (1) reducing prices to "drive" demand and (2) working on solution-centric platforms to deliver greater value to customers by providing solutions to travelers' total mobility requirements. These two areas are related, but they are not the same. As Warren Buffett, a business leader and investment authority, said, "Price is what you pay, value is what you get."

Consider the opportunity side of the challenge: reducing complexity to achieve massive reductions in costs, and, in turn, massive reductions in prices. This is an area most likely to be exploited by some pioneering low-cost carriers, given not only their lack of legacy systems and less fragmented data (as well as nonconventional mindsets) but also their ability to move fast, take more risks, and undertake fail-fast initiatives. The fundamental building block for a massive reduction in costs is the development of powerful internal data platforms that will enable management to transform internal operations, both on the commercial side as well as on the operations side. This capability will help management to overcome the challenge of planning with "old systems and new systems held together with duct tape." For example, the use of an internal data platform, coupled with new technologies, will enable management to find alternative ways of performing some tasks rather than continuing the use of older-generation systems, such as the older-generation passenger services systems (PSSs). Furthermore, emerging technologies will expand the capability of the internal data platforms. For example, the use of artificial intelligence will facilitate not only the integration of the data contained in multiple sets of systems but also its communication among different parties, and to offer customers relevant options – in other words, making the internal systems more intelligent.

With much lower costs, a new breed of airlines will be able to "drive" demand. Low-cost carriers as diverse as Norwegian and WOW Air are already driving demand in long-haul markets. Both are expanding their networks. WOW Air, based in Reykjavik, now offers service to San Francisco to the west and Delhi, to the east. To strengthen itself, WOW agreed to be merged with Icelandair in November 2018. This point is clearly not overlooked by full-service airlines, given the recently reported interest by the International Airlines Group and the Lufthansa Group to take equity in Norwegian. Consider also the decision by Scoot (a division of the Singapore Airlines' Group) to expand its services to points in Europe, now serving

Athens and Berlin. Jetstar, the low-cost division of Qantas, may not be far behind in its decision to serve Europe from its hubs in Asia. The concept of driving demand through lower prices is reasonable given that there are still segments of consumers who (1) do not travel, (2) could travel more if there was a significant reduction in prices, and (3) can afford to pay more but do not perceive the additional value. The low-cost carriers will expand in long-haul markets to accommodate growth in leisure travel, and vice versa. According to one estimate, while air travel is doubling every 15 years, 80 percent of the passengers, particularly in long-haul markets, are leisure travelers.[5] The new generation of low-cost airlines will start with lower prices but then add further value in such areas as simplicity and convenience, resulting from the development of a stronger bond between marketing and operations, as discussed in Chapter 3. Would the airlines pricing to drive demand be limited only to the low-cost sector? Not necessarily. What if a full-service airline group (such as IAG or Lufthansa) decides to separate its marketing function from its operations function? What if the airline's separated marketing group then puts out a request for proposal from different operational groups to bid on the services proposed by the marketing group, in competition with, in some cases, its internal operational groups or other bidders in the marketplace, for example, within the alliance?

In some ways, the aviation industry has always been at the forefront of the deployment of technology – advances in aircraft design on the technical side and the development of revenue management systems on the commercial side. On the other hand, when it comes to digital transformations, the movement in the aviation industry is in an early stage. Specifically, the management of technological innovation is in an early stage in both domains, marketing innovation and operational excellence. Such a situation exists because the effective implementation of emerging technologies requires changes in both systems and processes as well as the workforce. The sequential or the linear approach will not work. The workforce strategy needs to go hand-in-hand with the business strategy, which in turn needs to go hand-in-hand with the technology strategy.

Most airlines continue to invest in non-scalable business models. What is needed is a step change in investments to go from the analog to the digital framework to produce and offer, not just MaaS, but user-friendly MaaS. Consider this analogy: mainframe computers were business-transformative devices but required experts to operate them. Then the personal computer was developed based on the basic operating system. This device was more user friendly but still required some expertise in its use. Next came the development of Windows, an amazingly powerful capability to enhance user friendliness by placing a layer above the various user tools. Almost everyone could operate these devices. Finally, the mobile platform appeared, supporting everyone without requiring any computing capabilities. In the airline business, there were the linearly operated airline networks, operating with the legacy systems and within the bilateral framework that enabled travel for a small segment of the population. Then airlines developed hub-and-spoke systems, revenue management systems, strategic alliances, a wide variety of distribution channels, electronic tickets, and more, that expanded the marketplace for travel. Now, intelligent engagement platforms are about to appear that will enable user-friendly MaaS to expand travel to incredible levels. It is possible that airline managements are ready to bring about a step change in their mindsets to ride the digitalization wave, not just to manage in the ambiguous and unpredictable era but to create a new future.

Notes

1 "Future of the Airline Industry 2035," IATA, Geneva, Switzerland, 2017.
2 "European Aviation in 2040: Challenges of Growth," Eurocontrol, 2018, Edition 2.
3 Barbara H. Wixom and Jeanne W. Ross, "How to Monetize Your Data," *MIT Sloan Management Review*, Spring 2017, Vol. 58, No. 3, pp. 10–13; James E. Short and Steve Todd, "What's Your Data Worth?" *MIT Sloan Management Review*, Spring 2017, Vol. 58, No. 3, pp. 17–19.
4 A recent report by *Euromonitor International* provides some insightful information on how global consumers are challenging ageing. "Old Is the New Young: How Global Consumers Are Challenging Ageing," *Euromonitor International*, 2017.
5 Helen Massy-Beresford and Adrian Schofield, "In For the Long Haul," *AviationWeek & Space Technology*, August 20–September 2, 2018, p. 60.

8 Thought leadership pieces

Value added service/solutions partners for airlines

Ben Boehm

Executive Vice President, Business & Market Strategy
Wencor Group

Raisa Ferdinand

Marketing Manager
Wencor Group

The commercial air transport market has consistently ebbed and flowed between boom and bust. A renewed focus on the spread between revenue per available seat mile (RASM) and cost per available seat mile (CASM) has yielded positive net returns for the past several years. Network carriers and value airlines (a.k.a. low-cost carriers (LCCs)) have been in a market-share battle for years. Network carriers try to increase their yield per seat while value airlines add new routes and expand their revenue seat miles. No matter the strategy implemented, there is an increase in operating cost that airlines continue to ignore – the administrative, management, and logistics costs associated with widespread "bargain hunting" for materiel in support of flight operations.[1]

In today's aviation industry, airlines are working overtime to save as much money as possible through their procurement processes. Every part that is manufactured or supplied to the maintenance operations goes through a rigorous multi-vendor bidding war to try to save as many cents on the dollar as possible. From a historical viewpoint, this has been the main way of conducting business but is not the most efficient. Airlines should take a closer look at maintenance materiel service and solutions companies that offer greater savings through integrated supply chain management.

Maintenance materiel service and solution companies specialize in vendor management, aftermarket services, logistics, and much more. These are all critical functions needed for aircraft operations but do not need to all be handled by the airline. With almost 60 percent of airlines' cost already going to suppliers, it is a known fact that airline procurement teams do not operate at optimum levels[2]. Many airlines lack the skill set of category management and do not approach their buying process with a high-level strategy.[3]

Rather than the airlines attempting to hold inventory over numerous years as a result of high volume purchasing (chasing discounts); these value added service companies offer a more efficient, streamlined, JIT (just in time) approach that allows the airline to focus and excel at their core competency of providing transportation services. This in turn will enhance the airlines' customer experience and overall revenue intake.

The examples illustrated in Figures 8.1 and 8.2 show a comparison between the current "cherry picking" approach that airlines use (incurring excessive procurement costs and the need for warehousing and logistics teams) in an effort to buy quantities of airplane parts from multiple vendors after exhaustive RFPs – to in the end save a few cents on each part from different vendors – compared against a streamlined approach using an aftermarket service and supply integrator. It is important to note that: (1) there is rarely a single integrator that can serve the entire airline's needs, but rather a likely hood that 2–4 integrators would be needed to properly serve the various specialized materiel categories necessary to operate an airline, and (2) the business case for net cost reduction lies not just in the use of the integrator but in the optimization of the airline's infrastructure and staffing commensurate with the tasks being taken on by the aftermarket service and supply integrator.

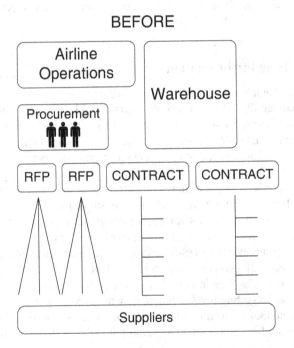

BEFORE

Figure 8.1 As Is: Typical Airline Procurement Structure and Supplier Relationship Map

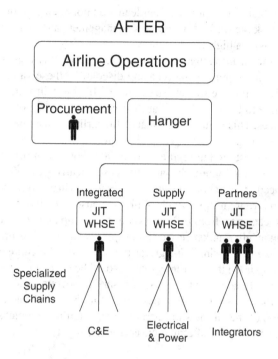

Figure 8.2 Future State: Integrated Maintenance Service Partners Streamline Material Flow to Airline Operations

Supply chain agility in aviation

Changes in the commercial air transport marketplace are demanding a higher level of supply chain agility. The best way for airlines and heavy maintenance companies to succeed is to grow and build global partnerships with reliable value added maintenance materiel service companies. These value added companies would be incentivized to find annual operating efficiency improvements and would focus on materiel services spread across the entire aircraft operations support value chain. By working directly with the airline's procurement teams, both parties can share synergies and create mutually beneficial relationships. Key logistics partners can help manage, store, and move spare parts through networks, monitor inventory, and establish operations in new regions to meet increased customer demand.[4]

A focus group survey of key US-based aerospace and defense firms showed that according to nearly 30 percent of survey respondents, the top challenge aerospace and defense companies face in optimizing their MRO supply chains is managing the complexities of getting parts to where they need to be on time.[5]

Airlines could look to the modern-day restaurant industry to see how partnering with reliable suppliers could alleviate some non-value added resource drains on the company. See Figures 8.3 and 8.4. In Figure 8.3, the restaurant is attempting to handle the supply chain and procurement for all operations themselves, thus spending valuable time, money, and effort on non-customer-facing, non-revenue activities including supplier relationships and quantity and quality control. In Figure 8.4, the restaurant is using a restaurant supply company (i.e., value added service company) to manage the sourcing of inputs. This now allows the restaurant to focus on its core competencies of providing quality food and top-notch customer service. This eliminates the need for the restauranteur to be chef, maître de, buyer, and logistics coordinator and allows the restaurant to see the supply company as a partner and work together to do what both parties do best, thus creating a mutually beneficial partnership.

In commercial aviation, value added service companies can work hand in hand to create innovative programs to improve service levels, custom part manufacturing, and delivery times and reduce staffing and warehouse requirements. This allows the airline to focus on customer-centric issues that ultimately drive their revenue and profit growth.

Restaurant Supply Chain

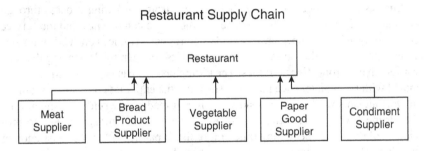

Figure 8.3 Restaurant Supply Chain – Without a Value Added Supply/Service Company

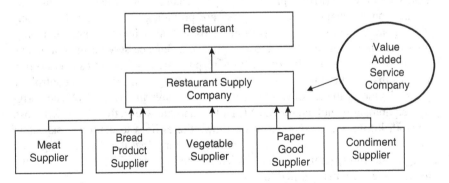

Figure 8.4 Simplified Restaurant Supply Chain – With a Value Added Supply/Service Company

The value added service model

Kitting and inventory management solutions are key examples of the benefit of value added service integrators for airlines. Just as the restaurant example shows a simplified and integrated logistic chain, the aviation industry can achieve similar efficiencies through the use of maintenance kits. Kits significantly reduce the number of touch points for parts while simultaneously increasing productivity. Airlines are losing money and time by dealing with multiple buyers that are handling numerous contracts, creating a web of inefficiencies and disorganization.

Time and efficiency are the main benefits derived from the kitting process. In the practical day to day of aircraft maintenance, technicians have to input requests for 20 parts and wait at a dispensing desk or for a trolley to come by and bring the parts needed to complete a maintenance task. The time and money that is wasted during this process is enormous and can be reduced tremendously with the use of a single kit. Additionally, airlines are stocking these parts in huge warehouses that could be better used for more profitable operations that lead directly to their bottom line.

Airlines and service companies both benefit from the kitting process through economies of scale. The airline focuses on their core competency and the service company provides a superior, consolidated product. Airlines can work with services companies to design these kits for repeat tasks, thereby decreasing the time wasted on nonproductive activities. The kitting process can be advanced and automated with the maintenance planning such that the entire kit could be available at the technician's work station beside the aircraft ready for service. By integrating the airline's weekly operational scheduling the service company begins to provide a solution, thus becoming much more like a partner rather than just another supplier. The airline begins to receive planned deliveries and sees a significant decrease in overall stock holding cost.

Airlines also have a gaping hole in the management of their third-party maintenance and repair (MRO) providers' supply chains. Since MROs are primarily focused on the maintenance work they are providing (labor efficiency), many airlines are being overcharged with markups and other fees for materiel supply, approval, and logistics. With the use of a maintenance service integrator that knows the tasks the third-party MRO is responsible for, airlines can set up prefab kits that can be shipped to the third-party MRO's. The airline can control the parts – including the use of surplus, parts manufacturer approval (PMA), and original equipment manufacturer (OEM) parts – and know exactly what it will cost. Overall, kitting for outsourced work allows the airlines to control costs rather than be subject to subcontractor markups, knowing that they are dealing with integrators who specialize in that particular category(ies) of parts needed for the maintenance task being kitted for.

See the value of kitting in Figure 8.5.

Without Kits	With Kits
Complex Procurement	Simplified Logistic Streams From Warehouse to Shop Floor
More Warehouse/ Process	Fewer Warehouse Tracking Storage Interfaces
Expensive Mechanic	Fewer Piece Parts for the Airline to Manage
Finding/ Waiting for Parts	Mechanic Time Focused on Hands on Repairs vs Chasing Parts
Possibly Cheaper Individual Piece Parts	

Figure 8.5 Kitting Value Flow

Reduction in accounting and paperwork, receiving/inspection expenses, and the elimination of the use of multiple purchase orders ultimately contributes directly to lower CASM, leading to more revenue for airlines.[6] With these management solutions, there is a reduction in the number of transactions and suppliers needed, which ultimately reduces processing costs and increases order accuracy. Ultimately, kits improve inventory management, reduce procurement steps and improve operational efficiency. By leaving the integration of kit parts to a company that has in-depth knowledge of the product category and is closer to the source of supply, airlines gain more time and resources to handle their core business.

Notes

1 Stalnaker, T., Usman, K., Taylor, A., and Alport, G. (2018). "Airline Economic Analysis," Oliver Wyman, 1(1). Retrieved from https://www.oliverwyman.com/content/dam/oliver-wyman/v2/publications/2018/January/Airline_Economic_Analysis_AEA_2017-18_web_FF.pdf.
2 Ditchter, A., Juul Sorensen, A., and Saxon, S. (2017, April). "Buying and Flying: Next-Generation Airline Procurement," Retrieved from https://www.mckinsey.com/industries/travel-transport-and-logistics/our-insights/buying-and-flying-next-generation-airline-procurement.
3 Elliott, J. (2018, July 4). "Commercial Aviation Aftermarket Heats Up – Skies Mag," Retrieved from http://www.skiesmag.com/news/commercial-aviation-aftermarket-heats-up/.
4 Grokhovskaya, V. (2018, February 23). "5 MRO Supply Chain Challenges Aviation Companies Need To Prepare For – The Network Effect," Retrieved from https://supplychainbeyond.com/5-mro-supply-chain-challenges-in-aviation/.
5 Insight on Market Dynamics. (2015). "Solutions to MRO Supply Chain Challenges [Inforgraphics]," Retrieved from http://aviationweek.com/datasheet/solutions-mro-supply-chain-challenges.
6 Bajaj, S. (2009, October 6). "Procurement Process in Aviation Industry | SAP Blogs [Web log post]," Retrieved from https://blogs.sap.com/2009/10/06/procurement-process-in-aviation-industry/.

Transforming of the airline business model through retailing and data

Kieron Branagan

CEO
OpenJaw Technologies

Historically, airlines view themselves as sellers of seats. This created a selling model focused around the seat and its associated pricing. The accepted frame of reference was: "I have this product – a seat on a flight, so how do I sell as much of this product as possible through a set of distribution channels, and how do I maximize my revenue using dynamic pricing of inventory?"

This "seat selling" approach led to price-driven competition, commoditizing the airline's offering and making it indistinguishable from the competition. Where airline seats are a commoditized product, the opportunity for revenue growth is limited. However, new revenue streams are needed for all airlines, as the rate of passenger growth plateaus and fares remain relatively static.

Outside of the airline industry, retailers across the globe have developed sophisticated retailing techniques to better serve their customers. These retailers don't see themselves as a provider of products but as a store designed to fulfill customer needs. Retailers guide shoppers through their stores (online and off-line) in a way that encourage them to add products and services to their real or virtual shopping carts. The future for airlines needs to be based on thinking about what they can sell beyond the seat.

Today's airlines look for inspiration outside of the airline industry and wish to emulate the success of online and off-line retailers such as Starbucks, Amazon, ASOS, eBay, Alibaba, JD.com and Netflix. While many airlines are now trying to sell new types of offerings to add value to their customers, many are selling these with a traditional airline mindset. Instead, airlines need to behave like retailers. By adopting a "retailing" mindset, airlines can flip their thinking about their customer on its head: "I have this set of customers, so how do fulfill the customer's travel requirements across the full customer journey?"

Retailing as the customer imperative for airlines

The primary need of an airline customer is organizing a trip, not buying a flight, and armed with this understanding, an airline can begin to sell the complete range of products and services relating to a trip.

Simply put, retailing is about providing the right product and service to the traveler, delivered through the right channel and at the right time, in a way that is visually appealing and easy to understand. The successful airline of the future will depend to a large extent on how quickly it can transform itself into a retailer dedicated to fulfilling all of a customer's needs.

The airline direct channel, whether it's a browser-based website, a mobile site, or an app, is the perfect storefront to sell the full itinerary from the air seat and air ancillaries to hotel booking, car rental, lounge, destination attractions, insurance, and airport transfers. The airline retains 100 percent control of the customer, books all of the revenue, and gets higher profit margins. In addition, the airline gets to own all of the customer behavioral and transactional data. Using this data gives the airline a competitive edge by being able to offer a more personalized, tailored experience for the total customer experience.

The framework of opportunity for airline retailers: the new customer journey

All airlines are facing a fundamental change in their relationship with customers. The rise of digital and, in particular, social media has meant that customers are increasingly connected not only with the business but with other customers, friends, and like-minded communities. Airline customers are just as likely to connect with and be guided by other customers as they are to be influenced directly by an airline. All you need to do to understand this is to look at the success of Tripadvisor or the exponential growth of the so-called sharing economy travel brands like Airbnb.

In this new world order, customers can shape brands, markets, and reputations. And for travel businesses to grow and to prosper, there needs to be a fundamental rethink of how the business interacts with potential customers and actual customers throughout the various stages of the customer purchase funnel.

What does the "new customer journey" look like?

There's a lot of planning that goes into traveling. And travelers are using devices for help right across the "new customer journey." Before making any purchase, travelers are taking time to get inspired, to dream, and to research all the possibilities. All the options are considered first before looking around ("shopping"). Once the dream destination has been explored, the research has been done, and it's only then that customer is ready to book.

Airline marketers usually think that getting the booking is the total opportunity when it comes to serving passenger needs. However, this is where the "airline as a retailer mindset" and the understand of the new customer journey enables airlines to deliver useful information to build your brand and offer great products and services.

Extending the new customer journey

Despite the opportunity of the new customer journey, the airline industry continues to struggle with the concept and practice of retailing. To deliver on a retail strategy, airlines must follow the lead of successful retailers by moving beyond thinking of a customer as a transaction and a seat. The goal should be to act like those retailers which have a laser-like focus on increasing their customers' "share of wallet."

Figure 8.6 A Customer Journey Map

Source: OpenJaw Technologies

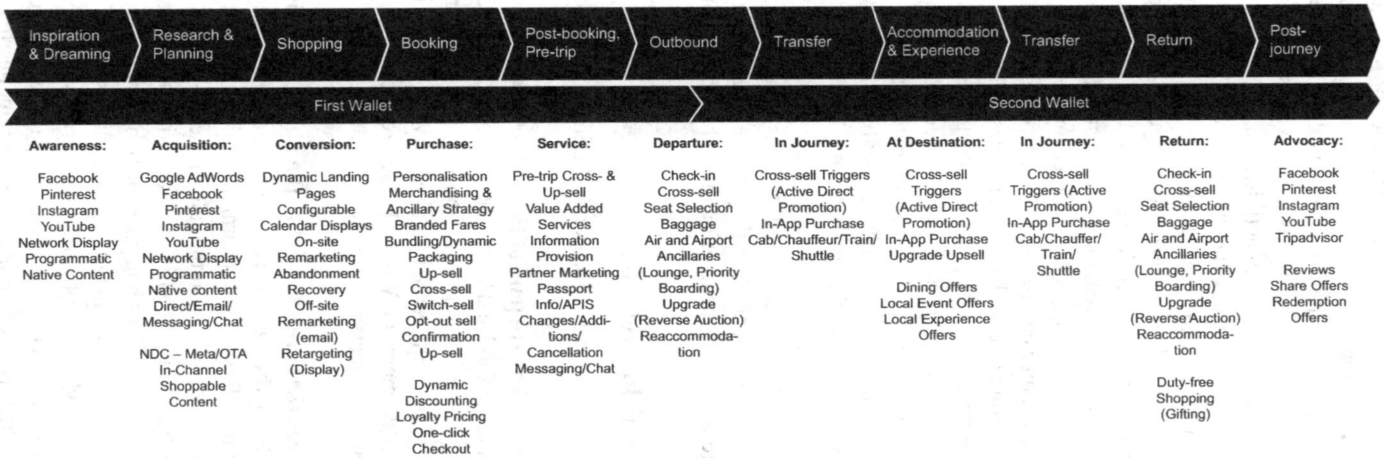

First Wallet: Inspiration & Dreaming | Research & Planning | Shopping | Booking | Post-booking, Pre-trip | Outbound

Second Wallet: Transfer | Accommodation & Experience | Transfer | Return | Post-journey

Awareness:
Facebook
Pinterest
Instagram
YouTube
Network Display
Programmatic
Native Content

Acquisition:
Google AdWords
Facebook
Pinterest
Instagram
YouTube
Network Display
Programmatic
Native content
Direct/Email/
Messaging/Chat
NDC – Meta/OTA
In-Channel
Shoppable
Content

Conversion:
Dynamic Landing
Pages
Configurable
Calendar Displays
On-site
Remarketing
Abandonment
Recovery
Off-site
Remarketing
(email)
Retargeting
(Display)

Purchase:
Personalisation
Merchandising &
Ancillary Strategy
Branded Fares
Bundling/Dynamic
Packaging
Up-sell
Cross-sell
Switch-sell
Opt-out sell
Confirmation
Up-sell

Dynamic
Discounting
Loyalty Pricing
One-click
Checkout

Service:
Pre-trip Cross- &
Up-sell
Value Added
Services
Information
Provision
Partner Marketing
Passport
Info/APIS
Changes/Addi-
tions/
Cancellation
Messaging/Chat

Departure:
Check-in
Cross-sell
Seat Selection
Baggage
Air and Airport
Ancillaries
(Lounge, Priority
Boarding)
Upgrade
(Reverse Auction)
Reaccommoda-
tion

In Journey:
Cross-sell Triggers
(Active Direct
Promotion)
In-App Purchase
Cab/Chauffeur/Train/
Shuttle

At Destination:
Cross-sell
Triggers
(Active Direct
Promotion)
In-App Purchase
Upgrade Upsell

Dining Offers
Local Event Offers
Local Experience
Offers

In Journey:
Cross-sell
Triggers (Active
Promotion)
In-App Purchase
Cab/Chauffeur/
Train/
Shuttle

Return:
Check-in
Cross-sell
Seat Selection
Baggage
Air and Airport
Ancillaries
(Lounge, Priority
Boarding)
Upgrade
(Reverse Auction)
Reaccommoda-
tion

Duty-free
Shopping
(Gifting)

Advocacy:
Facebook
Pinterest
Instagram
YouTube
Tripadvisor
Reviews
Share Offers
Redemption
Offers

Figure 8.7 A Detailed Customer Journey Map

Source: OpenJaw Technologies

This means airlines have to understand and provide for the end-to-end needs of the travel customer from the time they leave their home and the products they need to get to the airport, through the products that they need to transition smoothly through the airport and the products that travelers need at their destination, e.g., transfers, hotels, and destination activities.

Good retailers stock the shelf the way they want to, with their own products or with products that are curated to differentiate them from the competitors. Likewise, airline retailers can apply their unique knowledge of customer preferences, behavior, and purchase history to select the right product – for example, a boutique hotel, a specific car hire, or a great bundle of destination experiences – and "nudge" the customer right across the new customer journey.

The full scale of the customer can be visualized through a "customer journey map" that creates a true picture of travelers' experiences, behaviors and even preferences. The customer journey map helps you to visualize the journey of each type of customer, so airlines can create powerful tailored retail-driven interactions to both create value and capture a bigger share of the customer's wallet.

Applying a customer journey map and seeing through the lens of retailing means that you can make a distinction called the "first" and "second" wallet. With first wallet mindset, the customer is focused on getting the best deal – the best bang-for-their-buck. Once that task has been done, the customer's mindset changes: they focus on the quality of experience that they are getting in-journey and at the destination, and they are willing to spend more on higher-margin products.

The nuts and bolts of airline retailing

Airlines can think in terms of four categories of retailing opportunities:

1   **Products and services that are part of the airline's suite of offerings:** This includes onboard sales of food and beverages, baggage, assigned seats or seat upgrades (including extra legroom seats on exit rows), amenities, priority check-in, sporting equipment, early boarding privileges, in-flight entertainment, onboard entertainment, or Wi-Fi. These are often called "a la carte" products, as they can be selected like a menu by the customer to add to their air travel experience.
2   **Product and services that are external to the airline, but directly related to the travel needs of the customers:** hotel and resort accommodations, car rentals, ground transfers, travel insurance, and destination activities: the airline earns a commission based on the sale of these products.
3   **Fare packaging or bundling:** bundling the fare with one of the ancillary revenue products or services, such as baggage, early boarding, or extra legroom.
4   **Dynamic packaging:** the combination of the airline's flight inventory with hotel accommodation, which can then be combined with ground transfers, car hire, and destination activities, creating one packaged price. These packages are created "on the fly" depending on the origin, destination, and dates searched.

The challenge of retailing in an airline

Becoming a "retailer with wings" means that airlines need to become not just seat sellers but real merchandisers – good at the art and science of merchandising ancillary products. However, aspiring to be a retailer creates new and complex challenges for all types of airlines:

Customer expectations

The first challenge facing airlines to become better retailers is that customer expectations are formed outside of the world of airlines. Great brands outside of travel are setting the agenda. Airline customers expect immediacy from airlines because the conventions of retailing are formed outside of the world of travel. Airlines need to embed the conventions of retail shopping and booking to be closer to the incredible experiences of brands such as Starbucks, Amazon, ASOS, eBay, Alibaba, JD.com, Netflix, Facebook, WhatsApp and WeChat.

The retailing mindset

It is a challenge for airlines to think about merchandising the way a retailer would – in other words, understanding who the airlines' customers are and delivering highly personalized product and content to them. Each customer has a unique set of expectations for their interactions with an airline. Customers want better airline retailing experiences that can inspire them as they shop and book their trips – but most of all, they desire to be recognized as people, not passenger name records (PNR). And it is this level of personalization that is at the heart of the challenge of retailing.

Technology platforms

The third challenge confronting airlines is that access to ancillary products is made difficult due to different technology platforms operated by various providers. Hotel and resort room inventory are on property management systems, and many different systems, to boot. Golf courses have their own booking systems. The critical challenge for any airline is this: how to integrate retail ancillary products across all channels so that their customers can book and pay based on real-live confirmed inventory – whether this is hotel rooms, car hire, meals, or golf tee times. The ideal, of course, would be a single integrated platform approach that provides a seamless user experience for customers across their entire online journey.

Data silos

Traditionally, airlines have held customer data across multiple siloed databases and systems. This creates a real headache using all the transaction data already collected to recommend products or services for future trips. In a retailer, the people responsible for bringing in revenue, such as buyers, have access to a supply of real-time sales data. All the stock keeping units (SKU) have unique codes assigned to each item of merchandise and are tracked to an incredible level of detail. Digital retailers such as Amazon and Netflix have been renowned for their successful recommendation algorithms. These sorts of tools are very rarely available to airlines.

Retailers need data-driven insights

Great retailers know who their customers are – and also who they are not. A flat pack self-assembly furniture retailer will not waste time courting customers who can afford to buy ready-built furniture. Similarly, an airline who embraces retailing acquires, converts, and engages with its customer segments and then aims to develop a stronger relationship with its customers. Integrating data from all sources enables retailers to develop greater customer insight and personalize customer recommendations.

Airlines create huge quantities of data from different sources and different customer actions, including reservations, fares, itineraries, accommodations, PNRs, pricing, yields, cancelations, customer feedback, social media comments, and complaints. Your customer leaves a trail of data from multiple channels and devices right through the customer journey: during research, planning, price search, comparison, booking, in journey, and after their journey.

All of this data has the power to reshape an airline's customer proposition and transform your business. But this tsunami of data creates a real challenge to deliver on the promise of retailing. It is very difficult to identify market trends, understand patterns and preferences, create personalized offers, and foresee opportunities to create loyalty, increase margin, and grow revenue without insight.

And not just any insights. Airlines need three different type of insights created by three different perspectives on analytics:

- Descriptive analytics: Used to segment your customers based on past behaviors, providing insights on previous customer actions and activities, usually only simple metrics such as averages, totals, etc.
- Predictive analytics: Fewer organizations use this approach, mainly because it is more difficult, or large histories of good quality data are not available. With predictive analytics, the goal is usually to target individual customers based on predictions of their future behavior – for example, the propensity of your passenger to buy a basket of airline retailing products.
- Prescriptive analytics: Only a small number of very sophisticated airlines have deployed these solutions. In this scenario, very large quantities of high-quality data are required, along with powerful computing resources and cognitive/machine-learning expertise. The power of prescriptive analytics is that the ideal action for each passenger can be automatically taken. In this way, prescriptive analytics can either replace or augment a task that previously

required a human user to manage. A great use case here is Alexa or Siri: imagine AI assistants like Alexa or Siri proactively engage with a customer to manage a lost baggage situation, using predictions of customer behavior to determine the next best action.

It is the last type of analytics – prescriptive analytics – that offers the most powerful opportunity for airlines who wish to think like retailers. Predictive analytics help create propensity models that delivers the ideal "next best action" for each passenger automatically, determining what to do next and predicting the likely future outcome of an action, event, or activity. This propensity model is the key to unlocking the value of airline data. Propensity predictions can support very sophisticated retailing campaigns that target a "segment of one" with highly customized offers and super-personalized travel experiences to optimize conversion rates, online media spending, and revenue per visit to your e-commerce site.

A great example of this is travel insurance: A passenger could have a high propensity to purchase travel insurance if they are naturally risk averse and purchased insurance in the past. In many cases, travelers may not even have consciously registered that they have a propensity to purchase something, but a data-driven machine-learning algorithm can predict it.

Propensity is not a new idea, but it is only with the availability of large amounts of high-quality data, cloud infrastructure, and machine learning that the models are starting to generate predictive signals with reliable accuracy. In particular, some of the more sophisticated retail banks and insurance companies have used this approach with great effect over the past few years. A combination of demographics and personal financial circumstances can play important roles in determining the propensity to purchase a personal loan, mortgage, investment, or insurance product.

These same principles apply to airlines: propensity in travel is revealed by a combination of a consumer's demographics, their personality, their transactional history, and attitudes. The best marketing and product teams in travel retailing have realized that they must embed these insights and combine these with data insight to compete effectively as a retailer.

Some insights from best-in-class retailing

Thinking like a retailer opens up extensive new revenue opportunities for high margin ancillary product selling for airlines, as it enables consumers to discover and book a diverse range of products, sourced from a multitude of suppliers including hotels, car hire companies, insurance, destination activities, events, transfers, etc., all under the airline brand.

Airlines should be studying the playbooks of both legacy and pure play retailers to see what they can learn and what talents and technology will be needed to transform business operations. Successful retailing is based on fundamental principles, and technology has enabled these to be implemented more effectively and efficiently for maximum advantage.

Here are five key insights that OpenJaw has seen while working with some of the world's best airline retailers:

Product mix

Product retailing is an industry where the choice of product and the broader product mix is a strategic choice, defined by what the retail brand stands for and how the retailer wishes to differentiate their online store. The merchandise is placed to promote cross-selling, and the amount of display space is carefully allocated. Regardless of whether a retailer sells bolts or belts, nothing in a store is placed in a particular location by accident.

Merchandising

From window display to website, retailers show the breadth of their inventory and explain the value to customers. Retailers make deliberate merchandise and design choices that balance creative elements with commercial considerations, for instance, placing higher-margin products at the top of a web page or on aisle ends in-store, all guided by factors such as merchandise mix, sales trends, consumer research, and more. They have poured over the analytics on price sensitivity and promotional activity and know how to craft "call to action" messages that will trigger an action on the purchase path.

Cross-sell and up-sell

Retailing can be both complex and paradoxical. Many airlines report that they have to make their merchandising capabilities work hard to capture ancillary sales during the initial seat-booking phase. However, as the customer mindset changes when they get closer to their trip, products such as meals, seat upgrades, and destination activities may then be viewed as a valid affordable choice. When a customer is booking a flight, the emphasis is on getting the best fare. Ancillaries not related to the fare can be ignored. But by using a comprehensive customer journey touch point strategy before, during, and after the booking has been made, the same ancillary products are viewed differently, and the cross-sell and up-sell can be much easier.

Good retailing is an art

Henry Harteveldt of Atmosphere Research Group, a consultancy focused on the global travel industry, points out: "The concept of retail merchandising balances creative elements with commercial considerations. A good retailer will sell a customer just about anything in its store. As travel sellers intensify their emphasis on selling ancillary products, they are realizing that much of what they sell can be considered to be an ancillary product."

Get ready: the seven steps to transforming an airline into a retailer

How can an airline adapt the principles of retail? Airlines that embark on retail transformation projects with a view to capturing this opportunity have to fundamentally assess how to develop their strategic mindset, much more than deliver a series of technology infrastructure projects. Adopting the mindset of a good retailer means that you have to create a defined customer experience, personalize your approach, choose the right content by connecting with the right suppliers, differentiate your proposition, and develop the capability to control and orchestrate all of this directly.

Let's get ready to be a retailer – here's how, step by step:

1 **Get experience:** Customer experience is based upon the sum of all the interactions a person has with an airline – it is becoming the defining differentiator between companies. The consumer now has a set of expectations forged by their contact with the great retailers and the platform-based disruptor brands, including Uber and Airbnb. These businesses focus on delivering a consistently excellent customer experience (CX), and airlines need to respond by delivering a seamless experience across the new customer journey – across all devices, platforms, and touch points.

2 **Get personal:** The objective should be to personalize a customers' experience and by doing so make things as easy as possible in the online customer journey. Personalization is about offering the right product at the right time to customers based on their prior history and/or current context. This is particularly important in the world of mobile, where customers are looking to efficiently transact from the palm of their hand. Airlines already have an advantage in the wealth of customer data they possess and use profiling engines to identify the customer if they can collate it from their different sources of data and integrate it on one platform. Once the booking process is started; even if abandoned, the airline has already gathered incredibly useful data that puts it ahead of other travel sectors, and data gathering can continue with customer opt-ins for email updates, app downloads, etc.

3 **Get content:** The most crucial element of creating a retail capability is the ability to supply and support a broad range of products. This gives the airline leverage and supports the differentiated proposition. There are multiple supply models: connecting aggregators, connecting directly to hotels, or even individually selected destination attractions. Seamless API technology is now available that enables an airline to become a direct supplier of products, develop exclusive inventory to make more tailored recommendations, and support this across multiple channels.

4 **Get differentiated:** Good retailers stock the shelf the way they want to, with their own products or with partner products that are curated in such a way

so that they are differentiated from the competitors. Applying your airline's unique knowledge of customer preferences, behavior, and purchase history means that you can select the right product supply – for example, a chain of boutique hotels – and create combination retail offers for any flight and travel product. This can be your own products, or part of those products combined and made available.

5 **Get data:** There is no retailing strategy without data. Data-driven insights lead to better customer insight. With airlines able to collect and analyze more and more traveler data (including mobile app and social media behavior, session history from in-flight connections, travel history, and previous purchases), it is essential that this information be captured, stored and shared to create a single unified traveler profile. This will enable personalized search results so that the airline can merchandise the right products at the right time to the right person.

6 **Get control:** Integrating all data will enable an airline to develop greater customer insight and personalize customer recommendations. But it is the combination of insight, personalization, and recommendations that provides the "magic sauce" that enables airlines to use their data. Just like a retailer, an airline needs to ensure it has the correct tools at its fingertips to take contextual data and generate tailored offers specifically tailored to match the brand and funnel these products to the right segment of the customer demographic – across all channels.

7 **Get converting:** Adopting a retailer mindset means understanding that there is a long window of opportunity to sell relevant products to customers before departure. Research shows that the average booking window is 78 days, with a breakdown of 81 days for LCCs and 55 days for scheduled carriers. Within this timeline there will be optimal moments that matter for the customer; these will be the times when they are most receptive to recommendation of certain products during the new customer journey. The "secret sauce" is the potential for *a real time response* to a customer signal with the perfect product based on signals of intent and past purchase history.

Conclusion

Once an airline starts thinking about identifying and solving problems rather than selling seats, then it can realize the opportunity to become a retailer. Airlines need to view the flight seat as just one of many products that can be developed and offered to meet both the practical needs and the more emotional desires of travelers. By adopting a retail mindset, they will be better positioned to provide a superlative customer experience. This is how to generate incremental revenue, build loyalty, and engender the goodwill that translates into lifetime customer value. The right business partner and technology platform will put an airline in control of the product, the experience, and the consumer data, thereby unlocking the value beyond the selling of a seat.

Parallels seen from the insurance industry

Ian Czaja

Vice President, Office of Corporate Strategy
Nationwide Insurance

The news headlines covering the insurance and airline transportation industries are very different. However, operational parallels and similar high-level impacts of mega trends help to illustrate the strength of forces of change in the current landscape. These forces are so powerful that legacy industries like insurance and airline transportation are facing a high likelihood of transformation, along possibly common dimensions.

Consider these industry parallels:

Operationally, insurance and airline transportation are two highly regulated industries navigating competing and fragmented legal and regulatory regimes. Major competitors are ±100 years old and have the resultant legacy technology systems and siloed, static data.

Industry-specific skills, regulatory barriers, and capital intensity have protected both these industries, compared to many other customer-facing industries. Local market regulations have limited the intensity of global competition. Market shocks have enabled lower-cost competitors periodically, but safety and security concerns have kept these industries more like the pre-Uber taxi industry – seemingly unassailable at scale by a totally new entrant. Most industry executives have grown up in the industry and have deep operational knowledge; one untended result is limited visibility into what is possible today with ground-up digitalized operating models.

From an end user perspective, customers experience high effort processes, a bureaucratic feel, and difficult-to-understand pricing models. In the eyes of many consumers, these industries' services are often a "necessary evil" or a means to an end, with relatively few truly delighted customers/enthusiasts.

Signs of change starting to emerge

If an airline industry executive found him- or herself suddenly in a management meeting in an insurance company, the issues at hand might feel surprisingly parallel:

The potential of transformational technology still difficult to tap

From a technology perspective, the scale of a large airline or insurer lends itself to significant increases in efficiency and effectiveness through data and analytics. However, there are challenges in making the promise of data and analytics real. High on the list are fragmented legacy technology platforms and a cultural and operating emphasis on local experience over data-driven insights.

Customers' interactions through the Internet are an amplifying factor

As an example, self-service has the potential to significantly lower costs, but digital technology has also led to a new level of price transparency and price comparison. Customer-facing staff can feel more enriched because they are dealing with more complex problems that can't be handled online; however, this puts greater emphasis on skill, retention, and empathy and makes the failures more visible.

There are increasing conversations about technology platforms and startups – but disruptive models have not yet fully emerged

Like many industries, platforms have played a vital role but haven't disrupted industry leaders. For example, in the airline industry, there is Sabre for standardizing the process of finding flights and making reservations. In insurance there is the CLUE database in the US that is a repository of crash data used for auto insurance pricing and eligibility. However, there is a new type of experience platform (e.g., Facebook, Google, or Amazon) which has become the "front door" for consumer shopping in other categories. These platforms are unique in their influence because they are so dominant. For example, the No. 3 search engine has far less share than the No. 3 airline or insurer – a No. 1 platform company becomes a nearly impossible-to-assail strength. That scale could radically impact the airline or insurance industries if any one of these experience platforms becomes truly central to the consumer shopping value chain. At the same time, these platforms are enabling niche companies to operate without the infrastructure of a traditional company (e.g., services that use Facebook as their customer acquisition platform).

This combination of the very big and very small has the potential to squeeze the value chain of legacy insurers and airline transportation companies equally. By separating the customer experience from the capital-intensive part of the industry, both threaten to commoditize the legacy players if they aren't careful. While this dynamic has yet to fully emerge in either industry, the potential is clear.

A digital company at scale can attack legacy companies that are digitalizing

For example, not only has Amazon expanded far beyond their original category of goods into a broad range of categories and streaming services, they are also monetizing their more digitally efficient operating model as a service. AWS went from being an internal computing capability to a business unto itself. Given their actions to tackle the cost and complexity of health insurance and delivery logistics (including Amazon Air), it is entirely possible they could move these from internal capabilities to businesses as well. As the scale of these operations becomes so large, their infrastructure becomes more efficient. Selling access to that infrastructure creates a virtuous cycle with the potential to disrupt legacy companies that still reflect the costs of an "in house" operating model.

From operational excellence to strategic leadership?

Decades that rewarded industry operators may be in the rearview mirror

The airline and insurance industries have both been tested by the shocks of 2001 and 2008. These shocks emphasized strong financial and operational acumen in leaders – the strongest operators generally were best rewarded, especially if they happened to face toward the market segments that recovered more rapidly, including low-cost, high net worth, and emerging markets.

Mega-trends are unavoidable

The tech mega-trends are well known and widely covered, but they are being amplified by social factors including generational shifts, the gig economy, wealth bifurcation, and a volatile regulatory, political, and economic environment. The number of factors, and when they may "tip" – meaning, when a company that isn't leveraging becomes structurally disadvantaged – suggests that few executives today will have the option to avoid these trends during their career (see Figure 8.8). Investment capital is widely available and patient for profits when backing bold, disruptive models. Across many industries, this is touching off a race between legacy players and the disruptors (see Figure 8.9). The social platform companies and digitalized architectures were mentioned earlier. Not only do digitalized models provide agility, they also remake notions of scale – potentially making very big and very small experience and data-oriented companies more valuable than capital-intensive companies of medium scale.

The promise of forthcoming technology abundance through technologies such as 5G + IoT + quantum computing + blockchain is another unavoidable, potential

Trend	Description	When 'Tipping'?
Tech-enabled Distribution	Distribution completed or augmented by technology	Now
Digitization	Automating manual processes	Next 5 years
Big Data / Internet of Things	The widespread availability and analytical use of data	Next 10 years
Artificial Intelligence	Computerized tasks that normally require human intelligence	Next 10 years
Autonomous Vehicles	Control of critical functions shift from man to machine	Next 15 years

Figure 8.8 Mega-trends That Companies Must Leverage to Avoid Becoming Disadvantaged

Source: Nationwide Mutual Insurance Company

Trend	Description	Trend	Description
Generational Shifts	Aging Boomers; Rise of the Millennials	Platforms (GAFA)	What role will Google, Amazon, Apple, Facebook play
Gig Economy	Contract labor over full-time employment	Convergence (SMAC)	Hyper-extendable product & business architecture
Wealth Bifurcation	Hollowing of the middle class	Technology Abundance	Quantum computing and 5G leap to ubiquity
Regulatory & Political	New risk categories and / or transference of risk		
Economy	Volatility across the spectrum	Blockchain	Clear, streamlined, verifiable contracts

Figure 8.9 Social Factors Impacting Business Models, and Disruptive Forces That May Drive Change Faster Than Some Companies Can Adapt

Source: Nationwide Mutual Insurance Company

disruptor. Together, these four technology trends could vastly expand the amount of available, real-time information about our world while providing the pipes to transfer it (5G) and increased efficiency to process it automatically (quantum computing and blockchain). In insurance, the fundamental role of the industry is to price and aggregate individual risks into a pool and pay out when a loss occurs. Historically, the only way to do this well was to gather seasoned experts and years of data that together were proprietary to the company. Tomorrow, when the data is abundant and owned by others (e.g., your smart home, smart watch, or smart car), the business model could be disrupted. The leap in available data could well be that disruptor.

The coordination of people, luggage, parts, consumables, and planes is at least as operationally complex as insurance. The combination of gradual but powerful technology changes, social factors, and the wildcard role of potential "disruptors" is a seemingly unique confluence of challenges that both legacy industries face.

Consider the consumer lens: as consumers, our everyday actions are voting unequivocally for more digitized models that offer radically lower effort, greater efficiency, and more delight

It is difficult to think of a product or service that, once effectively translated into the digital world, has not taken over from its physical equivalent. Insurance features high effort, confusing pricing models, and low levels of delight. For most air travelers, the process of buying a ticket and getting to and through the airport is also high effort, with confusing pricing and low delight.

On the air transportation side, while a freight company thinks about the point-to-point logistics of a package, human travelers must work through a complicated patchwork in order to coordinate their trip. The power of the travel agent has been ceded to a patchwork, and the airline executive looking toward tomorrow will need to navigate how the patchwork gets reconnected digitally and who will capture value. The customers' total physical trip from discovery to fulfillment is the potential battleground, just as customers' total financial well-being across saving, spending, and protection is at play. In addition to the experience lens, there is the supply and demand lens. There is still quite a bit of uneven use of capacity in flights and in insurers' balance sheets awaiting tomorrow's greater disruption.

Another unique dynamic today is that these disruptions need not follow a traditional route into the competitive landscape (e.g., Clayton Christensen's low-end or high-end disruption paths). In the past, both airline transportation and insurance have seen low-cost providers attack margins. Both have seen high-end providers fight for the highest-paying customers. While these are challenging enough, new digitalized models, because they change efficiency and experience in fundamental ways, can attack all customer segments equally. Existing and new entrants alike have the power of transforming the experience of the highest-paying customers, the most price sensitive, and all those in between through these models.

More radical changes in effort, efficiency, and delight are ahead

The current and/or next leadership teams will navigate more radical changes

While these trends have yet to fully impact the insurance industry, it is easy to anticipate the potential trajectory and impacts by looking at other industries such as media and entertainment, retail, and banking. Changes such as customer choice, unbundling, new channels, "leasing" models, hyper-scale, and digital experiences that delight have proven to be keys to success.

Insurance is a virtual product (a contract) that is still largely purchased through a physical storefront and from a unique company called an insurance company. This makes it particularly susceptible to digital reinvention or disruption – especially when insurance is typically purchased alongside something else happening (e.g., buying a car, buying a home, materially expanding or moving a business). Today, the other things that are happening (the "life event" that the insurance relates to) could often generate the data needed to also underwrite and price the insurance. In the future, the IoT from the smart car, smart home, smart business, and/or wearable will provide an even richer data set. The insurance executive of tomorrow will need to think about where the product is sold, how it is underwritten and priced, and how it is operationally delivered in very different ways than the past.

To be sure, there will still be a regulated insurance product at the core of many transactions that requires industry knowledge to deliver – just as the technical know-how and capital to own and operate airplanes and airports won't go away. However, so much of the value chain can be reinvented that a different leadership lens will be needed to navigate change – one that can think about other industry players as partner, threat, or "frenemy."

Time to pick a strategic path

*At a minimum, all companies must sustain and enhance
their customers' experience and drive greater efficiency
through future transformations*

There is no escaping that digital will become part of every industry, and failure to anticipate what this means can lead to solutions that feel old before they are even rolled out. In air transportation, as an example, a mobile-first strategy can lead to customers downloading an airline's app to their phone and streaming content in-air vs. the choice to install screens in the back of every airline seat. Which is faster, cheaper, and provides the groundwork for more long-term customer intimacy while simultaneously feeling more contemporary?

*It remains to be seen whether the boundaries of what defines a
"company" or an "industry" will remain as historically defined*

Companies like Amazon, Apple, or Netflix are redefining what industry they are in, raising the question of whether "industry" is a construct that still makes sense or a legacy organizational blinder. Making future plans around the assumption that a company will continue to compete in a stable industry and against incremental changes is a strategic decision – one that is easiest in the short term but may risk unexpected surprises. Figure 8.10 is a high-level illustration of some of the choices that participants in the insurance industry are contemplating:

On the left of this chart are examples of continuous improvement – changes that can make an insurance company perform better while the industry overall would still feel like insurance – easier, more digitally integrated, but still the insurance industry. For most legacy participants, this is the default presumption and, while still challenging operationally, it is easiest to execute this vision.

In the middle are choices where the consumption of insurance becomes even more consumer-friendly – easier for the consumer to coordinate with other things

Play the game... or change the game?

Incremental ←——————————————————————→ Step Change

Incremental		Step Change
• Personalize (IoT, 3rd party data)	• Coordinate (home purchase)	• Imbed (auto lease, mobility)
• AI, chatbots, drones	• Reimagine offer (financial security)	• Hyper-scale (platforms, layers)
• Pricing sophistication	• Go cloud (GAFA)	• Crowd-fund

Figure 8.10 Examples of Strategic Responses – From Incremental to Step Change
Source: Nationwide Mutual Insurance Company

happing simultaneously in the consumer's life, easier to understand, and available through the online tools and brands most consumers love. Industry boundaries start to blur, and the integrated experience becomes the selling point. Today, some industry participants are contemplating these moves with more nervousness about what happens to the value chain and their ability to capture the same share of the profit pool. These changes are more difficult to predict and therefore more difficult for executives to commit to.

In other industries, we have seen existing companies who found themselves "boxed out" of a leadership position in the current business model try options like these as a way to leapfrog to future success. In insurance, the rise of GEICO and Progressive happened in part because companies like State Farm and Allstate had already secured the best agents in the right locations in most local markets. The disruptors had to leapfrog – trying direct advertising and phone sales to bypass their inability to compete locally. The middle column represents the potential next version of this play. Will we see an "Amazon home insurance company" that can offer you a one-click price when you purchase and install a Nest smart home bundle? It is quite possible that an existing insurance company – possibly one that is not a top company today – will take the pioneering path of using big data to populate and price a one-click insurance policy and allow Amazon to use its brand instead of theirs.

On the right are scenarios in which insurance (or an insurance company) disappears as a stand-alone construct relative to how many consumers would think of it today. While the insurance mechanisms may still exist (the need to transfer, manage, and remediate risk won't go away), they become imbedded or completely reimagined from an end-consumer point of view. Existing and new players are actively experimenting on this dimension – it is perhaps an even higher risk, higher reward alternative . . . and also perhaps where patient capital will back a disruptor who gains traction.

The right includes business models where you pay monthly for transportation and your insurance is included. It could be included in your mobility monthly payment or your mortgage or your alarm system in the future. There are also potential models where your peers provide your insurance. Hard to conceive of? I'm sure the same was true in the taxi industry and hotel industry before Uber and AirBnB created platform businesses. The power of these platforms is that the right customer experience and exchange doesn't actually require the business to own any of the assets – yet the platform can command greater scale and margins and grow far faster than traditional competitors. Those competitors may remain, but their margins and preferred access to customers may not.

We may also see a traditional insurer seek to take something they are good at and turn it into a platform service, as Amazon has done with AWS. Indeed, Allianz is already trying this. They have a policy administration system that they already use in 42 countries and are making it open to the competition. Why open this system up to competitors? Allianz lowers and further amortizes their development costs. Other insurers can reduce their development costs as well vs. rebuilding or updating custom systems. The more volume on the system, the more leverage they have over vendors (including, for example, those who provide servers and storage). Platform standardization can put pressure on those who choose to go it alone. A successful ecosystem can attract new innovators and service providers just as the Apple app store marketplace made the platform more compelling, creating that self-reinforcing virtuous cycle.

Are airlines facing a similar future?

It is always difficult to predict the future. Disruptive models can go from impossible, to imagine, to obvious once they are introduced. At the same time, many experiments that sound compelling fail, and it is easy to get distracted by the "noise" or the costs of dead-end paths.

Legacy participants in both insurance and airline transportation have many advantages to build on that both large platform companies and new startups do not. More positive reinvention is likely possible in the coming years than in the decades past. While it may be tempting and easy in the short run to assume traditional models will remain in the future with only incremental changes, that's not the only possible outcome. To sustain success, an executive must lean into the changes and trends, embrace a strategic lens, and reimagine the future.

A new revolution in the air travel industry

Chuck Evans

Vice President, Marketing, Communications, and Business Development

The aviation industry has experienced a small number of revolutionary changes throughout its short history. Most of these were driven by advances in aircraft design and have been brought forth by new materials, new engines, new navigation equipment, or changing market requirements. Of course, the most notable of these revolutions was the introduction of powered flight in 1903. By 1915, a revolutionary all-metal aircraft was first built, paving the way for more revolutionary aircraft designed and used during the Second World War. One aircraft in particular, the Douglas DC-3, revolutionized civil transportation in many ways to create the airlines that we know today. By the 1950s, jet engines began to appear on civil passenger aircraft, marking the beginning of another revolution in air travel. By the 1970s, the jumbo jet introduced high-capacity, long-haul capabilities and issued in another sea change for the industry.

From the 1970s to today, there have been several evolutionary advances that have made aircraft more efficient, cost-effective, more capable, and more comfortable. However, changes that would be described as revolutionary are not evident. In fact, aircraft designs have become more consistent, with the standard twin-engine wing mounted design from 70 seats up to 500 seats. From the operational perspective, operators are achieving readiness rates above 99 percent, engine removals above 6,000 hours and safety records at historical highs. The commercial aviation ecosystem has become a highly mature, though not revolutionary anymore.

As happens with other mature industries, a new wave is approaching the horizon. The next revolution in commercial aviation is coming from far outside the industry as we know it today. In fact, it's coming from multiple sources, many of which are unrelated. Some of these drivers have already matured, and others are quickly advancing.

The first driver of commercial aviation's next revolution is the development of carbon-fiber construction materials. By now, most are aware of carbon-fiber's ability to be molded into nearly any shape and that it can be stronger than steel. However, it wasn't until the mid-2000s that it became inexpensive enough to be used for everyday consumer products. Today, aircraft with carbon-fiber fuselages as small as two seats are being built at price tags less than US$200,000. Those aircraft are reinvigorating the general aviation market with very smooth aerodynamic surfaces (no rivets) that allow for high relative speeds and very light airframes powered by 100 hp engines (versus of 160 hp) using premium unleaded (versus avgas). The ability to inexpensively form aircraft fuselages, wings, and other structural elements using carbon-fiber is the first step of a revolutionary new aircraft design approach.

The second driver of the next revolution lies in battery technology. The smartphone revolution essentially presented a free gift to aviation and other industries with lithium-ion battery technology. The power density of these batteries have enabled cordless power tools, lawn mowers, tablet computers, and other consumer products that can run for long periods of time. The same batteries have powered dozens of successful aerial drones with varying functionality. Today, military personal, law enforcement personnel, movie studios, energy and powerline monitors, and search and rescue organizations are using these drones to replace work previously performed by airplanes or helicopters. Companies like Tesla Motors are building massive battery production capabilities and will continue to improve the power density. It is expected that the next step in battery technology will enable a new wave of electric-powered aircraft in parallel to the flood of electric cars.

The third driver of the revolution centers on electric motors. As with battery technology, the aviation industry did not have to invest R&D dollars for the newest generation of electric motors. The automobile industry, all-electric cars specifically, developed these high torque motors that have allowed for extreme acceleration as well as energy recovery systems when braking. The result for aviation is a series of motors that are fast to react to higher or lower inputs of electricity and are directly linked to propellers. This architecture removes the need for reduction gear boxes, transmissions, and variable-pitch blade mechanisms that add weight and complexity to turbine or piston airplanes and helicopters.

The fourth driver of the revolution is best captured in the "bucket" of remotely controlled drones. As previously mentioned, drones are already executing numerous functions that were once conducted by airplanes and/or helicopters. However, when you dissect the technologies that allow them to function, they are truly remarkable. The first technology to examine is the flight control algorithms. Fly-by-wire is the baseline, and even the least expensive drones have very advanced stability control in the air. More complex drones will also compensate for wind gusts to hold an exact position above the ground. Directional control is driven by differential thrust (speeding up and slowing down the various propellers), which makes the drones extremely maneuverable in three dimensions (up/down, forward/backward, side/side). Newer drone models are equipped with proximity sensors that keep the aircraft from colliding with structures, other drones, or the ground. During the 2018 Consumer Electronics Show (CES), Intel created a nighttime display using 100 individual drones acting in unison to create a 3-D lightshow. The "chips" and algorithms responsible for the flight controls are increasingly smart and are being mass produced in a very inexpensive way. Another technology driving the success of the drone market is GPS (or other names depending upon the region of the world you are in). Linking the flight controls to GPS opens the drone's navigation capability to operate with or without a person/pilot. Some drones can be programmed to fly a specific GPS routing without any pilot interaction. Powerline inspection, ground surveillance, and even crop-dusting missions are becoming more common based on the ability provided by GPS. Often the algorithms have fail-safe modes that return the aircraft to its origin if the GPS signal is lost. Some drones can link to a smart device and follow you wherever you go. As a relatively inexpensive consumer gadget, the rapidity of advancement in the flight control algorithms will create the opportunity for safe, autonomous flying functionality. By comparison, a hover-hold flight control box for a traditional helicopter costs well over $100,000, compared to a $50 drone that offers the same capability and more. The technology used in drones is being scaled up to for larger aircraft and systems. In the coming years, these technologies will pave the way for autonomous flight.

The four drivers discussed have developed over time and in parallel, some within the aviation industry and others outside. The next revolution in aviation will combine these to make air travel an everyday part of commuting. This revolution will happen quickly in the grand scheme of things, though it will likely take a decade or more to mature. There will be distinct phases driven by technology readiness and regulatory acceptance. By the 2030–2035 timeframe, the revolution will have happened and will be ramping up to maturity. Its effects on the automotive and airline industries will be significant, though not necessarily negative. The next revolution is the eVTOL revolution.

At this point in mid-2018, there are over 100 companies competing to develop the first mass-produced vertical takeoff and landing aircraft that use electric motors for propulsion. Some designs are reminiscent of small drones (quadcopters), while others use wings with fixed or rotating propellers. Most of the designs have four seats, which is very logical given its similarity to a standard sedan car. The companies competing range from aviation behemoths (Boeing and Airbus) to small startups with specialties in composites, propulsion technology, or general aviation. In addition, several automotive companies are either directly or indirectly competing. One of the most influential drivers of the eVTOL revolution is the ride-sharing company Uber. They have raised the visibility of this developing industry by creating and promoting a vision of the future where nearly everyone can travel by air and ground seamlessly. A key part of the vision is reducing travel time by flying over roadway traffic using electric vehicles with very low noise and emissions. The vision also includes that the aircraft and ground vehicles are driverless and pilotless. While Uber's vision may seem far reaching to many, the facts are that the technology readiness, as detailed in the four drivers of the revolution, is increasingly high. It is possible and practical that the first early adopters will have eVTOL aircraft carrying people by 2025.

The Uber vision will become reality in stages over the next decade and will happen on a global scale. The hurdles will involve technology readiness, significant changes to regulations and air traffic management, and infrastructure availability. The first stage of the eVTOL revolution is that of the flying car.

The dream of flying cars has existed since the 1940s, as Henry Ford himself predicted it. Some have successfully flown as proof of concepts, but none have experienced commercial success. The value that the flying car delivers is that of a single vehicle providing the ability to both drive and fly. The combination of the two means that the passengers and pilot board the vehicle once, and it can transport them in multiple modes from origin to destination. For the first time in 2012, the Transition, a vehicle produced by Terrafugia Inc., conducted a flight test of a flying car. To date, the Transition has accumulated around 250 flight hours and is close to receiving approval from the FAA as well as the National Highway Traffic Safety Administration. It will be the first vehicle to achieve multi-regulatory approval and bring the flying car to reality. With a carbon-fiber airframe, the Transition takes advantage of the advances in carbon-fiber technology described previously as a driver in the eVTOL revolution. The production version of the vehicle will also use electric motors for road driving and will be priced competitively with traditional single-engine general aviation aircraft. The Transition will certify under the light-sport category, has two seats for a pilot and passenger, and can fly 400 miles. In a typical operation, a pilot can step into their vehicle (fits in most home garages), drive to a nearby airstrip or municipal airport, unfold its wings for takeoff, fly to an airstrip near their destination, and drive the final leg of their journey. Terrafugia believes that the knowledge garnered from designing and producing the composite vehicle, use of hybrid-electric technology, and the data from Transition flight and road operations will be valuable as part of the first stage in the development of eVTOL. Of particular note are the airstrips that will be used by the Transition. These airstrips (public airports, municipal airports and private airports) will become the foundational infrastructure of eVTOL operations and are heavily underutilized today.

The second stage of the eVTOL revolution will come in the early and mid-2020s. The first dedicated eVTOL prototypes will begin flight testing while the regulators determine how to categorize them. The initial designs will make use of composite structures, electric propulsion, and varying levels of battery power. It's likely that the fully electric versions will have very limited operational capability, as battery technology will not yet meet the power requirements for sustained flight. Therefore, hybrid-electric designs will become the practical reality and rival the capability of traditional helicopters in terms of air-endurance time. It is also unlikely that pilotless navigation and flight controls will be accepted for passenger operations by regulators in stage two, driving the need for pilots for the eVTOL prototypes.

A potential "fast-track" for eVTOL operations lies with package freight and/ or cargo carriers. The possibility exists that autonomous unmanned operations of a cargo aircraft could be viewed by regulators as a testbed for both the aircraft technology and the airway/traffic management. With no people onboard and flight plan routings over unpopulated areas, significant proving data could be possible. Given that safety of operations is something that is demonstrated over thousands of hours and flights, this approach would be beneficial to both industry and regulators. In the case where collaboration exists, it's possible that the first autonomous eVTOL aircraft could begin operations in the 2020–2025 timeframe, thus expediting future manned autonomous operations.

Another challenge the eVTOL industry will face in the second stage is related to infrastructure. The dream of an aircraft landing in your driveway is unrealistic (unless your driveway is about one acre in size and has no trees nearby!). The facts are that the best infrastructure opportunities for eVTOL ops are existing airstrips. For example, airports like Hawthorne Municipal Airport, El Monte Airport,

Zamperini Airport, Van Nuys Airport, Oxnard Airport, and Riverside Municipal Airport could be targets for volume eVTOL operations around the Los Angeles area. In a scenario where a traveler flies from Riverside Municipal to Hawthorne Municipal, the flight time would be approximately 20–25 minutes. Given that Hawthorne Municipal is only 5 miles from LAX and 10 miles from downtown Los Angeles, the commute time is drastically reduced from today's standard highway commute.

Terrafugia believes that the most optimal and practical vision for the eVTOL revolution is built on combining air and ground/road transportation into a single vehicle or experience. Loading into multiple vehicles is not passenger friendly. In fact, there exist many years of data showing that airline passengers will choose nonstop travel over one-stop travel more than 80 percent of the time. Terrafugia and a few other OEMs recognize that eVTOL vehicles/systems will need the ability to seamlessly transport passengers from origin to final destination. To do so, eVTOL will have to have both air and road transportation capabilities in a single vehicle or a seamless system. This ability will be in high demand during the second stage of the revolution due to the fact that eVTOL infrastructure will yet to be fully developed.

Most of the 100 competing companies will not survive as competitors through the second stage of eVTOL. It's likely that companies developing piloted, hybrid-electric vehicles will be faster to market and will have the benefit of helping to shape the certification process while accumulating numerous hours of flight operations. Those looking to go fully autonomous and all-electric from the start will likely fall years behind the hybrid-electric adopters. As with any new technology, most competitors will be acquired by the more successful companies or cease to exist.

The third stage in the eVTOL revolution will see eVTOL operations become commonplace, eventually leading to economies of scale that afford most everyone the chance to fly. In stage three, the vehicle/systems migrate from hybrid electric to full electric and from piloted to autonomous. It's likely that this will begin in 2026 and accelerate throughout the 2030s. In stage three, the air vehicles become increasingly reliable, on a par with airliners like the Boeing 737 or Airbus A320. In addition, major cities known for heavy car traffic jams will begin to create eVTOL infrastructure to ease congestion. As costs diminish, daily commuters will have the option to live further outside of the cities they work in, thus expanding suburbs by another 50 miles in all directions. For example, a resident of the Hamptons, New York, could now travel to/from Manhattan in about 40 minutes as their normal daily commute (no longer a weekend trip).

As the eVTOL market matures, it's expected that operators of large fleets will emerge. As a disruptive trend/technology, it is not yet clear who those operators will be. As mentioned earlier, the automobile OEMs may be heavily impacted as more people begin to use eVTOL. In an attempt to defend their share of personal travel, automobile OEMs could become owners of eVTOL manufacturers and/or operators of eVTOL vehicles themselves. In addition to automobile OEMS, commercial airline operators and OEMs would have a vested interest in expanding their networks to include eVTOL routes and passengers. It is also worth noting that ride-sharing companies like Uber will have a keen interest in expanding their networks as well, specifically moving people quicker around cities or to nearby cities. Lastly, as the eVTOL industry is considered a high-tech industry, it's also likely that very large tech companies like Google, Apple, Amazon, or Microsoft would have an interest in operating in the eVTOL industry.

The third stage of the eVTOL revolution will see a change to the definition of daily travel and will reshape cities. It will also change urban and suburban infrastructure and give people more time for other activities. From the aviation perspective, the four drivers that create the opportunity are mature or almost mature from a technical readiness standpoint, and two of the four were free gifts from the smartphone battery industry and the electric car industry. It is also anticipated that the revolution will span a decade or more in three stages before achieving maturity. Altogether, the seeds of revolutions are sprouting and will change the way the world travels.

Hyper-personalization is the new oil

Antonio Figueiredo

Senior Director
Industry Solution at Salesforce

Organizations, in general, are trying to own the complete customer experience in whatever journey defines their industry, and for airline industry that is very much the case. Today, we are experiencing a dynamic digital disruption where disruptors of the past can be disrupted in this new competitive environment for customer attention. Consumers are becoming not just more connected but hyperconnected, and organizations need to better understand the individual preferences of customers and engage with them in more proactive and personalized ways throughout their journey.

In this section, we discuss how this "hyper-personalization" can be used to drive superior customer experiences in a way that impacts top-line growth in the airline industry. We'll also highlight key important approaches airlines should be pivoting into in order to support hyper-personalization, including the adoption of an agile customer engagement platform to keep up with changing customer expectations and the constant changes in the business and technological ecosystem. This also leads to cost reductions and the potential to increase revenue as a result of greater customer satisfaction, loyalty, advocacy[1] and improved revenue strategies.

Known challenges

According to Gartner[2] research, "for 75% of B2B organizations and 40% of B2C organizations, customer experience management is still an immature capability with a fragmented, uncoordinated approach," and depending on the industry, this is not clearly defined by leadership.

To most organizations, the need to own the complete end-to-end customer journey is their top priority. Some airlines may think their end-to-end customer journey is bounded by the actual time the customer is with them in air. But for their customers, everything starts days or even months earlier while they are still in the inspiration and research phase for their trip and certainly doesn't end when they arrive at their destination. Airlines need to own the entire journey – pre-trip, during the trip and post-trip.

Today, superior customer experience is the new battlefield for customer attention and loyalty. The customer experience is a cumulative impact and encompasses all the touch points of your company (physical and digital) and the relationships, or lack thereof, it fosters. Every touch point can be seen as an opportunity to delight your customer as well as a chance to put that relationship at risk. This new battlefield is fast approaching the airline industry, where every passenger carrier will be competing on how well it engages with customers and creates positive experiences. And the airlines that better engage with customers will see their market share and financials improve, including more revenue per seat, even though flights are full.

A recent Salesforce Research eBook[3] discussing trends shaping the future of travel and hospitality found that 50 percent of customers said that they would be likely to switch brands if a company didn't anticipate their needs, and 52 percent would be likely to switch brands if a company didn't make an effort to personalize communications. These findings were derived from surveying over 7,000 consumers and business buyers. Among US online adults, 62 percent have chosen, recommended, or paid more for a brand that provides a personalized service or experience, according to Forrester Research.[4]

A challenge commonly found among organizations seeking hyper-personalization is the lack of an agile and scalable platform to aggregate all the meaningful data (structured and unstructured) generated by customers across different touch points and other sources that directly or indirectly impact the customer experience. This includes third-party data not necessarily generated by the consumer, such as contextual data – like weather or events happening in the location (city or region) – that can be used in real-time decisions to optimize flight operations.

Addressing these challenges will enable airlines to deliver better experiences, stay closer to their customers, and uncover patterns that help them increase customer loyalty and the revenue stream.

The hyper-personalization hexagon – know your customer

The customer base is constantly changing. New generations, for instance, millennials and Gen Z, in the workforce are demanding modern, personalized customer experiences. They tend to be skeptical about interventions (offers, promotions, etc.) that are not contextualized or personalized, and they are comfortable engaging on social networks. They are tech savvy and deeply connected to their devices, and they tend to be financially prudent and look for brands and services that bring value for them. Also, these individuals are willing to share their data as long as they see value coming back.

Hyper-personalization, also known as extreme personalization,[5] utilizes data from all customer touch points, contextual and behavioral data, combined with artificial intelligence processes, to deliver a superior customer experience. Delivering hyper-personalized experience to individuals, like this increasingly tech savvy customer base, requires a combination of having the right data and engaging at the right time via an integrated cross-channel experience. The goal of this broader view of personalization is to use data effectively and intelligently to provide a seamless and smooth customer journey so the "customer can find and consume what they want, how they want and at the time they want."[6] Personalization can cover a broad range of capabilities – from self-service and assisted digital experiences to outbound and inbound marketing to learn more about a customer's intent. A persistent, high-quality customer experience will drive loyalty and ongoing advocacy for a brand.

The hyper-personalization hexagon presented (Figure 8.11) shows how the power of a customer relationship management (CRM) platform can elevate the

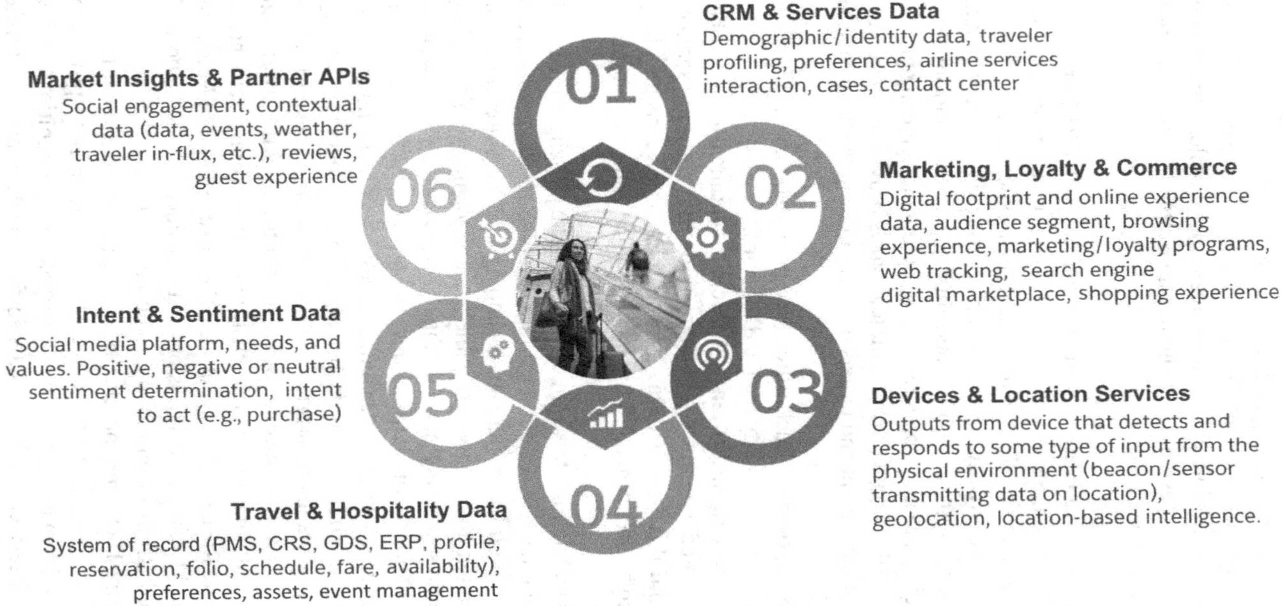

CRM & Services Data
Demographic/identity data, traveler profiling, preferences, airline services interaction, cases, contact center

Marketing, Loyalty & Commerce
Digital footprint and online experience data, audience segment, browsing experience, marketing/loyalty programs, web tracking, search engine digital marketplace, shopping experience

Devices & Location Services
Outputs from device that detects and responds to some type of input from the physical environment (beacon/sensor transmitting data on location), geolocation, location-based intelligence.

Market Insights & Partner APIs
Social engagement, contextual data (data, events, weather, traveler in-flux, etc.), reviews, guest experience

Intent & Sentiment Data
Social media platform, needs, and values. Positive, negative or neutral sentiment determination, intent to act (e.g., purchase)

Travel & Hospitality Data
System of record (PMS, CRS, GDS, ERP, profile, reservation, folio, schedule, fare, availability), preferences, assets, event management

Figure 8.11 Hyper-personalization

capabilities of your business to better anticipate customer needs and provide a complete, 360-degree view of each passenger. An agile and intelligent CRM platform helps companies deliver hyper-personalization by aggregating, orchestrating, analyzing, operationalizing and correlating data across different touch points. In doing so, companies can make this data actionable and customize experiences on both online and off-line channels to create memorable, contextually relevant experiences for each passenger, including understanding their intent and sentiment along the digital journey.

1   **CRM and service data** – Customer data in your CRM provides key customer information. Service integration between customer and call center as well as relevant critical cases that affect their experience.
2   **Marketing and loyalty** – Data from marketing (including data management platform data – first-, second-, and third party data) and loyalty programs offer insights into guest preferences, behavior, and spending potential.
3   **Devices** – Data captured from remote devices provides a geofence to understand guest movement and targets the right offer at the right time to the right individual.
4   **Enterprise systems** – Back-office enterprise data houses transactional data as well as internal property data and logistics.
5   **Social, sentiment, and intent** – Customer sentiment data can be gathered from social media, reviews, and interactions with customer services.
6   **Market and third-party data** – Market data can give insights into competitors and consumer demand, bringing additional contextual information.

Obtaining and maintaining this complete view of the passenger is the most powerful and foundational activity, but it could pose some challenges for many, as they don't have the right infrastructure and technology. This requires more than just the typical information commonly accessible, such as demographics and transaction history.[7] It requires knowing not only their preferences, such as window or aisle seat, and also their favorite destinations, frequented events, preferred packages, most-consumed products, preferred food, interests, sentiment, hobbies, family relationships and social circle. The more personal data passengers are willing and able to share, without violating their privacy, the better the travel experience will be.

"Long-term innovation success **doesn't revolve around what innovations 'do'**; it centers on what they **invite customers to become**" (emphasis mine) – Michael Schrage, Research Fellow at the MIT Sloan School of Management.

Airlines should expand their vision and consider all the opportunities and customers' needs from inspiration/research phases before the trip to during the trip and post-trip. There are opportunities to delight the customer throughout the entire journey. In every interaction, seek for opportunities to provide personalized services and engage with external services (see definitions and examples on mobility as a service – MaaS – later in this chapter) that could offer way to monetize the relationship and also a mechanism to develop innovation that are in line with strategies and goals.

The age of the customer powered by the age of the platform

In order to support new customer expectations, requirements, and business challenges, the airline industry needs to adopt a platform that allows them to understand and get closer to their customers than ever before. The growing need to be managing digital touch points understanding the customer interactions and experiences with the airline demands a platform that can bring together the disparate solutions that airlines currently use to manage interactions at every point of the customer journey.

Such a platform needs to be adopted by your business on a single and scalable environment that can easily be customized and upgraded regularly without breaking your customizations and applications. It's an intelligent engagement platform that not only offers personalization capabilities but the business agility to adapt quickly to dynamic technology and industry changes.

This architecture (in Figure 8.12) presents all the layers typically needed for business agility supported by engagement capabilities from the Salesforce Customer Success Platform. This brings a whole new way to leverage innovation, business agility, and new experience to delight your customers.

Takeaways

- Platform architecture delivers a comprehensive capability that uses technology to match data producers and consumers in a multisided marketplace, as identified in the hexagon and MaaS diagram (Figure 8.13), unlocking hidden resources and creating new forms of value proposition made available by its adoption.
- Amazon, Netflix, Airbnb, Uber, and other companies from different industries have figured out their need to leverage a foundation that allows them to continuously grow and expand their business as new functionalities, requirements, customer expectations, and technologies will evolve along the years. They have adopted the platform business model by building from the ground-up a specific platform that meets their need and keep continuously refining and adapting to new trends and technologies. The recommendation here is:

    - Leverage a platform as described in this section, like Salesforce Customer Success Platform, to build your own platform or just add new capabilities to your existing platform and expand these capabilities in an incremental approach, as defined in your road map or based on your strategies.
    - This is not a recommendation for airlines to revamp what they current have (well, there are some systems they may want to retire and save a substantial amount of money in operations and training costs), but bring this platform to build an engagement layer on top of your existing systems. This approach allows you to keep what you have, avoid interruption on your business, and add tremendous new capabilities and agility to build what your business and customers demand as your modern platform.

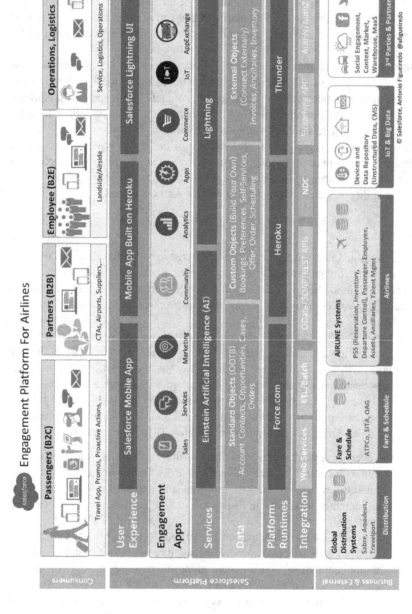

Figure 8.12 Engagement Platform Architecture

- Imagine if you get up in the morning and get to work without a transportation: that's much like trying to manage your business and customer interactions without a customer engagement platform – you're going to waste a lot of time and energy before you get to work for your first meeting.

- This platform would have capabilities, obviously, to gather all data needed and analyze and make them available with speed, empowering airlines to build their solutions in an integrated cloud environment using a declarative approach favoring clicks and configurations rather than an exhaustive code development with a lengthy, time-consuming process.
- Data collection and privacy – data authorization (consent data) and data regulations like GDPR are certainly supported.
- The platform is seamlessly updated three times a year without breaking anything in your applications.

Mobility as a service (MaaS) with extended flexibility

As mentioned earlier, airlines need to own the end-to-end customer experience. According to the MaaS Alliance,[8,9]

> Mobility as a Service (MaaS) puts users, both travelers and goods, at the core of transport services, offering them tailor-made mobility solutions based on their individual needs. This means that, for the first time, easy access to the most appropriate transport mode or service will be included in a bundle of flexible travel service options for end users.

These types of capabilities cannot be implemented easily and quickly if the airline does not have a platform that supports fast and robust integration with other systems and partners in their ecosystems – obviously some partnership agreement would need to take place from a business perspective. However, this MaaS approach can offer new ways and means for better mobility everywhere, and airlines should be part of that. Adding the "Extended Flexibility" term here to denote that the platform presented here has the capabilities to not only bring MaaS to live but also integrating with any other third-party solutions and/or services, like hotel, travel insurance, amenities, etc.

Imagine if you are flying from Boston to Dubai with a connecting flight in London, and due to some snow storm conditions in Boston your flight arrives late in London Heathrow Airport (LHR) and you miss the connecting flight to Dubai; there is no other flight to Dubai that arrives in a reasonable time compared to your original flight from LHR. What if your airline company could understand the situation because they are on top of the activities affecting your journey as they collect relevant and consensual information and are able to correlate them in the platform and automatically connect with a ground transportation service (Uber, for instance) that can take you to the Gatwick Airport in London and put you in the next flight to Dubai from there so you can be on time for your meetings or appointments. All this is happening without the passenger doing any work: just agree with this arrangement by one click on the mobile app or reply "YES" to the text message. All these can actually be done and causes a huge favorable impact on the customer experience, and the airline can actually make some extra money broking these transactions – this makes this customer one of your greatest advocates, expressing his experience at his business and in social media.

This is a quick scenario, not considering other organizations that could be playing an important role in the mix of this customer journey, like hotels, shopping, hospitals, etc., that "expand" the concept of MaaS and cover the total and thorough end-to-end experience of the passenger. A notional view of this ecosystem is depicted Figure 8.13:

This architecture brings an improved service to consumers, improved experiences, smooth transitions, and access to different players coordinated by the airline, reducing travelers' travel cost and time spent on trip planning.

NDC and personalization

The IATA's New Distribution Capability (NDC) brings a new data communication format between airlines and travel agents. As per IATA,[10]

> NDC will enable the travel industry to transform the way air products are retailed to corporations, leisure and business travelers, by addressing the industry's current distribution limitations: product differentiation and time-to-market, access to full and rich air content and finally, transparent shopping experience.

This is not mandatory, but it offers the possibility for airlines and travel organizations to switch from the existing data format Edifact to XML. We believe the support for both data formats will continue for quite some time. However, the risk of not adopting this new standard is that airlines will not be as competitive as the others who would be providing better and richer services.

NDC will allow travel agencies to have access to an airline's products and ancillaries like preassigned seats, baggage fees, food recommendations, boarding privileges, a potential 3-D view of your seat, etc. This certainly will bring an improved booking experience. Today, if a passenger wants to look for information like pre-boarding or prepay for their luggage, the agent or the agent system has to rely on additional queries to complete the transaction. With NDC, airlines will be enabled to have one single source of content across the entire booking and travel experience, which can be presented to consumer through different channels.

On the personalization hexagon in Figure 8.11, the NDC channel would be another data provider fostering,[11] among other benefits:

- **Personalized shopping experience:** Today, when an travel agent sends a search request to a global distribution system (GDS), no information about

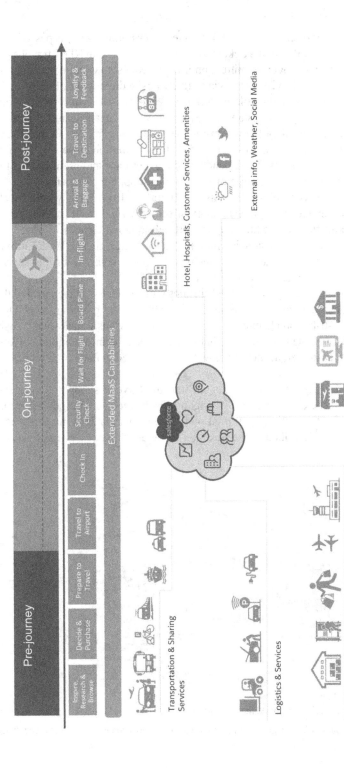

Figure 8.13 Mobility as a Service (MaaS) Architecture

Pre-journey

On-journey

Post-journey

Inspire, Research & Browse | Decide & Purchase | Prepare to Travel | Travel to Airport | Check In | Security Check | Wait for Flight | Board Plane | In-flight | Arrival & Baggage | Travel to Destination | Loyalty & Feedback

Extended MaaS Capabilities

Transportation & Sharing Services

Logistics & Services

Airports, Airlines, Shopping (airport merchants or outside), Storage

Hotel, Hospitals, Customer Services, Amenities

Travel Agencies, Payment, Financial Companies

External info, Weather, Social Media

© Salesforce, Antonio Figueiredo @afigueiredo

the passenger (e.g., passenger ID, frequent flier number, etc.) is passed down to the airline until after the ticket has been purchased. With NDC, travel agents can pass the passenger identification in their request to GDS in the same way as if the passenger were going via airline website directly (see Figure 18.14). Thus, airlines would be able to personalize the search results, as they know who is searching. For instance, they could show vegan dishes to Amy for purchase because they know Amy is vegetarian and free Wi-Fi to Olivia as a valued corporate traveler – with NDC, this attribution on search result can be totally dynamic, as this depends on the experience and preferences of the passenger and can certainly promote a better shopping experience.

- **Rich content (i.e., pictures, videos, virtual reality):** NDC would be able to display images and videos and even access virtual reality views for better visualization of product details, certainly helping airlines to better market their ancillaries (seat selection, access to lounge, meals, Wi-Fi, movies, boarding first, etc.). This opens huge possibilities to compare airlines services and products in one single page/view.
- **Content consistency:** With NDC, airlines will be to have total control of their own content and provide consistency on what they are providing via NDC to various distribution channels (GDS, OTA, and obviously their own website) as well as be able to customize that content based on information they know about the customer, as they are now being identified in the search request.

NDC will definitely bring a new insight into the traveler shopping experience, which can now be augmented by its capabilities to receive tailored content and be aggregated with additional information the consumer platform may have about the passenger, as described in the hexagon in Figure 8.11. The airlines can now

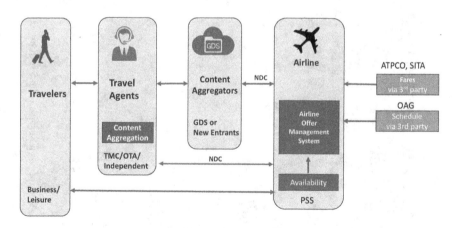

Figure 8.14 New Distribution Capability (NDC)

Source: Based on IATA's Diagram, https://www.iata.org/whatwedo/airline-distribution/ndc/Pages/default.aspx

support this rich and personalized content in a seamless omni-channel experience to travelers.

So how can this hyper-personalization help revenue management/strategy?

A platform supporting the hyper-personalization hexagon can use the information gathered in two different approaches – transactional operations creating **real-time personalization**, producing interactions that brings personalized offers and merchandise/products to customers via their preferred channels, and also leveraging the richness of this data by applying **segmentations** to extract value from the data and generate meaningful insights on selected groups of customers or segments.

Customer segmentation is an important practice in many industries, as this allows better identification of segments or groups of customers who have similar expectations, affinity, and behaviors and/or are looking for the similar levels of service and experience – so tailored offers and services can be generated. According to SearchSalesforce at TechTarget,[12] companies employing customer segmentation operate under the fact that every customer is different and that their marketing efforts would be better served if they target specific, smaller groups with messages that those consumers would find relevant and lead them to actually book their trip, for instance. Companies also hope to gain a deeper understanding of their customers' preferences, behaviors, and needs, with the idea of discovering what each segment finds most valuable to more accurately tailor marketing materials toward that segment.

Also, in SearchSalesforce at TechTarget,[13] it is presented that some key goals on customer segmentation are to use key differentiators that separate customers into targeted groups. Information such as a customers' demographics (age, race, gender, family size, income, education, location), home base (live near hub, any competitors), trip type (urgent travelers, business, leisure, budget conscious), loyalty level, sentiment insights, personality characteristics, and behavioral (travel destinations, vacation, spending patterns, and preferences) tendencies are taken into account when determining customer segmentation strategies. As we have this hyper-personalized view about the traveler, we can use this segmentation information to further recommend products and ancillaries that make more sense to a particular individual with a greater potential for increasing revenue per seat. This is typically an ongoing process applying intelligence on this data to better support revenue and marketing strategies.

Takeaways

- Traditionally revenue management creates strategies considering prices, inventory, and time, with different approach on the combinations of these dimensions – price and inventory must be managed in real time, as this information cannot be outdated.

- But airlines also need to consider personalization in their revenue strategy, which means offering a fare based on an individual traveler's preferences and other relevant information about that individual and travel behavior related to past, current behavior, and potentially expected in the future experience.
  - Legally, government may raise questions if a different price for the same seat is presented to different consumers.
  - However, if that price is offered along with a compelling ancillary, that it is personalized to that individual.

Blockchain for airlines

Look at the potential disruption coming this industry – blockchain. Airlines can take advantage of these capabilities that goes beyond the financial transactions; here are some considerations:[14]

- Ticketing – Blockchain can tokenize this asset and further dematerialize it via smart contracts. Airlines can add business logics and terms and conditions around how the ticket is sold and used. This opens the door for tickets to be sold by different partners, and in real time, from anywhere in the world, not only by OTAs.
- Loyalty – A big business for airlines. In traditional loyalty points schemes, travelers often have to wait until points settle and accrue to use them, and they are limited on where they can spend them.
  - By tokenizing loyalty points on the blockchain, travelers can get instant value by redeeming them on the spot. They can also use them more broadly through a specific user community of partners. Think of it as a marketplace or exchange model. With points accepted as "currency" among more providers, travelers get an easier and faster-to-use program that is more relevant to their personal preferences.
  - Adopting blockchain[15] would enable companies to rapidly add and maintain loyalty partnerships without adding complexity to their programs. A robust, frictionless partner network could mean many more redemption options outside of the core travel product, thereby creating a much-needed release valve for these growing balance-sheet pressures.
  - Here's what a passenger journey could look like in a blockchain world – This use case is based on "Making Blockchain Real for Customer Loyalty Rewards Programs," a Deloitte report[16] (Figure 8.15).
- Security and identity – Protecting data privacy is a clear issue when it comes to passenger records, flight manifests, and crew information, not to mention the security implications that are in play in today's world if this data is not properly protected. Blockchain technology with a security wrapper creates a very different and less risky way of managing and sharing this information through the use of authorized access requirements. Salesforce platform can extend the

1	✈	Amy buys airline tickets from Boston to San Francisco using her credit card	
		• Amy gets her tickets • Her credit card transfers loyalty tokens to Amy's loyalty rewards programs digital wallet • The airline transfers loyalty tokens to her wallet	• Amy gains current asset • The airline and credit card company have current liabilities
2	🏨	**Amy checks into a major hotel (a national chain) in San Francisco and realizes she can use points accumulated earlier**	
		• Amy checks into a chain hotel and uses her credit card points to upgrade to a suite • Hotels offer a drink at their theater if she buys ticket during her stay, as **Salesforce** provides her "plays" preferences • She also uses her airline points to rent a hotel limousine and posts pictures on social media	• Amy has a fantastic experience • The airline's and credit card company's liabilities are partly cleared while the hotel gets free advertising and a brand advocate
3	⬆⬇	Amy meets John, who wants to hop onto the last flight of the day to Boston after missing a flight with another airline	
		• Amy transfers her airline points to John in exchange for his points earned from the hotel chain – this depends on the blockchain aggregation strategy • She uses them to extend her holiday while John gets a discounted ticket back to Boston • Liability is cleared from the airline's book as the points have been completely used	• Amy gets an extended holiday while John gets a timely, discounted flight • Liabilities cleared from the airline's books while the hotel and airline get a happier and new customer, respectively

Source: Based on: Making blockchain real for customer loyalty rewards programs, a Deloitte report.

Figure 8.15 Use Case

Source: Based on "Making Blockchain Real for Customer Loyalty Rewards Programs," a Deloitte Report

trust of a blockchain business network, as it can control the end-to-end of the data until it is pushed to the blockchain network – the data that needs to reside there – and also protect the organization from policies like GDPR.

Requirements and use cases on the airline industry align well with the capabilities of the blockchain networks, whether is a private/permissioned, public, or hybrid blockchain network. Assets control (parts, inventory, status, etc.) and data sharing among multiple participants of the blockchain network fall within the airline blockchain realm. That may include players for a particular line of business, for instance, in a digital wallet case that would have consumers and other service partners or payment providers, among other players. Other participants (authorized partners or entities authorized to transact with that particular airline network) could be players commonly found on a MaaS ecosystem plus the extended vision presented earlier, like partners, online travel agencies, employees, airports, hotels, contractors, custom, car rental/sharing, etc.

Final remarks and recommendations

Personalization is hot topic today and will continue to be as the race for customers' loyalty will continue to be very active in this battlefield, as competition for their attention and business will continue strong. Some airlines may say my planes are full, and customer experience may not be their major focus. That may be the case today for some companies; they may even suggest using a competitor's flight when there's no competitor on that route. But this scenario may change, maybe sooner than expected. The more you know about your passenger, the more airlines can be creative, driving better services and personalized offers. Even if personalization and customer experience is not their top priority, this can pose an opportunity to rethink their revenue strategy and data segmentation processes to bring new insights into their current pricing strategy and consider a focus change from an approach based on seat assignment to passenger-centric.

This knowledge about the customer can support airlines to break the silos, in some cases, among different groups (marketing, sales, revenue management and customer services groups) inside the organizations and helps to have a macro view of their ecosystems. Here are some recommendations airlines should start moving forward:

- Leverage the value brought up by the hyper-personalization hexagon framework and start moving key components in an incremental approach to build this new platform, driving better support and personalization to customers across different and appropriate channels.

  - Imagine if a customer calls your contact center and is identified immediately, and fully comprehensive information about that customer is presented to the agent in one single screen – all their preferences, their demographics, loyalty point, their booking history and current reported and detected issues, their sentiment analysis (negative, neutral, or positive), and long-time value, among other pertinent information. Certainly, this bring more efficiency to the contact center and capabilities to address any issues, and intelligent insights can be readily available in one single view of the customer.

• Up-sell and/or cross-sell opportunities can be readily available for the contact center agent (obviously this can also be present on the online passenger app) – "Next Best Offer"[17] (via Einstein AI, see architecture diagram, Figure 8.12) is increasingly used for a proposal customized on the basis of passenger's attributes and behaviors (demographics, booking history, preferences, destinations, etc.).

• Use these capabilities to assess and analyze the customer-facing processes and touch points and improve them, creating a foundation to support the entire customer end-to-end journey, as highlighted in Figure 8.13.

• Look for a way to leverage this data available now (structured and unstructured) to leapfrog your competition with better revenue strategies on pricing optimizations – use the power of AI.

• Don't make personalization initiative as one shot only – create processes and metrics to keep constantly monitoring your personalization strategies in order to keep improving your customers' experiences.

• Airlines as well as hotel chains[18] recognized too late the power of online travel agencies (OTAs) to disrupt the industry and have been paying for that misstep ever since. The nascent state of blockchain for loyalty programs offers an opportunity to realize the value of disruption and shape its future impacts – if travel companies don't wait too long.

• Leverage the power of the integration capabilities of this platform – don't try reinvent the wheels. A platform should provide capabilities to integrate with your own systems and build the engagement leveraging the systems you already have.

The final results of all these is a better tailored and satisfying travel experience for the customers and a significant improved revenue opportunity for the airlines.

Be proactive and anticipate before your customer reaches out!

Notes

1 P. Gillespie and G. Bharaj, *Use Personalization to Enrich Customer Experience and Drive Revenue*, Gartner, https://www.gartner.com/doc/3839665/use-personalization-enrich-customer-experience, December 2017.

2 *How Supply Chain Can Drive Better Customer Experiences*, www.gartner.com/doc/368 8842?ref=ddisp, April 2017.

3 *Salesforce Research e-Book*, www.salesforce.com/content/dam/web/en_us/www/docu ments/e-books/industries/PR015027_Salesforce_Industry_Ebook.pdf.

4 *Customer Experience in Hospitality: Embrace Customer Data and Elevate the Guest Experience*, Forrester Research, http://hotelmarketing.com/index.php/content/article/ study_embrace_customer_data_and_elevate_the_guest_experience, December 2015.

5 Forbes, *Extreme Personalization Is the New Personalization: How to Use AI to Personalize Consumer Engagement*, www.forbes.com/sites/briansolis/2017/11/30/extreme-personalization-is-the-new-personalization-how-to-use-ai-to-personalize-consumer-engagement/#3c61d87829ad.

6 *The Power of Personalization*, www.accenture.com/t20170201T002423Z__w__/us-en/_acnmedia/PDF-39/Accenture-The-Power-of-Personalization-POV.pdf, Accenture, February 2017.

7 T. Davenport et al., "Know What Your Customers Want Before They Do," *Harvard Business Review*, https://hbr.org/2011/12/know-what-your-customers-want-before-they-do, December 2011.

8 *MaaS Alliance*, https://maas-alliance.eu/

9 *Mobility as a Service, National Aging and Disability Transportation Center*, www.nadtc.org/wp-content/uploads/Bringing-Mobility-as-a-Service-to-the-US-Accessibility-Considerations-Final.pdf.

10 *New Distribution Capability*, www.iata.org/whatwedo/airline-distribution/ndc/Pages/default.aspx.

11 *What Is New Distribution Capability? An NDC Primer for Travel Agents*, http://hostagencyreviews.com/what-is-new-distribution-capability-ndc-primer-travel-agents/, November 2017.

12 *Customer Segmentation*, https://searchsalesforce.techtarget.com/definition/customer-segmentation.

13 Ibid.

14 Accenture, *Beyond The Buzz: The Potential of Blockchain Technology for Airlines*, www.accenture.com/us-en/insight-potential-blockchain-technology-for-airlines.

15 D. Kowalewski et al., *Blockchain Will Transform Customer Loyalty Programs*, https://hbr.org/2017/03/blockchain-will-transform-customer-loyalty-programs?referral=03759&cm_vc=rr_item_page.bottom, March 2017.

16 "Making Blockchain Real," *Deloitte Report*, www2.deloitte.com/content/dam/Deloitte/us/Documents/financial-services/us-fsi-making-blockchain-real-for-loyalty-rewards-programs.pdf.

17 T. Davenport et al., "Know What Your Customers Want Before They Do," *Harvard Business Review*, https://hbr.org/2011/12/know-what-your-customers-want-before-they-do, December 2011.

18 D. Kowalewski et al., *Blockchain Will Transform Customer Loyalty Programs*, https://hbr.org/2017/03/blockchain-will-transform-customer-loyalty-programs?referral=03759&cm_vc=rr_item_page.bottom, March 2017.

Blockchain use – cases in travel

Maksim Izmaylov

CEO
Winding Tree

What is blockchain?

For people from the "blockchain space,"[1] the term blockchain is inseparably intertwined with Bitcoin. The Bitcoin creation story is short, yet profound in its consequences.

The year is 2008; Lehman Brothers has just collapsed, and a mere few weeks after that, in October, the now-famous "Bitcoin white paper"[2] was published by someone under a pseudonym Satoshi Nakamoto. The first sentence after the titles reads: "A *purely peer-to-peer* version of electronic cash would allow online payments to be sent directly from one party to another without going through a *financial institution*."[3] The goal and the motivation of this invention were further clarified when the first version of the Bitcoin software was released on January 3, 2009. In the coinbase parameter of the genesis block,[4] there was a message: "The Times 03/Jan/2009 Chancellor on brink of second bailout for banks."

The idea is straightforward. Instead of storing your money in a bank, and by doing so giving the banks an immense amount of power, which then can be used against you, you can now be your own bank. The Bitcoin software is open and transparent, the checks and balances designed for the system to be stable and resilient to attacks are introduced. The code is open-source, and the concept of chaining blocks[5] is just a part of the grand design for achieving the end goal, i.e., having a financial system that is not controlled by a third party or anyone but the community of its users. Despite that, there is a need for a word to express the idea of a "decentralized distributed network," so the term "blockchain" is coined.

Bitcoin goes virtually unnoticed for years, until reports about its ridiculously high price start circulating in the news, and Nouveau crypto riche start to appear. It is fascinating that what interests most people about Bitcoin until now is just a potential for making money on speculation and not the long-term vision that Bitcoin creators undoubtedly had.

Underestimated technology

The importance of the incarnation of these concepts in the physical reality – well, as physical as data bits can be – is easy to overlook.

First of all, none of the ideas behind Bitcoin were new. It just took a group of hackers outraged by injustice to put them together. For example, in 1998 a computer scientist and legal scholar Nick Szabo proposed a concept of a decentralized digital currency he called "bit gold" which today is considered a direct precursor of the Bitcoin architecture. A year before that Hashcash, a proof-of-work algorithm for solving email spam, was created by Adam Back, another prominent figure in crypto. It's hard to imagine that it didn't influence Szabo and Nakamoto's designs.

Quite a few thinkers anticipated the creation of Bitcoin. Some said that the government's monopoly on money would inevitably be displaced by "cybermoney," and that inflation wouldn't be a revenue option for nation-states anymore.[6] In a 1999 interview, Milton Friedman said that the role of government would be significantly reduced by the Internet, specifically mentioning the need for reliable electronic cash. Others warned that increasing centralization of financial systems leads to an appearance of stability while creating possibilities for system-wide devastating crises.[7]

The changes that are brought upon us by peer-to-peer technologies such as the Internet or Bitcoin are highly disruptive for centralized industries with high entry barriers, like telcos in 1993. Back then we probably had just one phone company to choose from if we wanted to make a phone call. Today I have a whole screen on my smartphone with apps that I can use to make video calls around the world *for free*. Because these applications use open technologies, new contenders can enter the market very easily. Music, TV, film industry, publishing, classifieds, and newspapers are just a few examples of industries that were entirely transformed by the Internet.

The blockchain revolution that started with Bitcoin and that is now well underway bears the same marks as the invention of the computer and the creation of the worldwide web. Most important, all of these inventions are in the public domain. There are no patents or any other barriers that could prevent us from using these technologies and creating new things on top of them. There are already thousands of projects under development, fueled by the crypto price surge and a sudden inflow of capital available to developers because of the borderless nature of cryptocurrencies. Even the VC market is being disrupted by ICOs (or initial coin offerings) that helped entrepreneurs raise $6.1 billion in 2017.[8]

Overhyped technology

The majority of the population has never heard about Bitcoin or blockchain, but the most vulnerable group out there is people who know something about them but still don't see the full picture. The recent example of that is Kodak's share price doubling after their announcement of creating a blockchain-based platform for photographers. Even more bizarre than that, now the Securities and Exchange Commission launched investigations of several US companies that added the word blockchain to their names, followed by an immediate stock price surge.

Does it mean that the public positively reacts to this technology? Not necessarily. I'm afraid it happens for all the wrong reasons. An average crypto-Joe wants to see the price of his favorite coins to go up. In other words, people want to make a quick buck, inspired by the stories of early adopters of Bitcoin and Ethereum who are now multimillionaires. A general assumption is that it's too late to buy BTC or ETH, so Joe is always looking for new cryptocurrencies to invest in. Unfortunately, the vast majority of all the new blockchain projects are utter nonsense designed to scam Joe, but with enough marketing money poured into them, Joe is convinced to give his BTC or ETH to the criminals. Bitconnect, a classic pyramid scheme, received multiple millions of dollars from people who should have known better. As Naval Ravikant said, "Bitcoin is a tool for freeing humanity from oligarchs and tyrants, dressed up as a get-rich-quick scheme."

Another dangerous fallacy is the idea of so-called private blockchains, i.e., a blockchain that is controlled by one company. But "centralized decentralization" is an oxymoron! If a blockchain is owned and controlled by one company, it is, by definition, centralized. Therefore, it is just a glorified database with some cryptographic magic sprinkled on top of it. As one of the most prominent thinkers of the blockchain revolution Andreas Antonopoulos[9] said, "if it ain't open, it ain't worth shit." Naturally, the businesses that are afraid to lose their market position have adopted the "let's just add the word blockchain to it" strategy. I attended several airline industry meetings where some big companies were trying to convince the audience to use their BaaS (blockchain-as-a-service), supporting their argument with illegible slides that consist of colorful circles and squares connected in complicated ways and inscriptions that are too small for anyone to read. Unfortunately, when I asked the audience about their knowledge of Bitcoin and blockchain, only three people out of 30 coyly raised their hands. No one knew what they were looking at, how blockchain could be used, or what it is. It was easy to see that the king was naked, but no one wanted to admit it first.

There is also an opinion that anything that uses the chained-blocks design can be called blockchain. It is as wrong as a statement that anything that uses the HTTP protocol is the Internet. Yes, HTTP is useful in many cases, but the groundbreaking change came from the combination of it with many other technologies that allow people to collaborate in large numbers effectively.[10] Similarly, you can use cryptographic proofs (a.k.a chained blocks) to assure your business partners of the validity of your data and increase the efficiency of your software by a few percentage points, but that improvement would be limited to your company only. Bitcoin, on the other hand, has already created a multi-billion dollar industry that anyone can participate in by building things on top of it: better wallets, faster payment networks, etc.

Blockchain benefits

The original sentiment behind Bitcoin goes against common business sense. It wasn't created so a few corporations could benefit from it – just the opposite. Bitcoin is public infrastructure that anyone can use anytime, anywhere on the planet. Everyone wins!

Again, it doesn't mean that chained blocks can't be applied in a context of one company, for the benefit of the reduced cost of audit. But only public blockchains can help us reduce the cost of networking[11] and increase social scalability, that is the ability of humans to effectively interact in large numbers, to transcend our Dunbar's number.[12] In other words, only networks with no entry barriers allow for massive network effects.

Peer-to-peer technologies, like public permissionless blockchains, could finally help us solve the tragedy of the commons. In today's capitalism, the goal of any business is to become a monopoly. But monopolies are bad for society as a whole – they should be avoided – so we've devised complicated antitrust laws. Big companies can work around them by moving to another jurisdiction and hiring the best lawyers money can buy, so we have to think of better laws, and so the struggle goes on and on.

With blockchain, mission-critical components of our society, like issuing currency or identity systems, could operate autonomously, so there is no risk that the party that controls those components would abuse their position. The transition will not be smooth. For example, venture capitalist Mike Maples' investment thesis reads:[13]

- Software-defined networks will be the most valuable businesses, displacing traditional corporations as central actors.
- Networks can bring exponential improvements in prosperity throughout the world.
- Networks will encounter fierce resistance from traditional businesses, governments, and other parts of society that don't want a different future.
- Tech leaders are part of the problem, and this needs to change for networks to realize their full potential.

A decentralized approach trumps the traditional one-entity-controls-all design on a few levels. First of all, a system like Bitcoin is unhackable. In 2017, Equifax, one of the largest credit agencies, was hacked, and the identities of 143 million people were stolen. With a decentralized identity system, it would be impossible to access that data. Yes, individual identities can and will be breached due to inadequate security measures, but there would be no way to access all the profiles of such networks. That's the difference between storing all your money in a bank or at home. If the bank is robbed, the money of all its depositors are lost, but there is no way for a criminal to break into every house in the country. That's precisely how Bitcoin works: there is no central storage of funds: you are your own bank, you control access to your Bitcoin "account," and if you have reasonable security measures in place, your funds and data will be safe.

Unauthorized access to information that should be protected is another threat that customers of traditional Internet businesses face. In a 2016 lawsuit, Uber executives were accused of spying on reporters' trips, and it was uncovered that some Uber employees were able to access information about their ex-partners and celebrities.[14]

Even in the most-secure centralized scenario, that kind of information will still be available to engineers that have access to the database where the sensitive data is stored. With the decentralized approach, you would have to explicitly permit another party to read your profile. Yes, all the Bitcoin transactions can be easily accessed by anyone, but it is an easy matter to use the system in such a way that would prevent anyone from deducing who is transacting and why.

Another important feature of distributed systems is their resilience to attacks. The Bitcoin network, for example, could never be stopped. About 12,000 nodes make up the Bitcoin network today, so even if it is banned in a whole country, its operation will not be affected significantly. Centralized systems fail all the time. Just in 2017 the airline industry experienced multiple system-wide disruptions due to technical failures of centralized systems.[15]

Most importantly, by delegating our power to one organization (whether it's money or sensitive data), we make those organizations extremely powerful. Let's say you put your money into a bank. What do they do with it? Bribe the economists and lobby the government so they allow for all sorts of gambling with your money. If the gamble is successful, the banks win big, and if it doesn't go too well, they know that they will be bailed out with your tax money.

Some theorize that even many functions of the governments can also be delegated to blockchains. For example, Ralph Merkle, the author of one of the technologies used in blockchains, Merkle trees, reasons that a new type of democracy, more stable and less prone to erratic behavior, could be built using what he calls "Distributed Autonomous Organizations."[16]

I would like the reader to decide for themselves whether the centralization of certain aspects of the airline industry has been beneficial or counterproductive.

Blockchain use cases

As I've shown above, blockchains can be used by almost any individual or organization, and therefore it is an ungrateful task to discuss its concrete use cases. If your business sends or receives payments, processes data in any way, or deals with customers, you can benefit from using blockchains, but you will have to decide how you're going to it based on the needs of your business.

I often use Conway's Game of Life[17] analogy to explain this. It's a mathematical game that has only four simple, carefully designed rules. The complexity that arises from those rules is fascinating! I encourage you to look up videos of Conway's Game of Life, I guarantee a few minutes of excitement if you are mathematically inclined.

The two important blockchain "games" today, Bitcoin and Ethereum, largely have just two "rules": they provide decentralized computation and decentralized immutable storage. Using these two properties, software engineers around the world have already devised projects like:

- peer-to-peer cash (Bitcoin);
- smart contracts (Ethereum, Rootstock);
- decentralized identity (uPort);
- tamper-proof voting systems (democracy.earth);
- dispute resolution (Kleros); and
- notary service (Proof of Existence).

Any business could benefit from, say, an effective dispute-resolution system or a lightning-fast online notary service. Certainly, a sovereign individual of the future will need some electronic cash and a decentralized identity.

Let's take a look at the travel industry. What problems can be solved with decentralized computation and immutable storage? What is centralized? What issues could go away if individuals and businesses adopted electronic cash and decentralized identities?

Fraud

Cryptocurrencies have far superior security compared to credit or debit cards, where the only piece of information that you need to authorize a transaction is revealed during every interaction with a merchant.

When we start paying for goods and services with cryptocurrencies, the fraud problem will be eliminated because if someone is able to access your private key[18] and send a transaction on your behalf, then you have a much bigger problem than one fraudulent transaction. The attacker won't spend your BTC, ETH or LIF on booking hotels, they will simply transfer all your funds to the account that they control as quickly as possible.

Customers could also have assurance that they are looking at a legitimate offer from an organization, if that offer is signed with that organization's private key. This could prevent criminals from creating phishing websites.

Reputation

Another general business problem is fake reviews. With decentralized identity systems, we will be able to have proof that the person praising your competition is indeed their customer and not a paid reviewer.[19] With blockchain, it is easy to prove that an account (e.g., passenger) is the initiator of a transaction with another account (airline), and it can be done in a completely anonymous manner; no details about the passenger need to be revealed.

Distribution

Travel distribution is a space dominated by just a few companies; in other words, it is highly centralized. Those companies have an immense amount of power they abuse.[20] They act as gatekeepers for both sides of the marketplace. It is a perfect example of where decentralized computation can help.

An autonomous algorithm that would match the traveler with the right hotel or airline is not just doable but is in its active development phase. For example, Winding Tree is a blockchain-based marketplace for travel inventory. Any supplier (airline, hotel, car rental, tour or activity provider) can connect to the marketplace via an API without asking anyone for permission, because the system is as open as the Internet itself. Travel agencies can access that data via another API, also in an entirely autonomous manner, no human interaction necessary.

This approach aims to radically lower barriers to entry into the travel industry, enable more innovation, and help streamline and standardize some business processes.

Settlement

Airline settlement in the US today is done by just one company, ARC. You can't get more centralized than that, so a smart contract run on a public permissionless blockchain could make it more efficient. Imagine that a complicated itinerary that involves a few legs with different airlines is reconciled not by the airline that initially received the payment but by an algorithm that sends the payments to the appropriate parties immediately.

Maintenance, repair, overhaul

The immutable storage feature of blockchains can improve the efficiency of businesses for which it is critical to store data in that way. For example, airplane maintenance and repair data can be stored on a blockchain[21] so that at any time the airline and other parties have full confidence that that information has not been tampered with; otherwise it would be very easy to detect.

Blockchain can assure the integrity of the data over time, but it doesn't guarantee its correctness. For this reason, using blockchain for supply chain management, for example, where information will inevitably be entered by third parties, is quite limited, though it could be vastly improved if used along with decentralized identities. It could be beneficial in the context of aircraft maintenance and airports, where every employee goes through extensive screening.

Airport operations

Blockchains are networks, and therefore they are useful when they achieve a critical mass. When airports, airlines, and governments agree to use the same data standard for decentralized identities, the efficiency of many processes around sharing passenger data or baggage tracking, for example, could be immensely improved.

The passenger, of course, should control their data at all times by explicitly allowing certain parties (airlines, governments, airports, even businesses located at airports) to read a specific subset of their profile. E.g., it would be useful for an airline to know the dietary preferences of their customers. The passenger will be able to choose to share that information or not.

The border control officers, perhaps, could prescreen arriving passengers even before landing. And then the duty-free shops could send personalized deals to passengers that explicitly wanted to receive them.

Loyalty

Blockchain looks like the perfect infrastructure for value transfer, and loyalty points could be represented as crypto-tokens. Creating a loyalty token for your business (whether it's an airline, hotel or a coffee shop) is extremely easy; it can be done with just a few lines of code. What prevents us from using tokens for loyalty is the high price of blockchain transactions. There are already several projects that aim to scale blockchain throughput and reduce transaction fees, like Lightning Network and Raiden Network. Once one of them is fully operational, a whole new range of possibilities will open up – if, of course, technology is one of the problems in the loyalty space at all.

Conclusion

According to Deloitte's 2018 survey,[22] the majority of executives they talked to claimed that their level of understanding of blockchain technology is "excellent" or "expert."[23] At the same time, those executives are sure that the main advantage of the blockchain technology is greater speed compared to the existing systems.[24]

It shows that the technology is still misunderstood, because Bitcoin was not created for faster payments. The transaction speed and the cost of executing were sacrificed for a higher ideal, to ensure Bitcoin's resistance to influence from any potential intermediary.

Blockchain means decentralization. This technology allows us to own and control our money and data without the help of an intermediary. Networks can exponentially improve the quality of life around the world, and the most successful networks are those with no barriers to entry. Some of today's most successful networks are centralized, and in many areas, the winner takes most of the market: Google, Amazon, Facebook, Uber, Amadeus, Expedia. Blockchain gives us a possibility to end this pattern.

Blockchain technology has yet to bring about products that would have as much utility as centralized networks. Nonetheless, there are hundreds of projects with billions in funding. Some of the smartest people on the planet believe that blockchain will radically transform business and society. How and when it's going to happen? It's for you to decide.

Notes

1 Sometimes also "crypto space," where "crypto" is derived from "cryptography."
2 "Bitcoin: A Peer-to-Peer Electronic Cash System," https://bitcoin.org/bitcoin.pdf.
3 Cursive is mine. Maksim Izmaylov.
4 Bitcoin Wiki contributors, "Genesis block," Bitcoin Wiki, https://en.bitcoin.it/wiki/Genesis_block (accessed October 31, 2018).
5 The term blockchain was never used in the original white paper; it came to prominence much later, around 2016.
6 James Dale Davidson and William Rees-Mogg, *The Sovereign Individual: Mastering the Transition to the Information Age* (Touchstone, 1999). New York.
7 Nassim Nicholas Taleb, *The Black Swan: The Impact of the Highly Improbable* (Random House, 2007). New York.
8 ICO 2017 Statistics. ICODATA.IO, https://www.icodata.io/stats/2017 (accessed October 31, 2018).
9 Andreas M. Antonopoulos is a best-selling author, speaker, and educator. In 2014, Antonopoulos authored the groundbreaking book, *Mastering Bitcoin* (O'Reilly Media), widely considered to be the best technical guide ever written about the technology.

10 Yuval Harari, in his bestselling book *Sapiens* (Harper, 2015, New York), argues that the ability of humans to collaborate effectively and in large numbers is what sets us apart from all other living beings.

11 Christian Catalini and Joshua Gans. "Some Simple Economics of the Blockchain," http://ide.mit.edu/publications/some-simple-economics-blockchain.

12 Nick Szabo, "Money, Blockchains and Social Scalability," https://unenumerated.blog spot.com/2017/02/money-blockchains-and-social-scalability.html.

13 Mike Maples, "Floodgate Partner Mike Maples: Network-Based Businesses Will Disrupt All Sectors of the Economy," *Fortune*, http://fortune.com/2018/08/16/floodgate-mike-maples-networks/ (accessed October 31, 2018).

14 Spangenberg, Samuel. SAMUEL WARD SPANGENBERG vs. UBER TECHNOLOGIES, INC. CGC-16-552156, October 5, 2016. Web. www.scribd.com/document/334009796/Spangenberg-Uber-lawsuit.

15 Christopher Jasper, Thomas Seal, Benjamin D Katz, "Airlines Suffer Worldwide Delays After Global Booking System Fails," Bloomberg, September 28, 2017, https://www.bloomberg.com/news/articles/2017-09-28/airlines-suffer-worldwide-delays-as-amadeus-booking-system-fails (accessed October 31, 2018).

16 Merkle, R., "DAOs, Democracy and Governance," *Cryonics Magazine*, July–August 2016, Vol. 37, No. 4, pp. 28–40; Alcor, www.alcor.org. https://alcor.org/cryonics/Cryonics2016-4.pdf#page=28.

17 Wikipedia contributors, "Conway's Game of Life," Wikipedia, The Free Encyclopedia, https://en.wikipedia.org/w/index.php?title=Conway%27s_Game_of_Life&oldid=866400002 (accessed October 31, 2018).

18 Simply put, it's the password that you need to send a transaction from your crypto-wallet.

19 Michael H. Keller, "The Flourishing Business of Fake YouTube Views," The New York Times, August 11, 2018, https://www.nytimes.com/interactive/2018/08/11/technology/youtube-fake-view-sellers.html (accessed October 31, 2018).

20 Winding Tree White Paper.

21 Storing data on a blockchain is very expensive, in the range of thousands of dollars per gigabyte. Instead of paying that much, you can create a cryptographic hash of the data and upload it to a blockchain instead. Now you have proof that certain data existed at a certain point in time, and any tampering with that data will be easily detectable. This concept lies behind services like Proof-of-Existence.

22 "Breaking blockchain open. Deloitte's 2018 global blockchain survey." www2.deloitte.com/us/en/pages/consulting/articles/innovation-blockchain-survey.html

23 P. 40 of the report.

24 P. 21.

The air cargo business models, or regaining customer relationship

Dietmar Kirchner

Senior Aviation Advisor
Frankfurt, Germany

Air cargo up to the '70s ("First Party Logistics")

Air cargo developed as a "by-product" of the passenger airlines. Belly space was not completely filled with passengers' baggage, and there was a demand for high-speed delivery when international trade started booming in the '60s. With the appearance of the jets, especially the B747s, selling cargo space became a substantial part of the airlines' business.

Cargo sales departments were established within the airlines' marketing organization. The ops team at the airport spun off their cargo team, located on separate premises at the airport. Some of the leading cargo airlines further extended their capacity by adding B747 freighters and by building large semi-automated cargo handling centers.

Processes were copied from the already established passenger workflows. Shipments were booked on specific flight numbers, equivalent to the PNR; the Airway Bill (AWB) was the underlying document. Reservations were done, similar to the passenger side, on large reservation systems ("USAS Cargo," etc,). Cargo had to be brought to the airport and was delivered at cargo centers at the destination.

Freight forwarders already played a role in these days. They used "blocked space agreements" to reserve capacity for their own business. However, more than often, they were not able to fill their blocked capacity, resulting in last minute cancelations, combined with an unwillingness to pay the "guaranteed" fare.[1]

Along came Fred Smith ("Second Party Logistics")

In the early '70s, Fred Smith invented FedEx and started to disrupt the air cargo business. He established a new air cargo system that changed a lot of the conventional wisdom:

- Service was door-to-door and no longer airport-to-airport, requiring a vast fleet of trucks to service the first and last mile.
- Shipments were managed with shipment numbers instead of AWBs.
- Rates for a city-pair were only driven by size/weight and urgency ("Overnite" vs. "Next Day") which required no published schedules.
- Shipments were always accepted, as capacity was driven by demand.
- The hub operation in Memphis (and later many other airports) was completely controlled by FedEx to guarantee maximum efficiency.

- FedEx provided four layers of airplane capacity:

  - year-round trunk long-range routes (operated by own fleet, mainly new and efficient aircraft);
  - short-range and seasonal capacity (operated by own fleet of older, written-off aircraft);
  - ad hoc capacity for unforeseeable "delayable" demand operated by third-party carriers on 24-hour notice; and
  - ad hoc capacity for unforeseeable "must-go" demand operated by third-party carriers on very short notice.

Over time the FedEx business model was copied, and now, after many mergers and acquisitions, there are only FedEx, UPS, and DHL sharing the global market for door-to-door services. With their fast growth starting in the US, most classic carriers (except Northwest) decided not to invest in B747 freighters.

The age of the forwarders ("Third Party Logistics")

Logistics companies started as specialists for short range (trucks), medium range (trains), or long range (shipping companies). Over time they added services from third parties to complement their offerings. Urgent freight was booked on air cargo carriers, continuous service on trunk routes provided by booking "pallet positions." In that case, business culture quickly deteriorated, as the forwarders very often did not stick to their commitments in case of unexpectedly low demand.

With the growth of complex international supply chains, the forwarders expanded their line of services:

- all means of transport;
- final assembly and storage;
- customs clearance;
- last mile distribution;
- relocation,
- waste handling; and
- fairs and events services.

In today's airline terms, "ancillaries" became part of the service chain.

Today, all the major forwarders have "pallet factories" near the major cargo hubs where they produce ready-to-fly pallets and then bring them to the most appropriate airline on a short-term basis.

The forwarders have managed to become the "owners" of the customers (=shippers), as they deliver fully integrated logistics solutions. Now it is common that they aggressively protect their customer relationship by prohibiting direct contacts between airlines and shippers.

Also, this market has consolidated. The largest 20 companies hold 60 percent of the global market.

Digital age logistics becomes "Forth Party Logistics" (4PLs)

Both disruptive customer-centric business models developed in the "pre-digital" age. No 21st-century technology was necessary to make the classic airlines "truckers in the sky."

Now the digital age starts producing "virtual integrators" who use ad hoc physical services by third parties without having those capabilities themselves. Their role is limited to "managing" the total process pretty much like Uber or Lyft manage taxi services without owning any cars.

This completely digital business model is intended to provide "best-in-class" solutions to the customer in every service component, as it is completely independent of the need to first fill own capacity. As of today we can observe three different approaches:

- Lead logistics providers (LLP) are forwarders (3PLs) who offer 4PL services. However, they have a credibility problem, as customers doubt their independence toward their in-house offerings.
- Customer-owned 4PLs are developed by companies with a large logistics budget. Germany's largest retail group, Metro, has established their in-house company MGL to organize all their logistics processes.
- The "true 4PL" company integrates, plans, and manages all the logistics processes of its customers without owning any assets. Pioneers are companies like Flexport (www.flexport.com) or Freightos (www.freightos.com). As the market still is very young and thus fragmented, it is still waiting for consolidation. Digital giants in the retail business (Alibaba, Amazon) will certainly play a role, as they are heading into the logistics business. Maybe logistics will be Amazon's next big offer after the establishment of their Cloud Services.

Lessons for the future passenger service providers

What can the airline passenger business learn from their cargo division's environment?

1   Even sales of air transport can work without reservations, yield management, and complex pricing, provided there is a smart combination of "storable demand" and flexible capacity. Today's passengers who are online even "on the road" certainly would accept ad hoc itineraries as part of an attractive price. Also, there are airlines specializing in providing "white label"[2] ad hoc capacity that could complement an airline's own capacity on short notice.

2   Also, passengers do not start or finish their trip in an airport. By adding door-to-plane services, airlines not only would increase their profile, but they could also use the pre- and post-flight ownership to select gateway airports in all those cases where there are multiple options for a passenger. It does not require a lot of fantasy to imagine a "**People FedExpress**" combining flights to fully integrated terminals with last mile services, whether by bus, minivan, car, or even drone.

3   "Ancillaries" should not be formerly **complimentary** services now sold at a price (meals, drinks, baggage, emergency seat rows, etc.) but rather services **complementary** to air transport (lodging, tours, ground transportation, visa services, data roaming access etc.). Certainly others will offer those services, including the air transportation, whether or not airlines will develop that sort of a business.

4   "Personal logistics" will come as "**mobility as a service** (MaaS)," either as 3PL by companies already owning some assets or as 4PL by companies who own just the process. It is still open whether these are customer-centric retailers with an already large customer base (Alibaba, Amazon) or travel and mobility disruptors (Uber, Airbnb), alliances of existing mobility providers (Daimler, BMW, and German Railways just started such a business for ground transportation in Germany), or even aggregators for large digital communities (Facebook).

So in the future we may see two new business models:

People FedExpress-type services will be provided by maybe three or four global network management systems. They will "soak up" the capacity of today's airlines (classics, LCCs, White Label). All these new networks connect the world's top 500 metropolitan areas with high frequencies and provide services to and from 90 percent+ of the world's markets for long distance transportation; thus, they have a really global presence. Around 60 percent of their capacity is deployed year-round, 20 percent on days with expectable higher demand, and 20 percent is operated on an ad hoc basis, when short-term unforeseeable demand is peaking. Passengers buy transportation on a door-to-door basis; prices are fixed and vary by three categories:

- Space (limousine vs. van transfer, sleeper vs. coach seats on the plane)
- Speed (as fast as possible vs. minimum time plus X hours)
- Flexibility (fixed arrival time vs. sometime within 48 hours)

Passengers are allocated to physical flights according to the category they have chosen. Those demanding maximum speed and no flexibility will be allocated first. Algorithms fill the planned capacity sequentially; overflow is allocated either on the same day's or next day's ad hoc capacity. This allocation process for most fare categories takes place within 24–48 hours before actual departure. Passengers are guided via mobile apps.

Yield management as a tool is discontinued, as demand and capacity are matched daily on an ad hoc basis. Fares per category are fixed and provide enough yield to even pay for an ad hoc airplane at a 80 percent load factor.

Over time, "fill-up" fares will disappear, as flying capacity will lose its "fixed cost" character.

Network management pays operators an ACMI rate per flight hour with some surcharge for short-term ad hoc capacity.

The three or four network providers maintain their own hub operations at airports to guarantee minimum check-in, connecting, and "air-to-land" times.

Airports will provide the operational airside infrastructure (runways, fuel, ATC, firefighting, fuel supply). As passengers are served door-to-door, waiting time at airports is drastically reduced; wherever possible, ground transportation connects right at the gate (with decentralized security checks). Typical airport ancillaries like parking, car rental, shops, and restaurants will either disappear or will be integrated into the services of the network providers.

"Mobility as a service" will be provided by quite a number of companies who provide smart self-explaining apps with voice-driven services on smartphones ("Mobile Alexa") to plan, organize, track, and support a traveler over his/her whole trip. Those services build on the "People FedEx" networks and combine them with all sorts of hospitality, event, and non-aviation mobility services. Other than today's GDS or OTA travel systems (or Amazon in the retail business), they do not only display purchasing options plus a web shop and a ticket/voucher delivery function, but they are supporting the traveler in every moment of his/her trip with online and "live" information to help navigate, to prepare a check-in at rental car stations or hotels, to facilitate transits between travel modes, to reroute in cases of delays, disruptions, or short-term itinerary changes, to advise of weather or traffic hazards, or to make reservations in restaurants (or even order meals before arrival).

Will today's airlines play a role?

Today's airlines will have two options:

1   **Follow the fate of their air cargo division**

    Provided their cost structure and locations are acceptable to the new network integrators, the airlines maintain their AOC, but sell most if not all of their capacity on an ACMI basis to the network integrators, pretty much like many of today's regional carriers sell their capacity to the large network carriers. Core competency will be the efficiency in operation.

2   **Become a global mobility provider (maybe together with others)**

    This highly innovative step would require the separation of the operational airline business from a completely new, customer-centric unit to provide mobility solutions independent of the capacity of the own "factory."

    "Culture eats strategy for breakfast" is an often cited quote (probably by Peter Drucker?). This fundamentally new strategy requires an innovation culture quite different to what we see at today's airlines:

Will even the ambitious airlines be able to fundamentally change their culture and innovate?

Table 8.1 The Innovation Culture Table[3]

	Status Quo Culture	Innovation Culture
1	Predictability	Un-predictability
2	Seek stability	Seek novelty
3	Focus on core competence	Focus on edge competence
4	High success rate	High failure rate
5	Reinforce the organizational hierarchy	Reinforce organizational networks
6	Fear the hierarchy	Focus on creative tension
7	Avoid surprises	Embrace surprises
8	Focus on inside knowledge	Combine inside and outside knowledge
9	Easy to live with	Hard to live with
10	Corporate politics	Moving the cheese
11	Efficiency through standardization	Efficiency through innovation
12	Extend the status quo	Abandon the status quo
13	Avoid change	Embrace change
14	Measure stability	Measure innovation
15	Look for data to confirm existing management models	Look for data to contradict existing management models
16	Senior managers have the critical knowledge	Everyone has critical knowledge
17	Look for certainty	Embrace ambiguity
18	Accept things as they are	Ask tough questions
19	Protect the past	Create the future

Notes

1 This "infidel" behavior was also common at tour operators on charter flights when the allotment figures could not be met.
2 Atlas Air is a well-known "White Label" operator of cargo airplanes. Besides many other customer airlines, they do all the flying on behalf of Amazon's "Prime" air cargo business.
3 The Agile Innovation Master Plan by Langdon Morris(p. 278), published by Future Lab Press 2011 & 2017.

Rethinking the airline platform

Soumit Nandi

Managing Director
Customer Technology Platforms, United Airlines

Introduction

Over the last 50 years, the travel industry has done an impressive job in investing in and modernizing the core technology platforms that power travel. Today we can book a flight and pay with our mobile apps, check in and board with our phones and even pay for upgrades and amenities from our smartphones. If we took the smartphones and apps away, the core building blocks that remain haven't changed significantly over the last five decades.

Early adoption of technology predictably led to early standardization, thanks to international organizations that have ensured that an airline in Ethiopia can connect seamlessly with one in Frankfurt, followed by one flying into Montana. PNRs, tickets, EMDs, and a series of standards that define integration between airline systems have enabled a global marketplace where passengers are no longer limited by the reach of an individual airline.

The PNR, ticket, and the messaging standards have served us well. However, the progress on digitizing and standardizing legacy paper-based processes is also an impediment as airlines look at transforming themselves to respond to accelerating shifts in consumer behavior and technology. These shifts, their implications, and potential technology strategies are the focus of this thought leadership piece. As with any future-focused strategy, it diminishes in relevance over time, and the industry will inevitably refine these strategies as market and consumer expectations evolve.

Understanding the shifts

Customer expectations

The effect of Amazon, amplified by a new generation of consumers that have accepted their level of customer service as the new normal, has meant that consumers expect to be in control of their experience, expect to be treated fairly, and are disappointed when companies do not go above and beyond. They also expect to be made whole when things go wrong, regardless of the fine print in the contracts they unwittingly agreed to.

Addressing customer-compatibility-related dissatisfaction is a significant challenge for airlines with broad product segmentation that cater to a growing and more diverse market. A local airline offering a no-frills travel service will typically attract and serve a specific customer profile. Deviations from that ideal profile can lead to customer dissatisfaction. This is a growing problem for larger, full-service carriers today. Aligning segmentation, marketing, and retail functions is critical to addressing this. How else could we make sure that a business executive on his weekly New York to Chicago flight is aware of the basic economy product he accidentally purchased? Or de-prioritize an offer to a frequent flyer used to picking a preferred seat from buying down to a product that doesn't allow him to select a seat?

Globalization

Globalization has extended the reach of global airlines in farflung markets around the world. As the world becomes a more connected marketplace, this creates opportunities for global airlines to cater to local markets better.

Unfortunately, many large global airlines are far too centralized in their outlook to local markets to effectively serve and grow these markets. Digital insights into consumer behavior, sales analytics by neighborhoods, and understanding of competitive forces all require a focused go-to-market strategy, built away from the head office but stitched together into a coherent plan.

Economic factors also play a role – generations growing up in a recession are more wary of credit, if, that is, they can get access to it. Expanding in such markets requires localized strategies – from marketing travel and experiences that are tailored to the local market, enabling popular, local forms of payment, to offering credit and installment payment options.

Social travel

Social sharing buttons are losing their relevance, but recent challenges around privacy notwithstanding, social cohesion continues to drive adoption and popularity of social media platforms. Airlines can help groups plan, shop, and book their travel – from flights to hotels to experiences – and extend this planning to tackling human factors – matching up potential travel partners, coordinating schedules, and sharing trip ideas, photos, and expenses.

Unlike the localization strategy, this demands a customer-centric perspective to understand how prospective customers plan, buy, and travel. This is outside the traditional "comfort zone" of creating a website where customers can search for flights. It shifts airlines farther left into the planning cycle and reduces friction in the planning and booking process for customers who plan to travel together.

While niche travel planning startups do not have a good success record, airlines and travel agencies can successfully play in this space and provide an end-to-end experience from planning to booking, and travel to social sharing.

Data privacy

As emerging regulatory activism around privacy and security become more prevalent, regulations like GDPR are driving the C-suite to pay greater attention to how their marketing, loyalty, and customer service departments leverage customer data.

Greater customer controls on how their data is captured, protected, and shared can be good news for emerging startups and platform companies like Google that can act as trusted custodians of customer biometric and profile data, enable customer-facing privacy controls, and share this information with partnering travel providers.

Airlines will have to step up their game and comply with these regulations across their marketing, sales, reservations, and travel systems or reorganize their business units and disparate systems to work with centralized customer data hubs that can better secure customer data and automatically apply rules driven by prevailing legislation.

Looking ahead

How do the newer generations think of travel? How have economic factors shaped their views on credit and luxury travel? How has the uneven nature of economic growth shaped the expectations of travel buyers? The more innovative airlines try to understand these shifts and refine their product, marketing, and customer strategies to cater to these changes.

Responding to business shifts leads to a framing opportunity.

As things evolve, an airline can put the urgent or emergent need at the center and leverage all available resources to solve the problem. This is certainly the only way to address a crisis, and an acceptable, if not scalable, way of doing business.

A reframed approach may serve airlines better in the long run. These emergent needs can be treated as transient, rapid innovations that are brought to market quickly, leveraging an adaptive, flexible underlying technology platform. As external influences change, airlines that invest in platforms may be in a better position to adapt quickly and effectively.

The new airline platform

Digital retail

Airlines are in danger of being relegated to becoming "suppliers" of travel – a majority of which is shopped, filtered, and sold on storefronts managed by large distributors and web-based travel agencies.

In this highly intermediated world of travel retail, airlines focus on two key strategies: improving their share of direct sales and improving conversion on direct sales channels. Capturing a larger portion of the pie will require more than an obsessive focus on flight shopping to booking conversion. Sometimes, making more money is just better than higher conversion.

Airline Internet commerce relies on a search-first mindset: you enter an origin, destination, and dates and initiate a search. This is travel supplier behavior at its best – it's simple, functional, and gets to results the quickest. Prospective customers know where they want to go, try a couple of searches, and either book or walk away. The advantage of this approach is simple – besides efficiency and higher conversion rates, once air travel is purchased, sales of ancillary services become easier based on the travel itinerary purchased – from seats to hotels.

In addition to a search-first pathway, a shop-first approach can expand the pie by creating a compelling, customer-centric retail experience. A customer picking a destination or an office location or just shopping for adventure travel creates more opportunities for up-selling and cross-selling. Even at lower conversion rates compared to the search-first path, shop-first pathways can expand the market size. Integration with travel partners in this new travel marketplace can translate to marginal revenue opportunities through commissions.

Expanding the funnel warrants an investment into travel curation beyond inclusion of syndicated travel content. Airlines will need to incubate digital agencies that develop and curate experiences. Combined with a travel planning platform, this new retail experience for airlines can expand the addressable market, inspiring more prospective customers into buying travel.

Offer management

Transitioning from top-down customer segmentation to choice modeling – dynamically building grounds-up customer micro-segments that are effective in predicting the likely retail behavior of customers – can allow for significant improvements in customer experience and revenue.

If 70 percent of all business travelers are likely to pick the 7:00 A.M. flight on Monday morning from Atlanta to New York, with a non-trivial number of close-in bookings forecasted, then offering incentives to move lower-yield customers to other flights during the day – or adjusting pricing in real time to shape demand – can serve as scenarios where revenue management, pricing, and digital channels can work in tandem. Airlines do this today by managing availability at various price points, but high fidelity customer data – including shopping, booking behavior, and competitive data – is crucial to making effective real-time pricing adjustments. Fortunately, some of this data is available, with varying degrees of quality, from an airline's customer-facing digital channels and other sources in the marketplace.

Dynamic pricing that optimizes revenue based on real-time channel and market feedback is the future of revenue management. Periodic willingness-to-pay-driven demand forecasts that drive adjustments to bid prices are important tools that get us part of the way. Being able to measure demand in real-time, test and tune total trip price, and refine offers to shape demand and optimize revenue is the end goal for most travel retailers. This requires bringing together two worlds that usually don't intersect: (1) Offer management – reviewing channel and customer attributes and leveraging analytics to construct personalized offers. (2) Revenue management – managing availability and pricing in order to optimize revenue.

Dynamic pricing is often met with skepticism due to the ability for an airline to differentiate pricing between customers. In reality, customers sitting side by side in the economy cabin of a major airline or booking similar rooms in the same hotel often pay different prices depending on a number of factors. Outside travel, aftermarket sales of Broadway tickets could vary widely based on demand for the same show and seat. A major donor to the theater or a celebrity may even get a ticket for free. Customers have come to expect to pay different prices at different times based on demand.

Centralized offer management and dynamic pricing are core capabilities in the airline platform of the future. In the heavily intermediated world of travel, ensuring all direct and indirect channels leverage common offer and pricing capabilities is a critical component of an airline's technology strategy.

Travel marketplace

Selling flights, hotels, and cars together isn't new. Expanding the PNR into "super PNRs" or other data formats and storing non-air travel merchandise takes us halfway there.

Enabling a retail marketplace, however, requires two additional capabilities: tracking fulfillment and financial settlement. Migrating from PNRs and tickets to a simpler and more extensible order management framework enables us to support both.

Once an order is sold, a hotel's property management system, for example, needs to be able to talk to an airline's order management system to mark an order item as fulfilled. A fulfillment trigger can kick off an automated process of financial settlement – either a manual process or one powered by blockchain.

The state transitions of an order item can be maintained in a blockchain smart contract – triggering automated financial remittances (with limited human oversight driven by threshold-based alerts) from the seller's account to the service provider's account or vice-versa. Since every participant in the transaction could host a few nodes of the blockchain, all parties to a transaction – and no one else – can share a common and always up-to-date status of settlement.

This deeper integration between travel partners goes beyond IATA's airline-focused One Order program. It enables travel and technology partners to create new ecosystems that can forge new alliances across the travel space including air, hotel and other travel companies.

Platforms play a central role in this ecosystem. An order management and settlement platform that enables partner integration beyond sales, and including fulfillment and settlement, greatly simplifies the current world of passenger service systems, accounting, and inter-line settlement.

The role of blockchain doesn't need to be limited to financial settlement. Enterprising startups are testing the application of blockchain in travel distribution – a travel mesh network – that allows a diverse range of travel providers and travel buyers to sell, fulfill and settle efficiently.

Customer centricity

In the world of travel technology, a customer is part of a PNR. This is another reframing opportunity for travel. PNRs are a transactional attribute of a customer, not the other way around. Customers come first, and a customer-centric approach is central to better understanding their travel needs and habits.

Identity

In an intermediated world, however, the customer is not very apparent. Is it the buyer? The agency? The GDS? The corporate department? Is it Alexa or Siri? Managing linked chains of identities across the travel ecosystem – for travel providers, aggregators, or buyers – is key to ensuring the right offer gets to the buyer at the end of the chain of intermediaries. Can an airline based in Ukraine trust an agency based in Ulan Bataar? If both were part of a global travel identity scheme, then yes, business partnerships can become a little bit easier.

The concept of authenticated travel buying – where a customer identifies himself prior to shopping – can lead to benefits for both airline and customer alike. Frequent travelers may gain access to better loyalty pricing or better inventory and be able to select services they are entitled to at the time of travel. Non-frequent travelers, once they identify themselves, may attract additional incentives from the airlines to try new products or services, and possibly incentives if they select alternate flights that aren't in high demand.

While this comes at a significant cost, customer data management is already in focus from emerging legislation around privacy and security. Well-written corporate policies that describe what kind of data is collected, what is shared, and what services are delivered are crucial to customer trust. Some basic customer data is crucial to the retail and fulfillment of travel products. Beyond that core set of customer data, customers may want to elect data they do not wish to share with an airline or customer data within an airline they do not want shared with the airline's partners.

Customer data hubs will have to store and manage these preferences as part of a customer's profile. Order management systems may need to restrict sales of products and services that cannot be fulfilled without access to the restricted data.

Assurance

Securing customer identity and data is the first step. A customer that shops, books, and travels still has to be able to validate his identity at progressively higher levels of assurance throughout the journey. It may be OK for someone to shop for her friend, but using a friend's credit card at the time of booking might not lead to a long-lasting relationship. Neither would the authorities appreciate impersonation of a friend when boarding the aircraft.

Biometrics usher in a high level of assurance in validating customer identities, enabling straight-through processing of orders, payments, many regulatory document checks, and boarding. Airports and airlines have been tentative adopters of this space and have started working with partners that act as custodians of customer biometric data to offer a better customer experience – from accessing lounges to speeding past long security lines. They may be right in taking a cautious approach. Over time, evolution of identity technologies is unpredictable and can take several paths: social platforms may dominate as the pre-eminent identity providers; governments may invest in digital identities for their citizens, from passports to driving licenses; and emergent customer identity management companies may grow and carve out broad regional or demographic niches in the market.

Identity assurance through digital identities and biometrics is best architected as a plug-and-play adapter that can connect with customer data management hubs within an airline. This offers the most flexibility as this area evolves further.

Context

With secure customer data management, and identity assurance, the next step in our journey toward customer centricity is context: Where is the customer in her journey? Is she in the dark space between the booking and travel, where airlines tend to forget about her till it's time for her to check in? Has she checked in but appears to have wandered into the wrong terminal, thanks to the beacon-based location capabilities of the airport and the airline's mobile app? Is she waiting for more than 15 minutes for her bag? Or is she flying on an aircraft without Wi-Fi capabilities? How do we prepare her for the next step? Location, travel context, and customer preferences are critical to improving customer experience.

What are the ways we can reach out to a customer about a critical travel issue impacting her journey? At the gate: notify the gate agent; on the flight: notify the flight attendants; in the club: send an alert on the customer's airline mobile app; and in the wrong terminal: SMS or call the customer directly. The message, the medium of delivery, and the target audience can vary widely depending on the importance and urgency of the message. The choices would be very different for a marketing promotion. Better context improves customer communication, and improving communication is core to a better customer experience.

Any platform, therefore, must put customer management at the very center of their ecosystem. Managing identities, customer profiles, and preferences, integrating with identity assurance providers, and tracking context are critical to a customer-centric platform.

Journey management

Despite advances in technology, travelers still endure a range of issues negotiating the physical world of travel. It is encouraging to see a range of industry initiatives currently underway to improve the customer experience at airports – from baggage tracking and automated bag drops to biometrics that can help de-stress security and boarding queues.

Airports are complex, confusing and overwhelming locations – and from experienced business travelers to seniors to those who are differently abled – governments, local chambers of commerce and airport authorities play a key role in improving the passenger experience.

It starts with preparing passengers for travel. Passengers are not always aware of the terminal they need to go to (particularly for codeshare/partner flights) or the state of congestion at the airport – at drop-off, bag-drop, security screening time – based on what they bought and entitlements they inherited. Flight information has been standardized and is accessible and largely accurate regardless of where we are. The same isn't true for vital airport information critical to travel. Add to this the complexity of globalization, and it isn't surprising that a Chinese airline would struggle to prepare their customers for travel commencing at an US airport.

Airports are travel platforms in their own right. But most airports have no real time view of their own "state." A mesh network of intelligent sensors that have the ability to identify passengers, monitor overall congestion and flow, and detect security threat patterns can provide real-time information to airlines, traveling passengers, and airport control systems alike.

An intelligent airport mesh network can serve four goals: (1) Security pattern identification and threat alerting (did a passenger leave his bag behind? is a young traveler seemingly unaccompanied/lost or in distress?). (2) Congestion and flow metrics (what is the processing time at security lane A?). (3) Real-time staff alerts (do we need to send a cleaning crew to gate 3?). (4) Personalized assisted travel (what is the best route to the gate? can we save time by using another security line?).

With the network in place, a couple of interesting possibilities open up. First, airports can generate real-time events or enable APIs that airlines and airport data exchanges can leverage to provide personalized assistance to customers. Second, digital signage at airports can tap into the network to provide real-time updates to passengers to balance out congested hot spots and even provide emergency information. As a further step, smart signs can identify a user with a smartphone and provide a range of personalized services – from help with navigation to providing tailored travel information.

Closer partnerships between governments, airports, airlines, and technology providers can reduce the stress of travel and deliver a frictionless travel experience for business and tourism alike.

The road ahead

Are we there yet?

The traditional airline isn't architected to take advantage of this rapidly evolving world. Peek under the covers and there are a set of B2C channels – websites, apps, contact centers – and large monolithic systems that manage frequent flyer accounts, revenue management, schedules, flight operations, and so on. At the core is the passenger service system (PSS) orchestrating the day-to-day customer-facing functions of an airline – managing schedules and revenue controls, pricing and selling tickets, and managing the airport functions. In addition to handling direct and NDC sales, the airline PSS today also serves as the storefront for GDS sales – the largest source of passenger revenue for the vast majority of airlines around the world.

This legacy architecture has developed over time to mirror how business units often work in a traditional airline: digital teams and marketing organizations pursue parallel marketing efforts; frequent flyer programs run in parallel to marketing organizations; and he customer experience is "owned" by several organizations across commercial and operations functions.

- Commercial teams create products that airports and contact centers struggle to fulfill.
- Country managers in other continents have no input into digital product management.
- Distribution teams struggle to prioritize digital investments that drive channel shifts.

To summarize, the shift toward a new platform requires us to reframe our priorities: (1) digital retail; (2) offer management and dynamic pricing; (3) travel marketplace; (4) customer centricity; and (5) journey management.

Each vector presents unique business opportunities in themselves – improving the customer experience, marginal revenue growth, and internal efficiencies.

Together, they help address the key shifts impacting the evolution of travel over the next few years – rising customer expectations, globalization, social travel, and data privacy.

A new business architecture

Airlines will need to focus on the core capabilities that are critical to their value chain. This shift away from the traditional PSS platform can dramatically simplify internal systems and drive collaboration across disparate business units.

The building blocks of a new airline platform will require cross-functional teams to focus on building five core capabilities:

- Customer: Unified view of the customer, including frequent flyers;
- Product: Centralized management of core, ancillary and partner products;
- Offers: Dynamically priced, personalized offers that span shopping and direct marketing initiatives;
- Orders: Booking, payments, fulfillment and settlement of travel marketplace orders; and
- Partners: Managing the partner ecosystem including travel and non-travel partners, distributors and agencies.

The immediate consumers of this new platform are APIs and B2C channels – APIs that can handle partner integration and B2C channels that enable a rich shopping and retail experience for customers.

If architected well, this new platform can open up new pathways for innovation. APIs and channels can rewire components of product, customer, and offers capabilities to create new services to drive local growth in a China market, while a different set of products, partners, and payment options may help capture higher market share in Brazil.

Bias toward action

Digitizing business processes has served airlines well over the last 50 years. It's easy to be comfortable in the world we know and grew up in. Changing the frame of reference and questioning the very building blocks of our current capabilities pushes us out of our comfort zone as airline leaders.

Creating a flexible, customer-centric airline platform that draws on the best thinking across the business units and builds on core airline capabilities presents a unique opportunity to invest in the future.

Two factors tip the scale in favor of airlines that adopt a platform approach: (1) Airlines are inherently technology companies. The physical world of airlines is mirrored by millions of lines of code in routing, scheduling, reservations, customer management, departure control, and flight planning systems. (2) Technology has transformed itself many times over in the last 50 years. Consumerization of enterprise-scale computing, and the ready availability of plug-and-play technologies are making platforms easier to build, maintain, and operate. Building platforms are no longer the domain of a chosen few mainframe programmers.

Shifts in consumer behavior and technology have created winners and losers in the market before. And it will happen again. Airlines that watch for points of inflection and adapt proactively will emerge as the next leaders in travel.

Flight plan to next-generation reliability: tomorrow's destination today

Bryan Terry

Managing Director and Global Aviation Leader, Deloitte

Mike Philipps

Commercial Director, McLaren Applied Technologies

The challenge today is to solve the problems of tomorrow with data-driven products that close the "physical-to-digital" divide for organizations. Facing this challenge requires going beyond the proof of concept and innovation to develop systems and processes that are robust enough to meet the demands of today and the future. McLaren, with expertise in simulation and analytics, and Deloitte, with its deep understanding on different industry domains, make it is possible to explore new opportunities for improvement in businesses to reach greater heights of performance, whether that's measured in customer experience, response to market, operational efficiency, or on the balance sheet. The goal is to address complex industry-wide problems and improve performance across businesses, combining specialist hardware and software with sophisticated algorithms. The idea is not just to measure what is unfolding right now and simply look back on events. Instead, it is necessary to create hundreds of thousands of alternate realities every second to guide the businesses toward the best available result. This is where an aviation business sector can capitalize on McLaren's expertise from the race track into the race for business performance to deliver competitive advantage.

Airline passenger numbers continue to grow exponentially, and the creation of new capacity trails behind the continued rising demand for air travel. How can stakeholders face challenges in different sectors of the aviation industry by developing a suite of solutions? Let us start with the need to predict airport operations performance.

Addressing critical industry challenges

Capacity utilization and asset maximization

Using data to make operational and efficiency gains

The aviation industry is going through an unprecedented level of growth, with predictions for Europe at 1.9 percent a year between now and 2040. That means 16.2 million flights a year, but crucially there won't be enough capacity for approximately 1.5 million flights – 160 million passengers – in 2040[1]. Historically, growth has been accommodated by investment and expansion in infrastructure. However, this approach is inefficient and unsustainable, particularly with increased environmental and economic pressures, not to mention political concerns around airport expansion.

Through August 2018, the European network has notched up over 14 million minutes of en route delay—year-to-year— an increase of more than 120 percent when compared with the same period last year, when the overall en route delay for the entire year was 9.3 million minutes.[2] The main causes have been capacity and staffing issues, as well as weather, followed by strikes and disruptive events.

In August 2018 alone, the average en route delay per flight was in the region of 3.35 minutes per flight (the EU-wide performance target for 2018 is 0.5 minutes), which represents an increase of 108 percent compared with the same period last year.[3] Longer term, the number of passengers delayed by one to two hours is predicted to grow from around the current figure of 50,000 each day to about 470,000 a day in 2040.[4]

To combat the increasing strain on the network, data needs to be used to make operational and efficiency gains. There needs to be a shift in focus toward optimizing the use of the infrastructure and assets already available, coupled with maximizing the opportunities and capabilities they present.

This change in source of growth should not be viewed as a limiting factor. Scope for asset maximization and capacity utilization resides in the resources currently present in the industry. Passengers can experience fewer delays and greater visibility of their journey as well as reduced transit and transfer anxiety.

Meanwhile, airports can increase their value proposition to airlines thanks to improved air performance and turnaround times. Further efficiency gains can free capacity to increase the number of flights operating in and out of the airport.

The disconnect between planning and operational reality

Closing the feedback loop

There is a frequent disconnect between planning and operational reality in aviation, leaving the industry to operate reactively as opposed to proactively. The object is to close this gap, moving the industry ahead of the curve by using simulation technology to determine outcomes and performance, as well as quantify the impact of factors beyond the plan.

Just as is the case in Formula 1, a closed loop system needs to be implemented to analyze performance using data tools, identify what could have been done better, learn from the internal approach and that of the wider aviation network, and rapidly implement improvements that can make a positive difference next time.

Currently in aviation, the day commences with a plan, and stakeholders execute that plan to the best of their ability using the knowledge, skills, and experience of the individuals. However, there isn't a closed loop system or a formal review process where what has happened and the decisions made are analyzed as to whether any different decisions would have contributed to a better outcome. There needs to be that feedback so that when that event happens again, the best possible outcome is realized.

The evolution of a Formula 1 race is highly dynamic and highly relevant here. Teams must manage their way through a race in the same way that it's necessary to navigate through the day at an airport to reach the best possible outcome. Each industry is highly regulated, the rules change on a continual basis, and they're both safety critical.

Within the Formula 1 environment, rapid change built upon the foundation of iterative feedback is fundamental to success. Although plenty of attention must be paid to how to operate within that regulated, safety critical, and dynamic landscape, fast-paced innovation and critical operations must be delivered. With the huge growth forecast in aviation, the opportunity exists to apply innovative, data-driven approaches continuously focused on performance to rise to this challenge.

Knowledge transfer

Fueling data-driven insight

The aviation industry, like many other industries, is guilty of basing most decision making on the knowledge of people working within it, this knowledge having been generated through years of loyalty and service. However, it needs to be shared and made readily available with enhanced access to enable a shift in reliance on knowledge to data-driven insight. By factoring in years of expertise into simulations, more accurate, reliable, robust, and meaningful predictions can be made.

The industry should recognize that data and technology can support, not replace, the human decision-making process. The principle in Formula 1 is to deliver decision making at the point of most expertise and provide those people with the intelligence to support those decisions. The principle holds for the aviation industry: to provide people with the tools to support their decision making rather than rely on gut feel and intuition.

The knowledge and experience of employees at an airport or airline is critical to support the data-driven adjustments being made over time. It is a holistic approach focused on delivering reduced delays, happier passengers, and saving millions of dollars for the industry along the way.

Harnessing the power of the network

The whole is greater than the sum of its parts

The core challenge faced by the aviation industry exists in the network, with a myriad of connected stakeholders needing to adopt change. The size of this network is considerable. It spans far beyond just aviation, which includes airports, airlines, and airspace, and branches out to a multifaceted, wider public transport network.

For aviation to overcome the challenges of tomorrow today, it must harness the power of this network to create a platform that drives synergies to deliver tangible and widespread benefits to stakeholders.

Aviation is part of a broader transport and mobility structure, as we take strides toward the concept of "smart cities." A smart airport for example, will link to road, rail and sea travel.

A smart city is one that uses technology to improve outcomes across every aspect of city operations and enhance the services it offers to its residents. It collects and uses data to drive its decision making, and creates networks of partners among governments, businesses, nonprofits, community groups, universities, and hospitals to expand and improve its ability to serve its residents.

The Formula 1 concept is already contributing to the development of smart operations, as it combines hardware and software with sophisticated algorithms to bridge the "physical-to-digital" divide by helping organizations make sense of data. This framework not only drives advantage and human benefit but begins to join the dots in a wider industry and ecosystem, which has become fragmented.

In response, the business needs to develop interconnected operations products. From the boardroom to the frontline, these products support people making critical decisions with the right data and help them make better decisions, while focusing on those that really drive performance.

Whether it's strategic planning or day-to-day operations, people supported by these solutions are empowered to make confident, proactive decisions. They can look beyond the immediate situation, traverse organizational boundaries, and understand the best options available as well as their most likely outcomes. It is in this way that an organization can remain agile and unified in its effort to achieve the best possible business results. This is, in essence, predictive operations.

Aviation is a dynamic industry. However, it is not always the most joined-up. Organizations that operate within it tend to exist in data siloes. This needs to change by feeding data into a central hub to provide an informed bigger picture that boasts detail and clarity.

The critical step is to look at overall performance. Just as each component on a Formula 1 car is optimized to deliver the best performance, it is the overall performance realized by all those components working in harmony where significant cumulative performance gain exists. The more stakeholders in the network that work in harmony with each other, the greater the performance.

Optimization on an individual and incremental basis, be it on a Formula 1 car or in an airport, can only go so far. The next step change in performance will come when previously separate worlds break out of siloes and start working together by sharing performance data, predicted future outcomes, and plans, as well as learnings and working methods in an open and collaborative manner. This will require the adoption of a high-performance culture, as in the case of Formula 1.

In aviation, we have identified where the high-performance culture and approaches that are used in terms of technology, people, and processes are relevant. We're taking that cultural mindset and exporting it into aviation. This is more than merely technology at play. It is not just about the data. The right operating model, processes, and, most importantly, culture are critical to implement change.

Although a cultural change is imperative, the catalyst for a step change in thinking can come from a cutting-edge simulation and analytic techniques to run millions of scenarios, often in real time, to take a data-driven approach to decision making. Technology will be the enabler for people across the industry to become agents of change.

Delivering results today

The airport operations performance predictor

Airline passenger numbers continue to increase and are set to do so for the fore-seeable future. No shortage of investment has been made in aviation capital infra-structure in response. However, creating new capacity naturally lags behind the pace of growth in demand for air travel. To maximize usage of these constrained resources, focus and investment has often been placed on airspace management and control systems. Meanwhile, airport operations have been left to rely on the skilled and dedicated efforts of operational teams to run these increasingly com-plex operations.

Deloitte and Mclaren are responding to the growing needs of airport opera-tors and developing a suite of solutions, starting with the development of our Airport Operations Performance Predictor (AOPP). This allows airport operators to deliver improved and robust on-time performance by enabling coordinated and focused delivery of the day's timetable.

Equipped with AOPP, operational leaders can look beyond the immediate situ-ation and manage the airfield toward the best available result while taking into consideration the most relevant internal and external stakeholder considerations. Analysis of schedules against actual performance over time is carried out to iden-tify areas ripe for improvement.

Designed to sit at the very heart of an integrated airport operations hub and based upon hundreds of thousands of simulations conducted during every second of the dynamic airfield environment, AOPP rapidly explores scenarios to improve predicted performance and provides a unified view of the remaining airport opera-tions for the day to answer the most pertinent questions. What is our projected end-of-day on-time performance? What are the forthcoming choke points in the operation, and what are our best available options to avoid or mitigate those?

The software-enabled system navigates airport operators through better decision-making and toward the best possible on-time performance. It can determine which arrivals and departures are most likely to operate out of schedule, which flights should be focused on to recover on-time performance, and how to decide the actions which best mitigate the impact of delay when there is disruption.

AOPP is now being used by the Manchester Airport (MAN). Rather than wait-ing for events to occur, the goal for AOPP is to combine the knowledge and expe-rience of employees with predictive algorithms to understand what is happening and, more importantly, what is likely to happen next. This is so that new and better plans can be formulated in advance to reduce operational impact the next time a similar situation arises.

The review process after events is a critical phase of improving performance and delivering a more streamlined airport or airline operation. By easing the decision-making process through prior planning, staff time is freed up to deliver post-event analysis. Incorporating this more formally into planning reduces the impact next time around. Crucially, the follow-up analysis includes both the data and the people involved.

What the industry should consider moving forward

On time and in for the long haul

Using the concepts described, it is possible to build an on-time aviation portfolio. It comprises an array of products designed to improve and optimize on-time performance derived from predicting airport, airline, and airspace performance. Working in tandem, the products can affect the change necessary in the industry to make a difference to people's lives, from those working in aviation to passengers. The portfolio includes on-time airside, on-time airspace, and on-time airport.

The progress made with AOPP and its tangible benefits, coupled with the development of the on-time aviation portfolio, underlines the resources required to plan within the dynamic the aviation industry. The success of the Formula 1 dynamic planning framework, when applied to the aviation industry, will shape the industry for decades to come.

Notes

1 "European Aviation in 2040: Challenges to Growth," Eurocontrol.
2 "Latest on Delays," Eurocontrol, August 23, 2018, (https:www.eurocontrol.int/news/latest-delays.
3 Ibid., "Latest on Delays."
4 Op. cit., "European Aviation in 2040."

Future of secondary market airports

Bernard Thiboutot

Vice President, Marketing and Development
Québec City Jean Lesage International Airport (YQB)

The purpose of this paper is to share ideas on the future of so-called "secondary" airports. Some might not feel at ease with this notion of a secondary airport. It is as if there were different levels of airports on the market. It is true, in fact, that there are various levels of airports if one considers the number of services provided, the number of flights available, or the relative investments made. However, when considered from the standpoint of a passenger, an airport is never "secondary." It is always the most important airport in the world, since it is that passenger's means to leave their region and to travel wherever they want to go.

Two other points need consideration. First of all, smaller airports face the same regulatory environment as larger airports (checkpoints, customs, etc.), which in itself tends to make all airports about the same in terms of security. Secondly, the size of an airport is more often than not related to the size and characteristics of its regional population and the proximity of a larger airport within a 2- to 3-hour drive.

With that in mind, it is worth putting into perspective how airports, especially regional airports, can better serve their passengers in the years ahead considering that new trends and new technologies are emerging on the market. Moreover, a proper diagnosis of the situation should impact the volume of passengers and how airports do business in general.

Introduction to Québec City and its airport

For those not familiar with Canada, Québec City is located in the eastern part of the country. It is a lovely city founded in 1608 by French settlers, and the majority of people still speak French as their mother tongue. It is a fortified and historic city and, as such, hosts some 4.7 million tourists annually. It is also a UNESCO World Heritage site. The tourist industry is therefore flourishing, as demonstrated by the numerous international accolades received. Québec City is also the capital of the Province of Québec, one of the ten Canadian provinces. This means that the National Assembly, the premier's and ministers' offices are all located within its boundaries, and there is a strong civil servant presence. Québec City is also a major educational center, with its three universities and six colleges, counting respectively 42,000 and 20,000 students. Its optics, photonics, health sciences, and video game industries are also flourishing businesses. In short, Québec City is a dynamic tourist destination and a growing business center.

For more than 75 years, the Québec City Jean Lesage International Airport (YQB) has been serving the Québec City area and other regions in its catchment areas. The airport is the 11th largest airport in Canada. YQB serves domestic, international, and US transborder passengers. YQB processes nearly 1.7 million passengers per year, with 121,700 movements annually. Almost all major international North American carriers are present at the airport, with flights to Canada, the US, Mexico, and the Caribbean as well as charter flights to Paris. YQB outbound traffic is 35 percent for business purposes and 65 percent for leisure, mostly to sun destinations. YQB is therefore an origin/destination airport. The traffic split is inbound 25 percent and outbound 75 percent. Even though the local population counts 812,000 people, potential traffic within its catchment area represents 2.7 million passengers, and YQB passenger traffic should double by 2030.

Passenger First®

YQB is ranked as one of the fastest-growing airports in Canada, with an annual compound growth rate of close to 7 percent a year for the last 15 years. Two reasons might explain this growth rate over the years, namely a clear focus on passenger needs and the fact that management has built a capacity to meet demand, as will be explored in further detail. About ten years ago, YQB adopted a *Passenger First*® focus, which explains a good deal of the airport's success today. The airport put passengers at the forefront of its concerns and, ever since, management has sought to build the business with passengers in mind. A second element of the strategy has been capacity development, with investments of close to $500 million over the past 15 years to build a domestic and international terminal, a 1,150-stall parkade, a new garage, and a fire station, all to provide passengers with a unique, efficient, and secure experience.

The results of those initiatives were almost immediate. According to various surveys conducted five years in a row, more than 90 percent of respondents either confirmed that they had a very good or good opinion of YQB or were in agreement with the YQB capital investment program. In 2010, 2011, and 2013, according to Airport Service Quality (ASQ) surveys, YQB was voted best airport in North America in the 0–2 million passenger category. YQB came second in 2012, 2014, and 2015. In short, this clear focus on the passengers has paid off, as shown in Figure 8.16, even though the volume of passengers is still only 1.7 million passengers per year.

This leads to the argument that YQB might be a "secondary" airport in size but definitively not in terms of the service it provides to passengers, as attested to by the various awards the airport has recently been granted. Let us now turn to the very point of this piece, i.e., what is the future for a passenger-oriented airport the size of YQB?

A change of mindset and focus for airlines

Keeping passengers in mind, it is obvious that airlines will need to better adapt to passenger needs and make some adjustments in their way of doing business. Airlines are major stakeholders of any airport and therefore key players in the game. In YQB's case, management expects airlines to offer more point-to-point flights when passenger traffic to a given destination has reached a certain level.

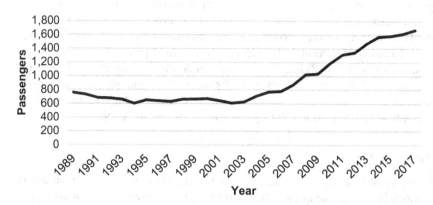

Figure 8.16 Québec City Jean Lesage International Airport Passengers Per Year (in thousands)

Currently, in Canada, some 66 percent of all traffic is funneled through only four hub airports, i.e., Vancouver, Calgary, Toronto and Montreal.

Carrying passengers through hubs gives rise to all sorts of seemingly unnecessary costs that are passed onto the passengers (multiple landing charges, baggage-handling costs at each airport, etc.) and is a major source of annoyance to travelers due in particular to unnecessary waiting time and longer travel days. It is suggested that airports (and airlines) would prosper more if airlines were to offer more point-to-point flights. Otherwise, regional airports are only there to feed major airports, with no reason to grow. They under-serve an existing market that actually has a strong growth potential. This is especially true in today's environment, considering that single-aisle aircraft are now available on the market to carry a smaller number of passengers across long-haul distances and that those aircraft feature impressive savings on energy, one of the highest expenses of the industry.

Generally speaking, legacy airlines have not necessarily been focusing on route development but rather on yield optimization and actual route optimization and on better use of their assets. They have also been reluctant to maintain regional services, as those are offered at hefty costs. Moreover, higher ticket prices and pilot shortages have eroded the services offered to regional airports, exacerbating even further the situation for passengers living in places other than large metropolitan areas.

Major hub airports are trying to improve their passengers-per-movement ratio in order to postpone for as long as possible costly expansion projects to cope with this capacity need. This may indeed drive large airports to optimize each movement by relying on moderate-to-large planes, especially if the airport faces a curfew. This further reduces service in the regions, since larger planes fly less frequently to spokes. Airlines need to reconsider this situation and think creatively to offer better services in places other than large metropolitan areas.

It is also interesting to note that in relatively slow-growing markets like North America or Europe, major airlines are consolidating to secure their market shares and reduce competition. On the other hand, in fast-growing markets like Asia, India, or Brazil, major airlines are investing in local airlines, not only to take advantage of their rapid growth but also to expand their network.

What's in store for the future?

The legacy airlines model is based on a hub-and-spoke network, with the bulk of their revenue coming from that network. Their stakes in such networks are so high that one can predict strong resistance to change on their part. One can also easily assume that the destination of the majority of passengers coming from the regions (the so-called secondary market) is not the hub city per se, which only acts as a connection airport.

From this perspective, the populations in all regions have the right to rely on equivalent or at least similar airline services as the populations living in large metropolitan areas. Thus, it can be argued that airports like YQB need to launch their second wave of development (i.e., point-to-point) to serve travelers seeking fast and convenient airline service. This, of course, should take place when a sufficient number of passengers travel from one place to another.

It is fairly clear that global air service will take advantage of "secondary" airport growth, because those under-served markets have room to develop. Keep in mind also that the propensity to travel is about the same as that in larger metropolitan areas.

Undeniably, passenger growth and improvements in technology will drive the industry to the point where air service will become a commodity with added value to fit each specific passenger's need. There are many factors, which will be described next, that lead us to believe that so-called secondary airports will be much better served in the future.

A shift in strategy and equipment

It is fairly evident that low-cost carriers (LCC) and ultra-low-cost carriers (ULCC) tend to serve large markets through other airports in the vicinity of large metropolitan areas. A carrier like Ryanair will serve Paris Beauvais rather than Paris Charles-de-Gaulle. It is possible that a similar phenomenon could take place at YQB, where tourists from Europe could easily land here with LCC or ULCC and visit Montréal later (only 300 km away). The same phenomenon could occur for, let's say, Toronto, Ontario, with vicinity airports such as Hamilton, London, and Kingston or Vancouver, British Columbia, with nearby Abbottsford, to name only those few.

With new single-aisle aircraft such as the Boeing 737 Max, the Airbus A320 neo or the Airbus A220 (formerly known as Bombardier CSeries) coming onto the market, it is expected that it will be technically feasible to better serve airports in mid-size markets. Those aircraft indeed have the capability to perform transatlantic flights, for instance with a load of 200 passengers. This is a real breakthrough, opening new possibilities for the various regional airports.

Hub weaknesses

Regions can also benefit from hub weaknesses. Many hubs in the world are totally congested. They are congested, first, because they lack gates at peak times and congested also because they have no physical ground to expand their facilities. Moreover, it is now also very difficult to expand airport facilities, as populations around airports tend to oppose this kind of move. This opposition is attributable to such factors as environmental and sustainability issues in general. Getting to hub airports is also becoming more and more difficult. For instance, roads are often highly congested, and parking space has become more prohibitive. Those factors tend to favor transiting through regional airports when need be and when it is feasible to do so.

Regional airports should also take into account the fact that flights to hubs from spokes are generally the first ones to be delayed or canceled to prioritize gate availability. Those factors reinforce the strengths of regional airports, especially when point-to-point flights are available and efficient. Regional airports also have the opportunity to create a unique experience for passengers that will make them want to avoid crowded hubs. A last point also needs consideration. Development projects at larger hubs need a considerable amount of time at the planning stage. Social acceptance is also often very long to achieve, which further delays the implementation stage. This provides a unique opportunity for regional airports, which generally show a greater agility in getting things done, thus "beating the competition," so to speak.

Technologies: key to airport growth and passenger satisfaction

Regional airports, like any other major airports, for that matter, will have to rely heavily in the future on technologies to improve passenger service. Traditionally, the passenger data collected by airlines and airports did not usually delve much into their primary clients, namely the passengers. This will have to change if airports really want to make breakthroughs in serving their passengers. How can this happen? First of all, through a willingness to share data among airlines and airports, as both actually serve the same person. It should be in everyone's interest to do this correctly.

It is also possible to innovate by relying on new technologies such as blockchains to make sure passenger data remain confidential but are used in a proper manner to improve service. The general idea here is to make sure airports know their passengers better. New technologies can also help reduce passenger processing times at all steps of the airport experience and, one might add, even before and after they spend time at the airport, considering that, for instance, luggage can now be picked up from and returned to the passenger's home.

Airlines and airports can also take advantage of new platforms created to gather data and provide a better experience to passengers. Think for instance how Uber, Airbnb and Amazon all changed traditional industries like taxis, hotels, or retail.

Closer to air service, note how car rental and hotel reservations have recently changed. At first, one could observe an aggregation of the offer on a search engine with better buying capability, then followed by an even higher level of service being offered. The fact is, now that passengers pay less for basic services, they can now tailor more options to fit their needs. It is time for this to also happen in our industry, to the passenger's benefit! The idea of limited services in order to keep airfares high should be discarded. Now is the time to put more seats on the market with as much direct service as possible so that more passengers fly more often. Finally, new technologies will even change the way people fly. Consider, for instance, how the Zunum hybrid aircraft will change the way regional communities are served. Smaller electrical aircraft will indeed allow for more frequent and more economical flights to regions.

The comparative advantages of regional airports

Regional airports do have comparative advantages, and they should make the most of them. For instance, it is easier for regional airports to reach out to their surrounding population, to seek custom solutions to problems, and to seize opportunities. Regional airports can also take better care of their own wider catchment area population. For instance, at YQB, the management designed a system by which a passenger living, let's say, 400 km away can board a small aircraft in a small airport with no screening facilities and be processed easily at YQB, taken immediately to the screening area upon arrival. Simply by rethinking how passengers are processed, the airport eliminated such things as landing at a fixed base operator, taking a taxi to come to the main terminal, or walking in the snow or rain before being screened.

Regional airports also have the opportunity of developing an entrepreneurial spirit among their relatively reduced number of employees. This allows them to see new opportunities, open closed doors, reject the status quo, and question the existing models and rules. It is with this sort of entrepreneurial spirit and a little bit of "stubbornness" that YQB has pursued, for over 15 years and against all odds, this idea of having a US preclearance facility. For the record, Prime Minister Justin Trudeau and President Barack Obama announced on March 10, 2016, that YQB would be one of the two Canadian airports allowed to open such a US preclearance facility.

Regional airports are also well positioned to test new airport and airline business models, thus allowing, among other things, for easier start-up of new airlines at their facilities or new projects with existing airlines.

Propensity to travel

It is sometime easier for a regional airport, in contrast to a larger one, to develop the propensity to travel of both its actual and future passengers. Consider some examples.

A regional airport has the option of developing its traffic by looking for potential inbound passengers that have an affinity for their city. Consider, for instance, the case of the novel *Anne of Green Gables*, which has been read all over the planet and which, every year, attracts thousands of visitors to the tiny province of Prince Edward Island in Canada, where this fictional story took place. The same is true for Memphis, Tennessee, where Graceland features Elvis Presley's life. Each region needs to be imaginative to discover what could attract the world. Regional airports can also more easily pinpoint the travel interests of their population so that it is relatively easier to develop direct services to some destinations. For instance, the Québec City population has direct affinities with such destinations as Fort Lauderdale and Paris, and YQB can count on that growth.

Regional airports should also exploit their "hidden" traffic leaking to other airports. Here is an illustration. Consider a regional airport located at only 250 km from major hub X. Suppose also that a large part of the population of this area comes from country Y. It is very possible that the population descending from Y often flies to that country because there is a direct flight from hub X. This is the "hidden traffic." Statistics will always show that there is no traffic between the airport and country Y, and yet there is indeed such traffic, except that it does not fly from that airport. Obtaining data on this hidden traffic is critical for anyone wishing to grow; otherwise it will leak forever to a competing airport. This phenomenon is even more acute today in all parts of the world because of the larger population movements between countries.

Propensity to travel, as measured by the number of passengers per the number of inhabitants of a given region, could also be increased by offers of better flights. The very fact that new destinations are offered at the smaller airport will of course increase the propensity to fly in the primary catchment area as well as in secondary or tertiary catchment areas.

Takeaways

The fact that technology could disrupt the aviation business will bring the whole industry to another level, and things that are taken for granted now might change. Technologies can indeed be a threat or an opportunity (by bringing new data sources, for instance). There is clear evidence that it will likely be the latter. Passengers around the world will benefit from the emerging breakthroughs in the market.

Airlines doing business in slow-growing markets like those in North America or Europe will have to find ways to stimulate their markets and better serve passengers in order to be competitive with emerging airlines (LCC-ULCC).

Air service will become increasingly mainstream. Remember the way air travel was in the '60s and '70s, with first-class services reserved only for rich people? Compare that to where we are now, with legacy airlines offering only a couple of first-class seats and charters/LCC/ULCC democratizing air service.

Regional (or "secondary") airports must stay proactive and entrepreneurial in order to "defend their turf." They need to create a new wave of development first and foremost with the passengers in mind. New technologies will make it feasible and cost-effective to achieve quality service to all travelers and not only to those living in large metropolitan areas.

To sum up, be patient and strategic, develop long-term vision, monitor the industry's disruptive events, prioritize passenger and population needs, develop agility to anticipate and face industry changes, develop added value for passengers, embrace technologies for hassle-free fluid passenger processing, and engage in big data. The opportunities are there to be seized, and the global population and air service as a whole will benefit and continue to thrive.

Index

About the author

Nawal K. Taneja, whose experience in the aviation industry spans five decades, has worked for and advised major airlines and related aviation businesses worldwide. His experience also includes the presidency of a small airline that provided schedule and charter service with jet aircraft and the presidency of a research organization that provided consulting services to the air transportation community throughout the world. On the government side, he has advised worldwide departments of civil aviation on matters relating to the role of government-owned or government-controlled airlines, and their management. Within the academic community, he has served on the faculties of the Massachusetts Institute of Technology (as an associate professor) and at the Ohio State University (professor, later as chair of the Department of Aviation, and finally, the Department of Aerospace Engineering).

He has served on the advisory boards of both public and private organizations. He continues to be invited to provide presentations at industry conferences worldwide and moderate panel discussions. He writes a Column in *Airline Leader: the Strategy Journal for Airlines CEOs* (published by CAPA – Centre for Aviation). He advises senior executives in airlines and related aviation businesses, as well as senior government policy makers, on the impact of following powerful and converging forces on the:

- profoundly changing behavior and expectations of connected, empowered, and increasingly divergent passengers in the on-demand and sharing economies;
- proliferation of smart technologies that facilitate the development of business intelligence and consumer intelligence;
- emergence of businesses with information, analytical skills, and CRM capabilities to market mobility-as-a-service, and support end-to-end journeys; and
- rapidly evolving aviation regulatory policies, making the market more dynamic and more unpredictable.

At the encouragement of, and for, practitioners in the global airline industry, he has authored ten other books:

- *Driving Airline Business Strategies through Emerging Technology* (2002)
- *AIRLINE SURVIVAL KIT: Breaking Out of the Zero Profit Game* (2003)

- *Simpli-Flying: Optimizing the Airline Business Model* (2004)
- *FASTEN YOUR SEATBELT: The Passenger is Flying the Plane* (2005)
- *Flying Ahead of the Airplane* (2008)
- *Looking Beyond the Runway: Airlines Innovating with Best Practices while Facing Realities (2010)*
- *The Passenger Has Gone Digital and Mobile: Accessing and Connecting through Information and Technology (2011)*
- *Designing Future-Oriented Airline Businesses (2014)*
- *AIRLINE INDUSTRY: Poised for Disruptive Innovation? (2016)*
- *21st CENTURY AIRLINES: Connecting the Dots (2018)*

The first eight books were published by the Ashgate Publishing Company (now part of Routledge) in the UK and the last two directly by Routledge.

He holds a Bachelor's degree in Aeronautical Engineering (First Class Honors) from the University of London, a Master's degree in Flight Transportation from MIT, a Master's degree in Business Administration from MIT's Sloan School of Management, and a Doctorate in Air Transportation from the University of London. He is a Fellow of the Royal Aeronautical Society of Great Britain.